THE OFFICIAL WAINWRIGHT GAZETTEER

Pictorial Guides to the Lakeland Fells

THE OFFICIAL WAINWRIGHT GAZETTEER

COMPILED BY
PETER LINNEY

Michael Joseph
London

MICHAEL JOSEPH LTD

Published by the Penguin Group
27 Wrights Lane, London W8 5TZ
Viking Penguin Inc., 375 Hudson Street, New York, New York 10014, USA
Penguin Books Australia Ltd, Ringwood, Victoria, Australia
Penguin Books Canada Ltd, 10 Alcorn Avenue, Toronto, Ontario,
Canada M4V 3B2
Penguin Books (NZ) Ltd, 182-190 Wairau Road,
Auckland 10, New Zealand

Penguin Books Ltd, Registered Offices: Harmondsworth, Middlesex, England

First published in Great Britain 1993

Compilation and original notes copyright © Peter Linney 1993
Data material, illustrations and maps from A. Wainwright's *Pictorial Guides*
copyright © Michael Joseph Ltd 1992

The material appearing in this book is based on works previously
published by the Westmorland Gazette, Kendal

Typeset in Monophoto Times
Made and printed in England by Clays Ltd, St Ives plc
Design and computer page make-up by Penny Mills

A CIP catalogue record for this book is available from the British Library

ISBN 0 7181 4070 2

The moral right of the author has been asserted

The logo printed on the title page of this book
is a trademark of Michael Joseph Ltd.

CONTENTS

ACKNOWLEDGEMENTS

In acknowledging the source of material for the Gazetteer, it is somewhat stating the obvious to acknowledge A. Wainwright's *Seven Pictorial Guides to the Lakeland Fells*, as without them there simply would be no Gazetteer. The guidebooks have often been referred to as the fellwalker's bible; for my part, if I were ever to find myself languishing on the ubiquitous desert island, I would want nothing more than my set of the Pictorial Guides.

The titles listed below are all Copyright © Michael Joseph 1992

THE PICTORIAL GUIDES TO THE LAKELAND FELLS
Book One: THE EASTERN FELLS 1955
Book Two: THE FAR EASTERN FELLS 1957
Book Three: THE CENTRAL FELLS 1958
Book Four: THE SOUTHERN FELLS 1960
Book Five: THE NORTHERN FELLS 1962
Book Six: THE NORTH WESTERN FELLS 1964
Book Seven: THE WESTERN FELLS 1966

The idea for the Gazetteer was my own but a number of people have, over the years, encouraged me to develop the original concept. A young colleague, John Adams, an experienced and enthusiastic Lake District fellwalker, initially turned me in the direction of the use of the databases and assisted in creating the first lists of ascents and starting points. Since those early days (circa 1985) and my retirement in 1986 I have been distracted by many fascinating activities, particularly with The Save The Children Fund and the Carr-Gomm Society, but the worm of the idea kept boring away until finally, in early 1992, I felt the urge to complete the database and write the introductions to support it.

At this point, I would like to thank a number of people who have been crucial to the book's publication: first, my good friend and colleague Geoffrey Myers, particularly for the conversations on 'Quality' and 'Value for Effort'; Andrew my son, who, with his skills of graphic design and illustration has been of inestimable help in producing the maps and diagrams, in addition to his welcome company on the fells; and Jenny Dereham, editor of the Wainwright Series, whose tolerance and enthusiasm for the book is matched only by her dogged persistence in requesting consistency and accuracy, and who has been a significant element in turning the original manuscript into the finished work for which I shall always be grateful.

Finally, my immense thanks to Margaret my wife, who has put up with this obsession and, despite a most healthy dislike and distrust of computers, has encouraged me to complete the Gazetteer. To her I dedicate this book.

INTRODUCTION

The seven guide books that A. Wainwright compiled between November 1952 and Christmas 1965 are an essential part of any Lake District fellwalker's equipment. The *Pictorial Guides to the Lakeland Fells* provide detailed descriptions of the ascents of 214 of the most significant fells of the Lake District, together with ridge walks connecting adjacent fells. Each description includes detailed maps, panoramic views of near and distant hills, unique pictorial elevations of the ascent routes, beautifully crafted line illustrations and a mass of interesting information, as well as much pithy and amusing comment.

For those who are fortunate enough to spend some days, or even weeks, in the Lake District, the seven Pictorial Guides are much more. As well as being carried on the fell, however, they are often read during the dark winter evenings, whilst walkers either reminisce about the previous season's achievements or contemplate future ventures.

The form and style of presentation, being completely hand-drawn and with justified left and right margins, are particularly pleasing from an aesthetic point of view. No attempt at copying this unique style – and, sadly, there have been a number – has come close to the character and knowledge of AW. (Wainwright is rarely referred to as 'Mr' and, indeed, until a few years before his death in January 1991, his first name was little known; he is invariably known as AW by the Lakeland fellwalkers.)

From the date of owning my first 'Wainwright', I have been impressed by the sheer quantity, as well as the quality, of the data contained within these guide books and it is with much of this database that this book is concerned. The Gazetteer can be used not only as a means to select and plan an expedition, but also as a directory and index *en route*. It will, I believe, widen the horizons of fellwalkers to identify 'long routes', 'horseshoes' and add generally to the enjoyment of both planning a journey and the actual walking.

USING THE DATA

Most people who visit the Lake District and who intend to spend some time fellwalking, may ask the following questions once they have chosen somewhere to stay:

* Which fells can be climbed conveniently from my base?
* Which group or groups of fells can be climbed in, say, an eight-hour day, using recognized ridge routes, at a speed I can cope with, and still return to, or near to, the starting point?
* For the 'peak bagger' (not the reader, I am sure) it is important to know which of the fells are 2000 or 2500 feet in height, although quantity should never be confused with quality.
* Which fell or group of fells within an area offers the best ascents, summits or views and which provides the best 'value for effort'?

CALCULATION OF ASCENT TIMES

Using the information presented in each ascent described, namely the height of ascent and the distance to the summit, it is possible to estimate the time required for the ascent. (These figures are given in miles and feet as AW would have wished; he did not believe in the metric system!) This calculation, involving both height of ascent and distance, is often referred to as 'Naismith's Rule' and there are as many values applied to the two variables as there are people to whom one may put the question. The following are some examples of those offered, set out in descending order of speed:

TABLE 1: 'Naismith's Rule'

SOURCE	DISTANCE COMPONENT	HEIGHT COMPONENT
Naismith	3 miles per hour	2000 feet per hour
Scout Association's Notes for Hill Walking	3 miles per hour	1500 feet per hour
Ordnance Survey's Leisure Guides	2½ miles per hour	1500 feet per hour

Of course, the correct value is the one which suits the walker personally, and it is relatively simple to test these 'models' against one's own experience and to choose accordingly. For the purposes of this book the first and last sets of values have been chosen to give the time dimension and appear as the Faster Ascent Rate and Slower Ascent Rate respectively. **These time values are shown in hours and decimal parts of an hour, enabling their easy addition and convenience for other calculations, rather than hours and minutes.**

It should be noted that these are walking times only, and extra should be added independently for lunch stops, and halts for taking photographs or just gazing at the incomparable Lakeland scenery.

THE COMPLETENESS OF THE SOURCE DATA

ASCENTS

The data provided by AW in his seven Pictorial Guides covers the ascents which he considered worth recording, but there are a number of occasions where, for unexplained reasons, AW chose not to quote the height or distance (or both) of ascent. Of these 94 incomplete ascents, 59 are simply deficient in data: 51 have neither height nor distance (e.g. ARTHUR'S PIKE from Howtown) and 8 have a quoted height but no mileage from the start point (e.g. MIDDLE DODD from Hartsop Hall). There are 35 cases where the Fell already has a number of ascents fully described with additional start points hinted at but not evaluated (e.g. HARRISON STICKLE from Borrowdale). The 4 ascents of PAVEY ARK are meticulously described from Stickle Tarn (which is given as 1250 feet and 1 mile from Dungeon Ghyll) but no overall heights or distances are given. Finally, the ascents of HIGH SEAT from Ashness Bridge and from Dale Bottom have a quoted distance from Keswick but are without the provision of a height component. The number of these 'calculated ascents' varies greatly from Book to Book and the table given below shows this variance.

Additionally, an examination of a number of fell descriptions will reveal that whilst an ascent may be described simply as (say) DOLLYWAGGON PIKE 'Ascent from Dunmail Raise', implying a single ascent, examination of the elevation will show at least two and possibly three routes to the summit. Other cases are even more complicated when AW mapped small detours within these various descriptions. In selecting those ascents which are displayed in the following chapters and tables, I have tried to be consistent in respecting real differences but avoiding trivial detours, conscious that if all possible combinations were included then we might reach the stage where we could not see the wood for the trees. If the reader's favourite ascent has been omitted I apologise but in presenting 759 ascents I feel the depths of detail in the Pictorial Guides have been plumbed.

TABLE 2: 'Missing' Ascent Data

BOOK	DATE FINISHED*	TOTAL NUMBER OF ASCENTS	ASCENTS WHERE DATA IS NOT GIVEN
1. EASTERN FELLS	Christmas 1954	107	24
2. FAR EASTERN FELLS	Autumn 1956	124	33
3. CENTRAL FELLS	New Year 1958	98	18
4. SOUTHERN FELLS	Christmas 1959	111	8
5. NORTHERN FELLS	Autumn 1961	106	5
6. NORTH WESTERN FELLS	Autumn 1963	95	1
7. WESTERN FELLS	Christmas 1965	118	5
TOTALS		**759**	**94**

* The dates AW gave at the end of each of the Pictorial Guides

It may be coincidental but it could be construed from the above that there is a link between the order in which AW wrote the books and the incidence of the 'missing' data as the three earliest books contain 75 of the 94 cases.

The tables in chapter 1 show an asterisk (*) adjacent to any height or distance which is not obtained by direct reference to the ascent height and/or distance quoted in the Pictorial Guides. Whilst the asterisk is not shown in Chapters 2 and 3 the data given there for height and distance of ascents is that which has been calculated for Chapter 1 since the database is common to all 'ascents' analyses in the Gazetteer. All calculations have been made using other material contained within the Fell description, such as the maps and elevations.

RIDGE ROUTES

Some 332 ridge routes are offered of which 4 have no height of ascent quoted and 2 have no distance: AW gave no reason. There are 152 ridge routes which are quoted in both directions making a total of 304. There are a further 14 in one direction only; one must presume that these ridge routes were not very worthwhile and my personal experience tends to support that judgement. For the sake of completeness, however, a return route has been added and is included in the database. These computed ridge routes and the missing data from the quoted routes have been added by reference to other source material in the Pictorial Guides and are shown in all relevant tables by an asterisk (*). The following table shows their incidence of occurrence in the seven guide books.

TABLE 3: **Calculated Ridge Route Data**

BOOK	RIDGE ROUTES IN BOOK	HEIGHT OF ASCENT CALCULATED	DISTANCE OF ASCENT CALCULATED	RETURN ROUTE NOT GIVEN	TOTAL CALCULATED RIDGE ROUTES
1. EASTERN FELLS	56	1	0	4	5
2. FAR EASTERN FELLS	62	1	0	1	2
3. CENTRAL FELLS	48	0	0	3	3
4. SOUTHERN FELLS	40	0	0	0	0
5. NORTHERN FELLS	36	1	2	2	5
6. NORTH WESTERN FELLS	38	0	0	1	1
7. WESTERN FELLS	52	1	0	3	4
TOTALS	**332**	**4**	**2**	**14**	**20**

There would seem to be little or no pattern emerging from the above data, particularly when the variation in the numbers of ridge routes between the books is taken into account. EASTERN and NORTHERN FELLS have, equally, the largest number of connecting ridge routes requiring some new data (5, or 9% of all ridges in that Book) but NORTHERN FELLS has the highest percentage (13% of all ridges) where some additional input has been necessary. Only SOUTHERN FELLS is totally without blemish!

THE FELLS OF THE PICTORIAL GUIDES

The tables which immediately follow this page list all 214 Fells depicted in the Pictorial Guides, in alphabetical order. The Book and Fell number is given for each fell (see page 21) and also the Ordnance Survey 6-figure Grid Reference. This latter information did not form part of the data provided by AW in the Pictorial Guides but is considered to be useful and therefore has been included in the Introduction rather than in the chapters containing the various analyses. The data for these OS Grid References has been kindly supplied by the Rev. Raymond W. Dent who, like the compiler, turned to his personal computer to make a list of fells to be climbed on a future holiday and found himself in a much bigger process of database construction. The Rev. Dent welcomes corrections but not to the extent of +/- 1 on the 3rd and 6th digits!

THE 214 FELLS OF THE PICTORIAL GUIDES
Listed in alphabetical order

FELL NAME	BOOK & FELL NUMBER	HEIGHT ABOVE SEA LEVEL (feet)	ORDNANCE SURVEY GRID REFERENCE
ALLEN CRAGS	4·12	2572	237085
ANGLETARN PIKES	2·26	1857	414148
ARD CRAGS	6·17	1860	207198
ARMBOTH FELL	3·18	1570	298157
ARNISON CRAG	1·35	1424	393150
ARTHUR'S PIKE	2·28	1747	461207
BAKESTALL	5·12	2189	266307
BANNERDALE CRAGS	5·10	2230	336291
BARF	6·22	1536	214267
BARROW	6·23	1494	227218
BASE BROWN	7·17	2120	225114
BEDA FELL	2·31	1664	429171
BINSEY	5·23	1466	225355
BIRKHOUSE MOOR	1·19	2350	363160
BIRKS	1·24	2040	382145
BLACK FELL	4·29	1056	340016
BLAKE FELL	7.23	1878	110197
BLEABERRY FELL	3·10	1932	286195
BLEA RIGG	3·14	1776	301078
BLENCATHRA	5·2	2847	323277
BONSCALE PIKE	2·29	1718	453200
BOWFELL	4·4	2960	245064
BOWSCALE FELL	5·8	2306	333305
BRAE FELL	5·17	1920	289351
BRANDRETH	7·12	2344	215119
BRANSTREE	2·13	2333	479099
BRIM FELL	4·10	2611	271986
BROCK CRAGS	2·27	1842	418136
BROOM FELL	6·21	1670	195271
BUCKBARROW	7·31	1410	136061
BURNBANK FELL	7·30	1580	110209
CALF CRAG	3·15	1762	301104
CARL SIDE	5·4	2420	254281
CARROCK FELL	5·13	2174	342336

FELL NAME	BOOK & FELL NUMBER	HEIGHT ABOVE SEA LEVEL (feet)	ORDNANCE SURVEY GRID REFERENCE
CASTLE CRAG	6·29	985	249159
CATBELLS	6·24	1481	244199
CATSTYCAM	1·3	2917	348158
CAUDALE MOOR	2·7	2502	418100
CAUSEY PIKE	6·14	2035	217209
CAW FELL	7·13	2288	132110
CLOUGH HEAD	1·18	2381	334225
COLD PIKE	4·19	2259	264035
CONISTON OLD MAN	4·8	2633	272978
CRAG FELL	7·26	1710	097143
CRINKLE CRAGS	4·6	2816	248049
DALE HEAD	6·7	2473	223153
DODD	5·21	1612	245273
DOLLYWAGGON PIKE	1·7	2810	346130
DOVE CRAG	1·12	2603	374104
DOW CRAG	4·14	2555	263978
EAGLE CRAG	3·17	1650	276121
EEL CRAG	6·2	2749	193203
ESK PIKE	4·5	2903	237075
FAIRFIELD	1·5	2863	358117
FELLBARROW	7·32	1363	132242
FLEETWITH PIKE	2·12	2126	206141
FROSWICK	2·12	2359	435085
GAVEL FELL	7·25	1720	117184
GIBSON KNOTT	3·21	1379	317100
GLARAMARA	4·13	2560	247105
GLENRIDDING DODD	1·34	1425	380175
GOWBARROW FELL	1·32	1579	407218
GRANGE FELL	3·22	1363	264162
GRASMOOR	6·1	2791	175203
GRAY CRAG	2·15	2286	427118
GRAYSTONES	6·25	1476	176266
GREAT BORNE	7·20	2019	124164
GREAT CALVA	5·9	2265	291312
GREAT CARRS	4·11	2575	270009
GREAT COCKUP	5·19	1720	273333
GREAT CRAG	3·20	1500	270147

FELL NAME	BOOK & FELL NUMBER	HEIGHT ABOVE SEA LEVEL (feet)	ORDNANCE SURVEY GRID REFERENCE
GREAT DODD	1·8	2807	342204
GREAT END	4·3	2984	227084
GREAT GABLE	7·1	2949	212103
GREAT MELL FELL	1·27	1760	397254
GREAT RIGG	1·15	2513	356104
GREAT SCA FELL	5·15	2131	291339
GREEN CRAG	4·27	1602	201982
GREEN GABLE	7·9	2603	214107
GREY CRAG	2·22	2093	497072
GREY FRIAR	4·15	2536	260003
GREY KNOTTS	7·14	2287	218126
GRIKE	7·29	1596	085141
GRISEDALE PIKE	6·3	2593	198225
HALLIN FELL	2·35	1271	433198
HARD KNOTT	4·25	1803	232024
HARRISON STICKLE	3·3	2403	282074
HART CRAG	1·11	2698	369112
HART SIDE	1·16	2481	359197
HARTER FELL	2·6	2539	459093
HARTER FELL	4·20	2140	219997
HARTSOP ABOVE HOW	1·26	1870	385121
HARTSOP DODD	2·23	2018	411118
HAYCOCK	7·8	2618	145107
HAYSTACKS	7·22	1900	194132
HELM CRAG	3·23	1299	327093
HELVELLYN	1·1	3118	342151
HEN COMB	7·28	1661	132181
HERON PIKE	1·25	2003	356083
HIGH CRAG	7·11	2443	181141
HIGH HARTSOP DODD	1·28	1702	393107
HIGH PIKE	1·21	2155	374088
HIGH PIKE	5·14	2157	318350
HIGH RAISE	2·2	2634	448134
HIGH RAISE	3·1	2500	281095
HIGH RIGG	3·26	1163	309220
HIGH SEAT	3·9	1995	287180
HIGH SPY	6·13	2143	234162

FELL NAME	BOOK & FELL NUMBER	HEIGHT ABOVE SEA LEVEL (feet)	ORDNANCE SURVEY GRID REFERENCE
HIGH STILE	7·6	2644	169147
HIGH STREET	2·1	2718	441111
HIGH TOVE	3·16	1665	288166
HINDSCARTH	6·9	2385	215165
HOLME FELL	4·30	1040	315006
HOPEGILL HEAD	6·6	2525	185221
ILL BELL	2·9	2476	436077
ILLGILL HEAD	4·22	1983	169049
KENTMERE PIKE	2·11	2397	465078
KIDSTY PIKE	2·5	2560	447126
KIRK FELL	7·7	2630	195105
KNOTT	5·7	2329	296330
KNOTT RIGG	6·19	1790	197187
THE KNOTT	2·10	2423	437127
LANK RIGG	7·24	1775	092119
LATRIGG	5·24	1203	279247
LING FELL	6·26	1224	179286
LINGMELL	4·7	2649	209082
LINGMOOR FELL	4·28	1530	302046
LITTLE HART CRAG	1·23	2091	388100
LITTLE MELL FELL	1·29	1657	423240
LOADPOT HILL	2·18	2201	457181
LOFT CRAG	3·8	2270	277071
LONGLANDS FELL	5·22	1580	276354
LONG SIDE	5·5	2405	248284
LONSCALE FELL	5·6	2344	286271
LORD'S SEAT	6·18	1811	204265
LOUGHRIGG FELL	3·27	1101	347051
LOW FELL	7·33	1360	137227
LOW PIKE	1·30	1657	373078
MAIDEN MOOR	6·15	1887	237182
MARDALE ILL BELL	2·8	2496	448101
MEAL FELL	5·18	1770	283337
MELLBREAK	7·27	1676	148186
MIDDLE DODD	1·22	2106	397096
MIDDLE FELL	7·21	1908	151072
MUNGRISDALE COMMON	5·16	2068	311293

FELL NAME	BOOK & FELL NUMBER	HEIGHT ABOVE SEA LEVEL (feet)	ORDNANCE SURVEY GRID REFERENCE
NAB SCAR	1·33	1450	356068
THE NAB	2·25	1887	434152
NETHERMOST PIKE	1·2	2920	344141
OUTERSIDE	6·16	1863	211215
PAVEY ARK	3·7	2288	285080
PIKE O'BLISCO	4·18	2304	272042
PIKE O'STICKLE	3·6	2323	274073
PILLAR	7·2	2927	171121
PLACE FELL	2·20	2154	406169
RAISE	1·4	2889	343174
RAMPSGILL HEAD	2·3	2581	444128
RANNERDALE KNOTTS	6·28	1160	167183
RAVEN CRAG	3·19	1520	303188
RED PIKE (Buttermere)	7·10	2479	160154
RED PIKE (Wasdale)	7·4	2707	165106
RED SCREES	1·14	2541	396088
REST DODD	2·16	2278	433137
ROBINSON	6·8	2417	202168
ROSSETT PIKE	4·21	2106	249076
ROSTHWAITE FELL	4·24	1807	258125
SAIL	6·5	2530	199203
SAINT SUNDAY CRAG	1·10	2756	369134
SALE FELL	6·27	1170	195297
SALLOWS	2·30	1691	436040
SCAFELL	4·2	3162	207064
SCAFELL PIKE	4·1	3210	215072
SCAR CRAGS	6·11	2205	208206
SCOAT FELL	7·3	2760	159113
SEAT SANDAL	1·17	2415	344115
SEATALLAN	7·15	2266	140084
SEATHWAITE FELL	4·23	1970	229102
SELSIDE PIKE	2·21	2142	491112
SERGEANT MAN	3·2	2414	286089
SERGEANT'S CRAG	3·11	1873	274113
SHEFFIELD PIKE	1·20	2232	369182
SHIPMAN KNOTTS	2·24	1926	473062
SILVER HOW	3·24	1292	325066

FELL NAME	BOOK & FELL NUMBER	HEIGHT ABOVE SEA LEVEL (feet)	ORDNANCE SURVEY GRID REFERENCE
SKIDDAW	5·1	3053	261288
SKIDDAW LITTLE MAN	5·3	2837	267278
SLIGHT SIDE	4·17	2499	210050
SOUR HOWES	2·33	1568	426031
SOUTHER FELL	5·20	1680	355291
STARLING DODD	7·18	2085	142157
STEEL FELL	3·12	1811	320111
STEEL KNOTTS	2·34	1414	440182
STEEPLE	7·5	2687	157117
STONE ARTHUR	1·31	1652	347092
STYBARROW DODD	1·9	2770	343189
SWIRL HOW	4·9	2630	272005
TARN CRAG	2·19	2176	488078
TARN CRAG	3·13	1801	304093
THORNTHWAITE CRAG	2·4	2569	431100
THUNACAR KNOTT	3·5	2351	279080
TROUTBECK TONGUE	2·36	1191	422064
ULLOCK PIKE	5·11	2230	244288
ULLSCARF	3·4	2370	292122
WALLA CRAG	3·25	1234	277213
WANDOPE	6·4	2533	188197
WANSFELL	2·32	1597	403051
WATSON'S DODD	1·13	2584	335195
WETHER HILL	2·17	2210	456167
WETHERLAM	4·16	2502	288011
WHIN RIGG	4·26	1755	152034
WHINLATTER	6·20	1696	191251
WHITELESS PIKE	6·12	2159	180190
WHITESIDE	6·10	2317	170219
WHITE SIDE	1·6	2832	338167
YEWBARROW	7·19	2058	173085
YOKE	2·14	2309	438067

CHAPTER 1

THE SEVEN PICTORIAL GUIDES TO THE LAKELAND FELLS

In compiling the comprehensive guide books, Wainwright recognised the geophysical distribution of the higher ground in the Lake District and perceived that there were at least seven blocks of fells which could be treated independently. From studying the Pictorial Guides it is significant to note that there are no instances of ridge walks connecting the fells of different books, thus indicating the separation between groups of fells in adjacent books.

AW also recognised that in order to use one of the guide books as reference material during a walk, the fells should appear in alphabetical order rather than by geographical location or height above sea level. On the two pages which immediately precede the description of the first individual fell in each Book, the fells are shown firstly on a map, indicating the natural boundaries and then – whilst being listed in alphabetical order – they are given a number which refers to the order of height above sea level and these numbers are included in the tables which follow: i.e. Arnison Crag is Fell number 35 in Book 1. The double-page spread, from each of the seven Pictorial Guides, is shown at the beginning of each section of tables given at the end of this chapter.

AW wrote these books before transparent map cases were as commonplace as they are today, when the fell walker was meant to put the guide book into his or her pocket. Because it was necessary to take out the book to refer frequently to the specific walk in progress, an easy design was essential. AW's design has stood the test of time, and this Gazetteer has been designed similarly to make it easily accessible.

The principal measurable variables are the heights and the distances of ascents of the 759 described climbs. It is interesting to examine their distribution over the seven guide books and the following tables show these together with the distribution of the computed ascent times.

TABLE 4: **Distribution of Numbers of Ascents – By Heights of Ascent**

GUIDE BOOK NUMBER

FEET OF ASCENT	1	2	3	4	5	6	7	ALL
0–500	0	1	1	0	0	0	0	2
501–1000	6	8	12	4	11	19	2	62
1001–1500	10	30	31	11	29	21	40	172
1501–2000	26	58	26	14	24	23	23	194
2001–2500	36	27	28	41	28	28	35	223
2501–3000	28	0	0	27	14	4	18	91
3001–3500	1	0	0	14	0	0	0	15
ALL ASCENTS	107	124	98	111	106	95	118	759

TABLE 5: **Distribution of Numbers of Ascents – By Distances of Ascent**

GUIDE BOOK NUMBER

MILES OF ASCENT	1	2	3	4	5	6	7	ALL
0–1	4	5	1	1	1	5	3	20
1–2	15	21	35	15	19	32	28	165
2–3	30	29	25	17	44	31	44	220
3–4	12	24	17	33	26	20	25	157
4–5	22	14	11	25	13	7	15	107
5–6	20	19	8	5	3	0	1	56
6–7	3	8	1	4	0	0	1	17
7–8	1	4	0	7	0	0	1	13
8–9	0	0	0	3	0	0	0	3
9–10	0	0	0	1	0	0	0	1
ALL ASCENTS	107	124	98	111	106	95	118	759

TABLE 6: **Distribution of Numbers of Ascents – By Times of Ascent (using Faster Rate)**

GUIDE BOOK NUMBER

FEET OF ASCENT	1	2	3	4	5	6	7	ALL
0–1	9	8	14	6	5	21	8	71
1–2	35	61	60	26	68	47	72	369
2–3	51	45	20	60	31	27	37	271
3–4	12	10	4	14	2	0	1	43
4–5	0	0	0	5	0	0	0	5
ALL ASCENTS	107	124	98	111	106	95	118	759

In this chapter, the ascents are listed in Book and Fell order and, as in the Pictorial Guides, they start with Book 1, EASTERN FELLS (Arnison Crag) and end with Book 7, WESTERN FELLS (Yewbarrow). The order in which AW produced the Pictorial Guides was, according to his widow Betty Wainwright, determined by the proximity to Kendal by public transport. The order of presentation of the individual ascents within each Fell is more difficult to understand, however. It is clear that it is not alphabetical, nor in height order, nor in clockwise or anti-clockwise order around the fell; nor, apparently, is it in any other systematic method. It would seem that AW simply selected the ascent he either knew best or perhaps preferred and then moved to another. It may be that, as with the order of the Books themselves, the availability of public transport assisted with the order of selection of starting point. Whatever the method was, we shall probably never know.

The individual ascents set below each Fell listed in this chapter are therefore arranged in the order of starting points given by AW. Each section of the chapter, one for each Book, is accompanied by a map drawn to approximately 4 miles to 1 inch, illustrating, diagrammatically, the ascents (shown by dotted lines) between the listed starting points (shown as a solid dot) and the fell summit (shown as a solid triangle).

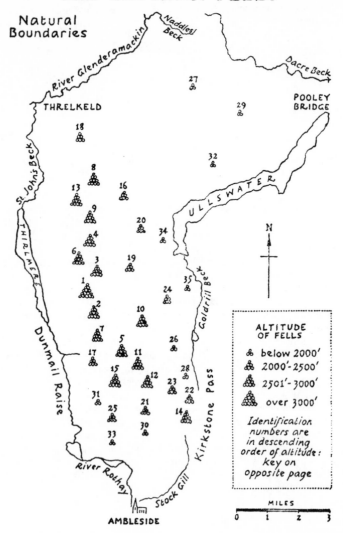

THE EASTERN FELLS

Natural Boundaries

Naddles Beck

River Glenderamackin

Dacre Beck

THRELKELD

POOLEY BRIDGE

St. John's Beck

27

29

18

32

8

13

16

ULLSWATER

9

20

34

4

N

6

3

19

1

35

24

2

10

THIRLMERE

7

26

17

5

11

28

15

12

23

22

Goldrill Beck

31

25

21

30

14

33

Dunmail Raise

River Rothay

Stock Gill

Kirkstone Pass

AMBLESIDE

ALTITUDE OF FELLS

⛰ below 2000'
⛰ 2000'–2500'
⛰ 2501'–3000'
⛰ over 3000'

Identification numbers are in descending order of altitude: key on opposite page

MILES

0   1   2   3

THE EASTERN FELLS

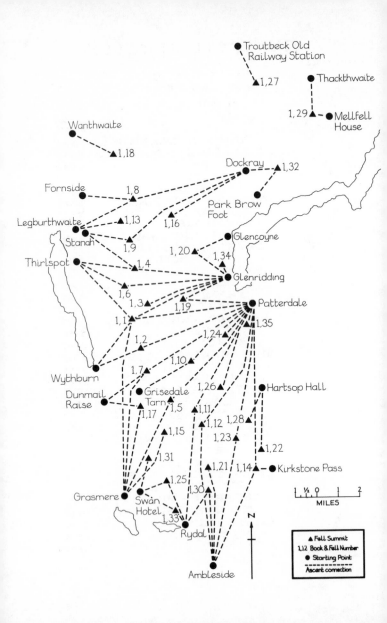

THE SEVEN PICTORIAL GUIDES TO THE LAKELAND FELLS
listed in order of Book and Fell

BOOK 1   THE EASTERN FELLS

FELL NUMBER & FELL NAME

STARTING POINT & ROUTE	HEIGHT ABOVE SEA LEVEL (feet)	HEIGHT OF ASCENT (feet)	DISTANCE OF ASCENT (miles)	ASCENT TIME FASTER (hours)	ASCENT TIME SLOWER (hours)
35 ARNISON CRAG	1424				
Patterdale direct *		900	0·67	0·67	0·87
Patterdale via Trough Head *		900	1·75	1·03	1·30
19 BIRKHOUSE MOOR	2350				
Patterdale via Grisedale		1900	3·50	2·12	2·67
Glenridding via Mires Beck		1900	2·00	1·62	2·07
Glenridding via north-east ridge *		1900	1·50	1·45	1·87
24 BIRKS	2040				
Patterdale via Trough Head		1600	2·50	1·63	2·07
Patterdale via Thornhow End		1600	1·75	1·38	1·77
3 CATSTYCAM	2917				
Glenridding via Redtarn Beck		2500	4·00	2·58	3·27
Glenridding via north-west ridge		2500	4·00	2·58	3·27
18 CLOUGH HEAD	2381				
Wanthwaite direct		1900	2·00	1·62	2·07
Wanthwaite via Hause Well		1900	3·00	1·95	2·47
7 DOLLYWAGGON PIKE	2810				
Grasmere via Little Tongue Gill		2700	5·00	3·02	3·80
Grasmere via Tongue Gill		2700	5·00	3·02	3·80
Dunmail Raise via Birkside Gill		2100	2·00	1·72	2·20
Dunmail Raise via Reggle Knott		2100	2·00	1·72	2·20
Dunmail Raise via Raise Beck		2100	2·00	1·72	2·20
Patterdale via Grisedale		2400	5·00	2·87	3·60
12 DOVE CRAG	2603				
Patterdale via Black Brow		2200	5·00	2·77	3·47
Patterdale direct		2200	5·00	2·77	3·47
Ambleside via HIGH PIKE		2500	5·00	2·92	3·67
Ambleside via Scandale		2500	5·00	2·92	3·67
Ambleside via Scandale and High Bakestones *		2500	4·75	2·83	3·57
5 FAIRFIELD	2863				
Grasmere via Little Tongue Gill		2650	4·25	2·74	3·47
Grasmere via Tongue Gill		2650	4·25	2·74	3·47
Patterdale via Greenhow End		2400	5·50	3·03	3·80
Patterdale via Deepdale Hause		2400	5·50	3·03	3·80

All ascents shown with an * following the Starting Points were not evaluated explicitly by Wainwright in his guidebooks but have been computed for the Gazetteer from data given therein.

FELL NUMBER & FELL NAME					
STARTING POINT & ROUTE	HEIGHT ABOVE SEA LEVEL (feet)	HEIGHT OF ASCENT (feet)	DISTANCE OF ASCENT (miles)	ASCENT TIME	
				FASTER (hours)	SLOWER (hours)
34 GLENRIDDING DODD	1425				
Glenridding *		1000	1·00	0·83	1·07
32 GOWBARROW FELL	1579				
Park Brow Foot via Yew Crag *		1000	2·50	1·33	1·67
Park Brow Foot via Aira Force *		1000	1·50	1·00	1·27
Dockray direct *		650	1·00	0·66	0·83
8 GREAT DODD	2807				
Dockray direct		2000	4·75	2·58	3·23
Dockray via Groove Beck		2000	4·75	2·58	3·23
Fornside		2300	2·50	1·98	2·53
Legburthwaite		2300	2·25	1·90	2·43
27 GREAT MELL FELL	1760				
Troutbeck Old Railway Station *		850	1·00	0·76	0·97
15 GREAT RIGG	2513				
Grasmere via Greenhead Gill		2300	3·00	2·15	2·73
Grasmere via STONE ARTHUR		2300	3·00	2·15	2·73
11 HART CRAG	2698				
Rydal via Rydal Head		2600	4·50	2·80	3·53
Rydal direct		2600	4·50	2·80	3·53
Patterdale via Wallend		2300	4·50	2·65	3·33
Patterdale via HARTSOP ABOVE HOW		2300	4·50	2·65	3·33
16 HART SIDE	2481				
Dockray via Brown Hills		1600	4·00	2·13	2·67
Dockray via Dowthwaitehead		1600	4·00	2·13	2·67
26 HARTSOP ABOVE HOW	1870				
Patterdale		1400	3·00	1·70	2·13
1 HELVELLYN	3118				
Thirlspot via the old pony-route		2600	4·00	2·63	3·33
Thirlspot via the 'White Stones' Route		2600	3·50	2·47	3·13
Thirlspot via Helvellyn Gill		2600	3·50	2·47	3·13
Wythburn via old lead mine		2550	2·50	2·11	2·70
Wythburn via Whelpside Gill		2550	2·25	2·02	2·60
Wythburn via Comb Gill		2550	2·25	2·02	2·60
Wythburn via Birk Side		2550	2·75	2·19	2·80
Patterdale via Grisedale Tarn		2700	7·25	3·77	4·70
Patterdale via Ruthwaite cove and DOLLYWAGGON PIKE		2700	6·25	3·43	4·30
Patterdale via Nethermost Cove and NETHERMOST PIKE		2700	5·00	3·02	3·80
Patterdale via Striding Edge		2700	5·25	3·10	3·90
Patterdale via Red Tarn and Swirral Edge		2700	5·50	3·18	4·00
Glenridding via Red Tarn and Swirral Edge		2750	4·50	2·88	3·63

FELL NUMBER & FELL NAME					
STARTING POINT & ROUTE	HEIGHT ABOVE SEA LEVEL (feet)	HEIGHT OF ASCENT (feet)	DISTANCE OF ASCENT (miles)	ASCENT TIME	
				FASTER (hours)	SLOWER (hours)
1 HELVELLYN *(continued)*	3118				
Glenridding via the old pony-route and Keppel Cove		2750	5·50	3·21	4·03
Grasmere		3050	6·50	3·69	4·63

NATURAL FEATURES

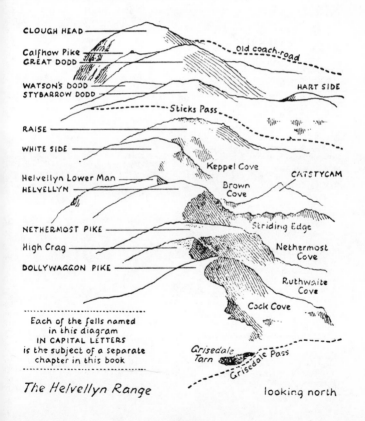

CLOUGH HEAD

Calfhow Pike
GREAT DODD

Old coach-road

WATSON'S DODD
STYBARROW DODD

HART SIDE

Sticks Pass

RAISE

WHITE SIDE

Keppel Cove

Helvellyn Lower Man
HELVELLYN

CATSTYCAM

Brown Cove

NETHERMOST PIKE

Striding Edge

High Crag

Nethermost Cove

DOLLYWAGGON PIKE

Ruthwaite Cove

Cock Cove

Each of the fells named
in this diagram
IN CAPITAL LETTERS
is the subject of a separate
chapter in this book

Grisedale Tarn

Grisedale Pass

The Helvellyn Range

looking north

FELL NUMBER & FELL NAME					
STARTING POINT & ROUTE	HEIGHT ABOVE SEA LEVEL (feet)	HEIGHT OF ASCENT (feet)	DISTANCE OF ASCENT (miles)	ASCENT TIME	
				FASTER (hours)	SLOWER (hours)
25 HERON PIKE	2003				
Grasmere, Swan Hotel via Alcock Tarn *		1750	1·25	1·29	1·67
Rydal via NAB SCAR *		1750	1·67	1·43	1·83
Rydal via Blind Cove *		1750	2·50	1·71	2·17
28 HIGH HARTSOP DODD	1702				
Hartsop Hall *		1200	0·75	0·85	1·10
21 HIGH PIKE	2155				
Ambleside		2000	4·00	2·33	2·93
23 LITTLE HART CRAG	2091				
Patterdale via Scandale Pass		1700	5·00	2·52	3·13
Patterdale via HIGH HARTSOP DODD		1700	5·00	2·52	3·13
Patterdale via Hogget Gill		1700	5·00	2·52	3·13
Ambleside		2000	4·25	2·42	3·03
29 LITTLE MELL FELL	1657				
Mellfell House *		650	0·50	0·49	0·63
Thackthwaite *		750	1·00	0·71	0·90
30 LOW PIKE	1657				
Ambleside via Low Sweden Bridge *		1500	2·25	1·50	1·90
Ambleside via High Sweden Bridge *		1500	2·25	1·50	1·90
Rydal *		1500	2·00	1·42	1·80
22 MIDDLE DODD	2106				
Hartsop Hall *		1650	2·00	1·49	1·90
33 NAB SCAR	1450				
Rydal *		1200	1·00	0·93	1·20
Grasmere, Swan Hotel *		1200	1·50	1·10	1·40
2 NETHERMOST PIKE	2920				
Wythburn		2400	2·00	1·87	2·40
Patterdale via Grisedale		2500	5·00	2·92	3·67
4 RAISE	2889				
Stanah		2400	2·50	2·03	2·60
Thirlspot direct		2400	2·50	2·03	2·60
Thirlspot via Brund Gill		2400	2·50	2·03	2·60
Glenridding direct		2500	4·00	2·58	3·27
Glenridding via Sticks Pass		2500	4·00	2·58	3·27
14 RED SCREES	2541				
Ambleside via Kirkstone Pass road		2400	4·00	2·53	3·20
Ambleside via Scandale Pass		2400	5·00	2·87	3·60
Kirkstone Pass *		1050	0·75	0·78	1·00
Patterdale		2200	6·50	3·27	4·07

FELL NUMBER & FELL NAME					
STARTING POINT & ROUTE	HEIGHT ABOVE SEA LEVEL (feet)	HEIGHT OF ASCENT (feet)	DISTANCE OF ASCENT (miles)	ASCENT TIME	
				FASTER (hours)	SLOWER (hours)
10 SAINT SUNDAY CRAG	2756				
Patterdale via Trough Head		2300	3·00	2·15	2·73
Patterdale via Thornhow End		2300	3·00	2·15	2·73
Patterdale via east ridge		2300	4·00	2·48	3·13
Grisedale Tarn		1000	1·75	1·08	1·37
17 SEAT SANDAL	2415				
Grasmere via south ridge *		2200	2·75	2·02	2·57
Grasmere via Little Tongue Gill		2200	3·50	2·27	2·87
Grasmere via Tongue Gill		2200	3·50	2·27	2·87
Dunmail Raise		1700	1·50	1·35	1·73
20 SHEFFIELD PIKE	2232				
Glenridding via south-east ridge		1800	2·00	1·57	2·00
Glenridding via Lead Mine		1800	3·25	1·98	2·50
Glencoyne via HERON PIKE		1800	2·50	1·73	2·20
Glencoyne via Nick Head		1800	2·50	1·73	2·20
31 STONE ARTHUR	1652				
Grasmere, Swan Hotel *		1400	1·00	1·03	1·33
9 STYBARROW DODD	2770				
Stanah via Stanah Gill		2300	2·50	1·98	2·53
Stanah via Sticks Pass		2300	2·50	1·98	2·53
Dockray via Green Side		1900	5·50	2·78	3·47
Dockray via Deep Dale		1900	5·50	2·78	3·47
13 WATSON'S DODD	2584				
Legburthwaite		2050	1·75	1·61	2·07
6 WHITE SIDE	2832				
Thirlspot		2300	2·50	1·98	2·53
Glenridding		2400	4·00	2·53	3·20

THE FAR EASTERN FELLS

Natural Boundaries

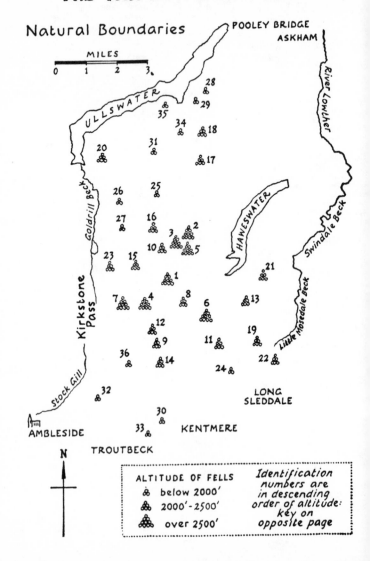

MILES
0 1 2 3

POOLEY BRIDGE
ASKHAM

River Lowther

ULLSWATER

28
29
35
34
18
31
17
20

Goldrill Beck

26
25
27
16
2
3
10
5
23
15
1
7
4
8
6
13
12
9
11
19
36
14
24
22

HAWESWATER

Swindale Beck

Little Mosedale Beck

21

Kirkstone Pass

Stock Gill

32
30
33
KENTMERE

LONG
SLEDDALE

AMBLESIDE

N

TROUTBECK

ALTITUDE OF FELLS
  below 2000'
  2000'-2500'
  over 2500'

*Identification
numbers are
in descending
order of altitude:
key on
opposite page*

THE FAR EASTERN FELLS

in the order of
their appearance
in this book

7 16 13

36

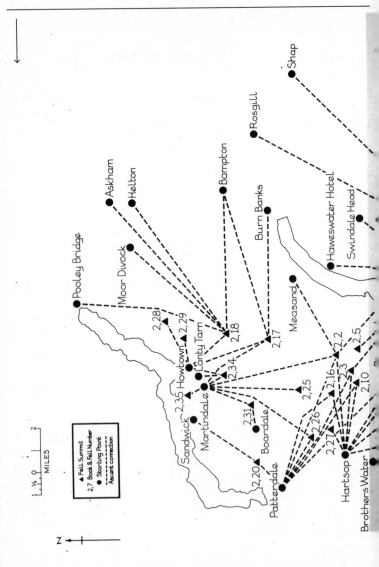

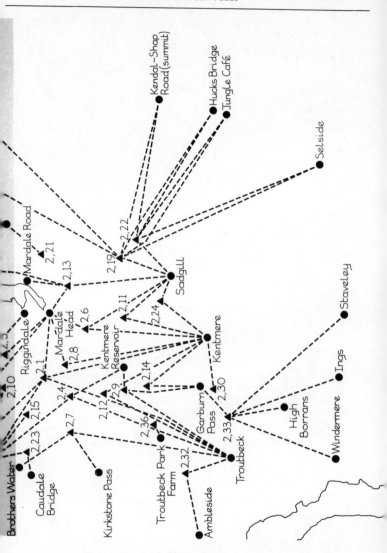

FELL NUMBER & FELL NAME STARTING POINT & ROUTE	HEIGHT ABOVE SEA LEVEL (feet)	HEIGHT OF ASCENT (feet)	DISTANCE OF ASCENT (miles)	ASCENT TIME FASTER (hours)	SLOWER (hours)
26 ANGLETARN PIKES	1857				
Patterdale via Freeze Beck		1400	1·75	1·28	1·63
Patterdale direct		1400	1·75	1·28	1·63
Martindale via Angle Tarn		1300	3·50	1·82	2·27
Martindale via Bedafell Knott		1300	3·50	1·82	2·27
28 ARTHUR'S PIKE	1747				
Howtown *		1200	3·50	1·77	2·20
31 BEDA FELL	1664				
Martindale		1100	1·75	1·13	1·43
Boardale		1100	1·75	1·13	1·43
29 BONSCALE PIKE	1718				
Howtown via the breast		1200	1·25	1·02	1·30
Howtown direct		1200	1·25	1·02	1·30
13 BRANSTREE	2333				
Mardale Head		1500	1·50	1·25	1·60
Mardale road		1500	1·50	1·25	1·60
Haweswater Hotel		1500	3·00	1·75	2·20
Sadgill		1750	3·50	2·04	2·57
27 BROCK CRAGS	1842				
Hartsop direct		1300	1·00	0·98	1·27
Hartsop via the filter house *		1300	2·00	1·32	1·67
7 CAUDALE MOOR	2502				
Kirkstone Pass		1150	2·50	1·41	1·77
Brothers Water		2000	2·50	1·83	2·33
Troutbeck via Sad Gill		2200	5·00	2·77	3·47
Troutbeck via Woundale		2200	5·50	2·93	3·67
Troutbeck via St Ravens Edge		2350	6·00	3·17	3·97
Troutbeck via Threshthwaite Mouth		2350	6·00	3·17	3·97
12 FROSWICK	2359				
Troutbeck via Blue Gill *		1850	3·75	2·17	2·73
Kentmere via the reservoir *		1850	5·00	2·59	3·23
15 GRAY CRAG	2286				
Hartsop direct		1800	2·00	1·57	2·00
Hartsop via Threshthwaite Mouth		1950	4·00	2·31	2·90
22 GREY CRAG	2093				
Sadgill		1500	1·50	1·25	1·60
Selside		1700	7·00	3·18	3·93
Jungle Cafe		1650	6·00	2·83	3·50
Hucks Bridge		1700	5·00	2·52	3·13
Kendal-Shap road (summit)		1000	5·00	2·17	2·67

All ascents shown with an * following the Starting Points were not evaluated explicitly
by Wainwright in his guidebooks but have been computed for the Gazetteer from data given therein.

FELL NUMBER & FELL NAME					
STARTING POINT & ROUTE	HEIGHT ABOVE SEA LEVEL (feet)	HEIGHT OF ASCENT (feet)	DISTANCE OF ASCENT (miles)	ASCENT TIME FASTER (hours)	SLOWER (hours)
35 HALLIN FELL	1271				
Martindale *		600	0·67	0·52	0·67
6 HARTER FELL	2539				
Kentmere via Nan Bield Pass		2200	5·25	2·85	3·57
Kentmere via KENTMERE PIKE		2200	4·25	2·52	3·17
Sadgill via Wren Gill		1950	4·25	2·39	3·00
Sadgill via Gatescarth Pass		1950	4·25	2·39	3·00
Mardale Head		1750	2·00	1·54	1·97
23 HARTSOP DODD	2018				
Hartsop *		1450	1·25	1·14	1·47
Caudale Bridge direct *		1400	0·75	0·95	1·23
Caudale Bridge via Caudale Beck *		1400	1·50	1·20	1·53
2 HIGH RAISE	2634				
Patterdale		2400	5·25	2·95	3·70
Hartsop		2250	3·50	2·29	2·90
Martindale		2100	5·00	2·72	3·40
Riggindale via Mardale		1900	2·50	1·78	2·27
Measand via Long Grain		1900	3·50	2·12	2·67
1 HIGH STREET	2718				
Patterdale		2450	5·50	3·06	3·83
Hartsop		2300	3·75	2·40	3·03
Mardale Head via Blea Water		2050	3·00	2·02	2·57
Mardale Head via Rough Crag *		2050	3·75	2·27	2·87
Troutbeck		2350	6·00	3·17	3·97
Kentmere via Hall Cove		2300	5·50	2·98	3·73
Kentmere via Lingmell End		2300	5·50	2·98	3·73
Kentmere via Nan Bield Pass		2300	6·00	3·15	3·93
9 ILL BELL	2476				
Garburn Pass		1050	2·50	1·36	1·70
Troutbeck via Hagg Gill *		1700	3·75	2·10	2·63
Kentmere Reservoir *		1500	0·75	1·00	1·30
11 KENTMERE PIKE	2397				
Kentmere		1900	3·00	1·95	2·47
Sadgill		1850	3·00	1·93	2·43
5 KIDSTY PIKE	2560				
Mardale Head		1900	3·00	1·95	2·47
10 THE KNOTT	2423				
Hartsop		1850	2·00	1·59	2·03
Patterdale *		1850	4·00	2·26	2·83
18 LOADPOT HILL	2201				
Bampton		1650	4·50	2·33	2·90
Helton		1650	5·50	2·66	3·30

FELL NUMBER & FELL NAME STARTING POINT & ROUTE	HEIGHT ABOVE SEA LEVEL (feet)	HEIGHT OF ASCENT (feet)	DISTANCE OF ASCENT (miles)	ASCENT TIME	
				FASTER (hours)	SLOWER (hours)
18 LOADPOT HILL *(continued)*	2201				
Moor Divock		1300	4·50	2·15	2·67
Pooley Bridge		1800	6·00	2·90	3·60
Askham		1600	6·50	2·97	3·67
Howtown		1750	2·25	1·63	2·07
8 MARDALE ILL BELL	2496				
Mardale Head via Small Water		1700	2·00	1·52	1·93
Mardale Head via Blea Water *		1700	2·50	1·68	2·13
Kentmere via Lingmell End		2100	4·75	2·63	3·30
Kentmere via Nan Bield Pass		2100	4·75	2·63	3·30
25 THE NAB	1887				
Martindale *		1300	4·00	1·98	2·47
20 PLACE FELL	2154				
Patterdale via The Knight *		1700	2·00	1·52	1·93
Patterdale direct		1700	1·75	1·43	1·83
Patterdale via Boardale Hause *		1700	2·00	1·52	1·93
Sandwick via Nettleslack *		1700	3·00	1·85	2·33
Sandwick via High Dodd		1700	2·50	1·68	2·13
Sandwick via Sleet Fell		1700	2·50	1·68	2·13
Sandwick via Scalehow Beck		1700	2·50	1·68	2·13
3 RAMPSGILL HEAD	2581				
Patterdale		2200	4·50	2·60	3·27
Hartsop		2050	2·75	1·94	2·47
Mardale Head		1950	3·50	2·14	2·70

The Ill Bell ridge, from Stile End

FELL NUMBER & FELL NAME					
STARTING POINT & ROUTE	HEIGHT ABOVE SEA LEVEL (feet)	HEIGHT OF ASCENT (feet)	DISTANCE OF ASCENT (miles)	ASCENT TIME	
				FASTER (hours)	SLOWER (hours)
16 REST DODD	2278				
Hartsop		1700	2·00	1·52	1·93
Patterdale		1900	3·50	2·12	2·67
30 SALLOWS	1691				
Kentmere *		1100	2·00	1·22	1·53
21 SELSIDE PIKE	2142				
Swindale Head via north-east ridge		1200	1·50	1·10	1·40
Swindale Head via Mosedale path		1350	2·25	1·43	1·80
24 SHIPMAN KNOTTS	1926				
Kentmere		1400	2·25	1·45	1·83
Sadgill		1300	1·50	1·15	1·47
33 SOUR HOWES	1568				
Windermere *		1200	4·25	2·02	2·50
Ings via Grassgarth *		1150	3·75	1·82	2·27
Ings via Hugill Hall *		1150	3·75	1·82	2·27
Staveley via Browfoot *		1250	5·25	2·38	2·93
High Borrans *		850	2·00	1·09	1·37
Garburn Pass *		100	1·00	0·38	0·47
34 STEEL KNOTTS	1414				
Howtown *		900	1·00	0·78	1·00
Lanty Tarn *		750	1·00	0·71	0·90
Martindale *		750	0·75	0·63	0·80
19 TARN CRAG	2176				
Sadgill		1600	2·00	1·47	1·87
Rosgill					
via Swindale and Brunt Tongue *		1730	7·00	3·20	3·95
Shap via Peat Hill and Brunt Tongue *		1680	7·00	3·17	3·92
Selside via GREY CRAG		1950	7·75	3·56	4·40
Jungle Cafe via GREY CRAG		1900	6·75	3·20	3·97
Hucks Bridge via GREY CRAG		1950	5·75	2·89	3·60
Kendal-Shap road (summit)					
via GREY CRAG		1250	5·75	2·54	3·13
4 THORNTHWAITE CRAG	2569				
Hartsop via GRAY CRAG		2000	3·25	2·08	2·63
Hartsop via Threshthwaite Mouth		2000	3·25	2·08	2·63
Hartsop via Hayeswater Gill *		2000	3·75	2·25	2·83
Troutbeck via Scot Rake		2200	5·00	2·77	3·47
Troutbeck via Threshthwaite Mouth		2200	5·50	2·93	3·67
Kentmere Reservoir via Gavel Crag		1650	2·00	1·49	1·90
Kentmere Reservoir via Hall Cove *		1650	2·25	1·57	2·00

NATURAL FEATURES

The main High Street range
illustrating the complexity of the valley systems

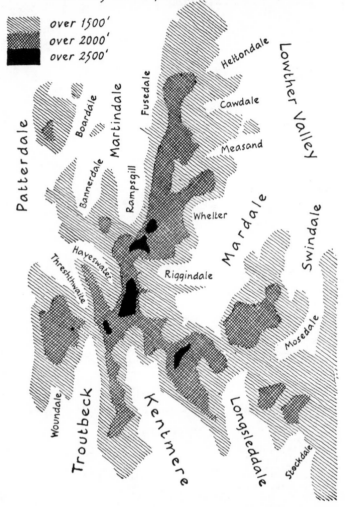

over 1500'
over 2000'
over 2500'

Patterdale

Boardale

Martindale

Bannerdale

Rampsgill

Fusedale

Hettondale

Lowther Valley

Cawdale

Measand

Whelter

Mardale

Swindale

Hayeswater

Threshthwaite

Riggindale

Mosedale

Woundale

Troutbeck

Kentmere

Longsleddale

Stockdale

FELL NUMBER & FELL NAME					
STARTING POINT & ROUTE	HEIGHT ABOVE SEA LEVEL (feet)	HEIGHT OF ASCENT (feet)	DISTANCE OF ASCENT (miles)	ASCENT TIME	
				FASTER (hours)	SLOWER (hours)
36 TROUTBECK TONGUE	1191				
Troutbeck Park Farm *		650	0·75	0·57	0·73
Troutbeck Park Farm via the Tongue *		650	3·00	1·32	1·63
32 WANSFELL	1597				
Ambleside via Stock Ghyll Force		1500	2·50	1·58	2·00
Ambleside via Blue Hill road		1500	2·50	1·58	2·00
Troutbeck		1100	1·75	1·13	1·43
17 WETHER HILL	2210				
Howtown		1750	3·00	1·88	2·37
Martindale		1550	2·50	1·61	2·03
Burn Banks direct		1550	4·50	2·27	2·83
Burn Banks via Measand Beck		1550	5·00	2·44	3·03
Bampton		1750	5·00	2·54	3·17
14 YOKE	2309				
Garburn Pass		850	1·75	1·01	1·27
Kentmere direct		1800	2·50	1·73	2·20
Kentmere via Garburn Pass		1800	3·00	1·90	2·40

THE CENTRAL FELLS

Natural Boundaries

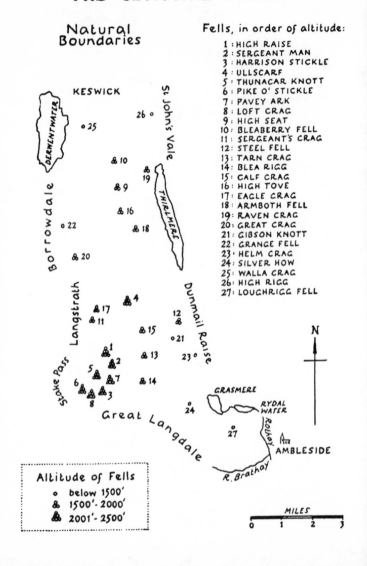

Fells, in order of altitude:

1: HIGH RAISE
2: SERGEANT MAN
3: HARRISON STICKLE
4: ULLSCARF
5: THUNACAR KNOTT
6: PIKE O' STICKLE
7: PAVEY ARK
8: LOFT CRAG
9: HIGH SEAT
10: BLEABERRY FELL
11: SERGEANT'S CRAG
12: STEEL FELL
13: TARN CRAG
14: BLEA RIGG
15: CALF CRAG
16: HIGH TOVE
17: EAGLE CRAG
18: ARMBOTH FELL
19: RAVEN CRAG
20: GREAT CRAG
21: GIBSON KNOTT
22: GRANGE FELL
23: HELM CRAG
24: SILVER HOW
25: WALLA CRAG
26: HIGH RIGG
27: LOUGHRIGG FELL

KESWICK

DERWENTWATER

St John's Vale

Borrowdale

THIRLMERE

Langstrath

Stake Pass

Dunmail Raise

GRASMERE

RYDAL WATER

Rothay

Great Langdale

AMBLESIDE

R. Brathay

N

Altitude of Fells

∘ below 1500'

🌢 1500'- 2000'

🌢 2001'- 2500'

MILES

0   1   2   3

THE CENTRAL FELLS

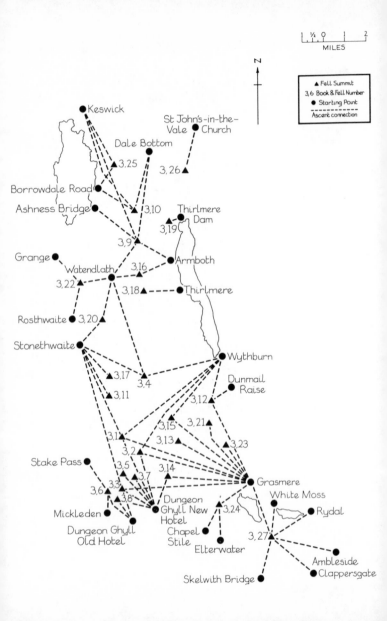

MILES

▲ Fell Summit
3,6 Book & Fell Number
● Starting Point
- - - - Ascent connection

N

Keswick

St John's-in-the-
Vale Church

Dale Bottom

3,25

3,26 ▲

Borrowdale Road

Ashness Bridge

3,10 ▲

3,9 ▲

Thirlmere
Dam

3,19 ▲

Grange

Watendlath

3,16 ▲

Armboth

3,22 ▲

3,18 ▲

Thirlmere

Rosthwaite ● 3,20 ▲

Stonethwaite

Wythburn

3,17 ▲

3,4

3,11 ▲

Dunmail
Raise

3,12 ▲

3,1 ▲

Stake Pass

3,15 ▲

3,21 ▲

3,13 ▲

3,23 ▲

3,2 ▲

3,5 ▲

3,14 ▲

3,3 ▲

3,7 ▲

3,6 ▲

3,8 ▲

Mickleden

Grasmere

White Moss

Rydal

Dungeon
Ghyll New
Hotel

3,24 ▲

3,27 ▲

Dungeon Ghyll
Old Hotel

Chapel
Stile

Elterwater

Ambleside

Clappersgate

Skelwith Bridge

FELL NUMBER & FELL NAME

STARTING POINT & ROUTE	HEIGHT ABOVE SEA LEVEL (feet)	HEIGHT OF ASCENT (feet)	DISTANCE OF ASCENT (miles)	ASCENT TIME FASTER (hours)	ASCENT TIME SLOWER (hours)
18 ARMBOTH FELL	1570				
Thirlmere via Dob Gill *		850	2·50	1·26	1·57
Thirlmere via Brown Rigg *		850	1·75	1·01	1·27
Thirlmere via Launchy Gill *		850	1·25	0·84	1·07
Thirlmere via Fisher Gill *		850	1·25	0·84	1·07
10 BLEABERRY FELL	1932				
Borrowdale road		1650	1·75	1·41	1·80
Keswick direct		1650	3·50	1·99	2·50
Keswick via Brown Knotts		1650	3·50	1·99	2·50
Dale Bottom		1600	3·00	1·80	2·27
Keswick via Dale Bottom		1650	5·50	2·66	3·30
14 BLEA RIGG	1776				
Grasmere		1600	3·50	1·97	2·47
Dungeon Ghyll New Hotel via Tarn Crag		1550	2·00	1·44	1·83
Dungeon Ghyll New Hotel via Whitegill Crag		1500	1·50	1·25	1·60
15 CALF CRAG	1762				
Grasmere via Far Easedale		1650	4·50	2·33	2·90
Grasmere via Green Burn		1650	4·50	2·33	2·90
Wythburn		1250	4·00	1·96	2·43
17 EAGLE CRAG	1650				
Stonethwaite direct		1300	2·00	1·32	1·67
Stonethwaite via Greenup path *		1300	3·00	1·65	2·07
21 GIBSON KNOTT	1379				
Grasmere		1300	4·50	2·15	2·67
22 GRANGE FELL	1363				
Grange to Brund Fell via King's How		1300	2·00	1·32	1·67
Grange to Brund Fell via Troutdale and King's How		1300	2·50	1·48	1·87
Grange to King's How only		1050	1·25	0·94	1·20
Grange to King's How via Troutdale		1050	2·00	1·19	1·50
Rosthwaite to Brund Fell via Hazel Bank		1100	1·50	1·05	1·33
Rosthwaite to Brund Fell via the bridle path		1100	2·00	1·22	1·53
Rosthwaite to King's How, direct		1000	1·50	1·00	1·27
Watendlath to Brund Fell		550	1·00	0·61	0·77
20 GREAT CRAG	1500				
Stonethwaite via Knotts		1200	1·50	1·10	1·40
Stonethwaite via Dock Tarn		1200	1·50	1·10	1·40
Watendlath		700	1·50	0·85	1·07

All ascents shown with an * following the Starting Points were not evaluated explicitly by Wainwright in his guidebooks but have been computed for the Gazetteer from data given therein.

| FELL NUMBER & FELL NAME | | | | ASCENT TIME | |
STARTING POINT & ROUTE	HEIGHT ABOVE SEA LEVEL (feet)	HEIGHT OF ASCENT (feet)	DISTANCE OF ASCENT (miles)	FASTER (hours)	SLOWE (hours
3 HARRISON STICKLE	2403				
Dungeon Ghyll Old Hotel via Thorn Crag		2150	2·00	1·74	2·23
Dungeon Ghyll Old Hotel via The Ravines		2150	1·75	1·66	2·13
Dungeon Ghyll New Hotel via Pike How		2100	1·50	1·55	2·00
Dungeon Ghyll New Hotel via Stickle Tarn		2100	1·75	1·63	2·10
Dungeon Ghyll Old Hotel via Stickle Tarn		2100	2·25	1·80	2·30
Stonethwaite via HIGH RAISE and THUNACAR KNOTT		2410	4·75	2·79	3·51
Stonethwaite via Langstrath, Stake Pass and PIKE O'STICKLE *		2360	5·83	3·12	3·91
Grasmere via SERGEANT MAN and THUNACAR KNOTT *		2450	5·50	3·06	3·83
Grasmere via BLEA RIGG and Stickle Tarn *		2450	5·16	2·95	3·70
23 HELM CRAG	1299				
Grasmere		1100	1·50	1·05	1·33
1 HIGH RAISE	2500				
Dungeon Ghyll New Hotel		2250	2·50	1·96	2·50
Grasmere		2350	5·50	3·01	3·77
Wythburn		1950	5·00	2·64	3·30
Stonethwaite		2200	3·75	2·35	2·97
26 HIGH RIGG	1163				
St John's-in-the-Vale Church		450	0·50	0·39	0·50
9 HIGH SEAT	1995				
Ashness Bridge via the falls		1500	2·00	1·42	1·80
Ashness Bridge via Dodd		1500	2·00	1·42	1·80
Keswick via Ashness Bridge *		1750	4·50	2·38	2·97
Watendlath via HIGH TOVE		1200	2·00	1·27	1·60
Watendlath via Raise Gill		1200	2·00	1·27	1·60
Dale Bottom via Mere Gill		1600	4·00	2·13	2·67
Dale Bottom via Litt's Memorial		1600	4·00	2·13	2·67
Keswick via Dale Bottom *		1750	6·50	3·04	3·77
Armboth		1450	2·00	1·39	1·77
16 HIGH TOVE	1665				
Armboth		1100	1·33	0·99	1·27
Watendlath		800	1·00	0·73	0·93
8 LOFT CRAG	2270				
Dungeon Ghyll Old Hotel		2000	1·25	1·42	1·83
Dungeon Ghyll New Hotel		2000	1·75	1·58	2·03

FELL NUMBER & FELL NAME STARTING POINT & ROUTE	HEIGHT ABOVE SEA LEVEL (feet)	HEIGHT OF ASCENT (feet)	DISTANCE OF ASCENT (miles)	ASCENT TIME FASTER (hours)	SLOWER (hours)
27 LOUGHRIGG FELL	1101				
Grasmere		920	2·25	1·21	1·51
Ambleside via Browhead Farm		1050	2·50	1·36	1·70
Ambleside via Fox Gill *		1050	3·00	1·52	1·90
Rydal		1000	2·50	1·33	1·67
White Moss		925	1·50	0·96	1·22
Clappersgate		1050	2·50	1·36	1·70
Skelwith Bridge		1000	1·75	1·08	1·37

*Grasmere
from Loughrigg Terrace*

7 PAVEY ARK	2288				
Dungeon Ghyll New Hotel via south-west ridge *		2050	1·75	1·61	2·07
Dungeon Ghyll New Hotel via Jack's Rake *		2050	1·50	1·52	1·97
Dungeon Ghyll New Hotel via Easy Gully *		2050	1·75	1·61	2·07
Dungeon Ghyll New Hotel via North Rake *		2050	1·75	1·61	2·07
6 PIKE O'STICKLE	2323				
Mickleden via Troughton Beck		2000	3·25	2·08	2·63
Dungeon Ghyll Old Hotel via Mickleden		2000	1·75	1·58	2·03
Stake Pass		800	1·33	0·84	1·07
19 RAVEN CRAG	1520				
Thirlmere Dam		950	1·00	0·81	1·03

Sour Milk Gill

| FELL NUMBER & FELL NAME | | | | ASCENT TIME | |
STARTING POINT & ROUTE	HEIGHT ABOVE SEA LEVEL (feet)	HEIGHT OF ASCENT (feet)	DISTANCE OF ASCENT (miles)	FASTER (hours)	SLOWER (hours)
2 SERGEANT MAN	2414				
Dungeon Ghyll New Hotel direct		2200	2·25	1·85	2·37
Dungeon Ghyll New Hotel via Stickle Tarn *		2200	2·00	1·77	2·27
Grasmere via Easedale Tarn		2200	4·00	2·43	3·07
Grasmere by Codale Tarn		2200	4·25	2·52	3·17
Grasmere via Far Easedale		2200	5·50	2·93	3·67
Wythburn via Far Easedale		1850	5·00	2·59	3·23
11 SERGEANT'S CRAG	1873				
Stonethwaite		1600	4·50	2·30	2·87
24 SILVER HOW	1292				
Grasmere direct		1100	1·50	1·05	1·33
Grasmere via Wray Gill		1100	1·50	1·05	1·33
Elterwater		1200	2·25	1·35	1·70
Chapel Stile direct		1050	1·25	0·94	1·20
Chapel Stile via Spedding Crag *		1050	1·75	1·11	1·40
12 STEEL FELL	1811				
Grasmere		1650	3·25	1·91	2·40
Wythburn		1250	2·00	1·29	1·63
Dunmail Raise		1050	1·00	0·86	1·10
13 TARN CRAG	1801				
Grasmere via Sour Milk Gill		1600	3·00	1·80	2·27
Grasmere via the east ridge		1600	3·00	1·80	2·27
Grasmere via Stythwaite Steps		1650	3·50	1·99	2·50
Grasmere via Deer Bield Crag		1650	3·50	1·99	2·50
5 THUNACAR KNOTT	2351				
Dungeon Ghyll New Hotel *		2100	2·00	1·72	2·20
4 ULLSCARF	2370				
Wythburn via West Head		1800	3·50	2·07	2·60
Watendlath		1600	3·50	1·97	2·47
Stonethwaite via Coldbarrow Fell		2100	3·25	2·13	2·70
Stonethwaite via Lining Crag		2100	3·25	2·13	2·70
25 WALLA CRAG	1234				
Keswick		1000	2·50	1·33	1·67
Borrowdale road		950	1·00	0·81	1·03

THE SOUTHERN FELLS

Natural Boundaries

MILES
0 1 2 3 4

The Fells
in order of
altitude

1: SCAFELL PIKE
2: SCAFELL
3: GREAT END
4: BOWFELL
5: ESK PIKE
6: CRINKLE CRAGS
7: LINGMELL
8: CONISTON OLD MAN
9: SWIRL HOW
10: BRIM FELL
11: GREAT CARRS
12: ALLEN CRAGS
13: GLARAMARA
14: DOW CRAG
15: GREY FRIAR
16: WETHERLAM
17: SLIGHT SIDE
18: PIKE O' BLISCO
19: COLD PIKE
20: HARTER FELL

21: ROSSETT PIKE
22: ILLGILL HEAD
23: SEATHWAITE FELL
24: ROSTHWAITE FELL
25: HARD KNOTT
26: WHIN RIGG
27: GREEN CRAG
28: LINGMOOR FELL
29: BLACK FELL
30: HOLME FELL

Altitude
of fells

• below 1500'
▲ 1500'-2000'
▲ 2001'-2500'
▲ 2501'-3000'
▲ over 3000'

THE SOUTHERN FELLS

in the order of their appearance in this book

over 3000'	2501-3000'	2001-2500'	1500-2000'	below 1500'		Altitude in feet
	12				ALLEN CRAGS	2572
				29	BLACK FELL	1056
	4				BOWFELL	2960
	10				BRIM FELL	2611
		19			COLD PIKE	2259
	8				CONISTON OLD MAN	2633
	6				CRINKLE CRAGS	2816
	14				DOW CRAG	2555
	5				ESK PIKE	2903
	13				GLARAMARA	2560
	11				GREAT CARRS	2575
	3				GREAT END	2984
			27		GREEN CRAG	1602
	15				GREY FRIAR	2536
			25		HARD KNOTT	1803
		20			HARTER FELL	2140
				30	HOLME FELL	1040
			22		ILLGILL HEAD	1983
	7				LINGMELL	2649
			28		LINGMOOR FELL	1530
		18			PIKE O' BLISCO	2304
		21			ROSSETT PIKE	2106
			24		ROSTHWAITE FELL	1807
2					SCAFELL	3162
1					SCAFELL PIKE	3210
			23		SEATHWAITE FELL	1970
		17			SLIGHT SIDE	2499
	9				SWIRL HOW	2630
	16				WETHERLAM	2502
				26	WHIN RIGG	1755
2	14	5	7	2		

30

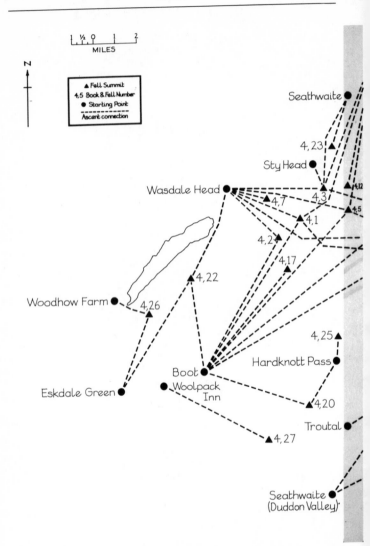

MILES

▲ Fell Summit
4,5 Book & Fell Number
● Starting Point
----- Ascent connection

N

Seathwaite ●

4,23 ▲

Sty Head ●

Wasdale Head ●

4,7 ▲   4,3 ▲   ▲ 4,12

▲ 4,1   ▲ 4,5

4,2 ▲

4,17 ▲

▲ 4,22

Woodhow Farm ●

4,26 ▲

4,25 ▲

Hardknott Pass ●

Boot ●

● Woolpack
   Inn

▲ 4,20

Eskdale Green ●

Troutal ●

▲ 4,27

Seathwaite ●
(Duddon Valley)

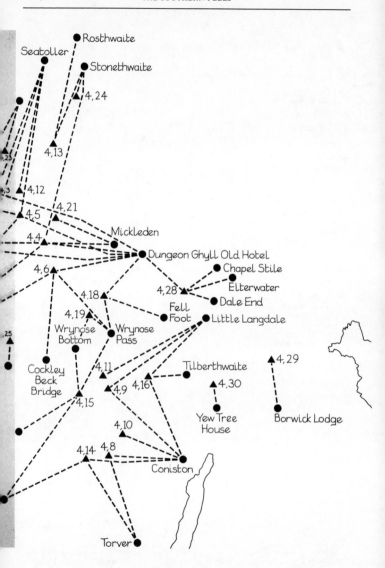

FELL NUMBER & FELL NAME STARTING POINT & ROUTE	HEIGHT ABOVE SEA LEVEL (feet)	HEIGHT OF ASCENT (feet)	DISTANCE OF ASCENT (miles)	ASCENT TIME FASTER (hours)	ASCENT TIME SLOWER (hours)
12 ALLEN CRAGS	2572				
Seatoller direct		2250	4·50	2·63	3·30
Seatoller via Allen Gill		2250	4·00	2·46	3·10
29 BLACK FELL	1056				
Borwick Lodge via Iron Keld *		600	1·33	0·74	0·93
4 BOWFELL	2960				
Dungeon Ghyll Old Hotel direct		2700	3·00	2·35	3·00
Dungeon Ghyll Old Hotel via Three Tarns		2700	3·25	2·43	3·10
Mickleden sheepfold		2500	1·75	1·83	2·37
Boot via Three Tarns		2900	7·50	3·95	4·93
Boot via Ore Gap		2900	8·00	4·12	5·13
Stonethwaite via Stake Beck		2650	6·50	3·49	4·37
Stonethwaite via Angletarn Gill		2650	6·50	3·49	4·37
Wasdale Head via ESK PIKE		3100	5·25	3·30	4·17
10 BRIM FELL	2611				
Coniston direct		2450	3·00	2·23	2·83
Coniston via Gill Cove		2450	3·50	2·39	3·03
19 COLD PIKE	2259				
Wrynose Bottom		1500	1·25	1·17	1·50
Wrynose Pass		1000	1·25	0·92	1·17
8 CONISTON OLD MAN	2633				
Coniston via Boo Tarn		2400	3·00	2·20	2·80
Coniston direct		2450	3·00	2·23	2·83
Coniston via Church Beck		2450	2·50	2·06	2·63
Torver direct		2350	3·25	2·26	2·87
Torver via Goat's Hause		2350	3·75	2·42	3·07
6 CRINKLE CRAGS	2816				
Dungeon Ghyll Old Hotel via Red Tarn direct		2600	4·00	2·63	3·33
Dungeon Ghyll Old Hotel via Red Tarn and Isaac Gill		2600	4·00	2·63	3·33
Dungeon Ghyll Old Hotel via Hell Gill and Three Tarns		2650	4·00	2·66	3·37
Dungeon Ghyll Old Hotel via The Band and Three Tarns		2650	4·00	2·66	3·37
Dungeon Ghyll Old Hotel via Oxendale		2550	3·50	2·44	3·10
Boot via Rest Gill		2650	7·50	3·83	4·77
Boot via Swinsty Gill		2650	7·50	3·83	4·77
Boot via Three Tarns		2650	8·00	3·99	4·97
Cockley Beck Bridge		2350	3·00	2·17	2·77
Wrynose Pass		1650	2·75	1·74	2·20

All ascents shown with an * following the Starting Points were not evaluated explicitly by Wainwright in his guidebooks but have been computed for the Gazetteer from data given therein.

FELL NUMBER & FELL NAME					
STARTING POINT & ROUTE	HEIGHT ABOVE SEA LEVEL (feet)	HEIGHT OF ASCENT (feet)	DISTANCE OF ASCENT (miles)	ASCENT TIME	
				FASTER (hours)	SLOWER (hours)
14 DOW CRAG	2555				
Torver via Walna Scar Pass *		2250	3·50	2·29	2·90
Torver via Goat's Hause		2250	3·75	2·38	3·00
Coniston via Walna Scar Pass *		2350	4·25	2·59	3·27
Coniston via Goat's Hause		2350	4·00	2·51	3·17
Seathwaite (Duddon Valley) via Seathwaite Tarn *		2300	4·50	2·65	3·33
Seathwaite (Duddon Valley) via Walna Scar Pass		2300	3·75	2·40	3·03
5 ESK PIKE	2903				
Boot via Lingcove Bridge		2800	8·50	4·23	5·27
Boot via Cam Spout *		2800	9·50	4·57	5·67
Wasdale Head		2700	4·25	2·77	3·50
Seatoller		2550	4·75	2·86	3·60
Dungeon Ghyll Old Hotel via Ore Gap		2800	4·25	2·82	3·57
Dungeon Ghyll Old Hotel via Esk Hause		2800	4·25	2·82	3·57
13 GLARAMARA	2560				
Rosthwaite via Comb Gill		2300	3·75	2·40	3·03
Rosthwaite via Thornythwaite Fell		2300	3·75	2·40	3·03
Stonethwaite via Langstrath and Tray Dub		2300	4·50	2·65	3·33
Stonethwaite via Langstrath and shepherd's track		2300	4·50	2·65	3·33
11 GREAT CARRS	2575				
Little Langdale village via Broad Slack		2350	4·00	2·51	3·17
Little Langdale village via Wet Side Edge		2350	4·00	2·51	3·17
3 GREAT END	2984				
Sty Head		1450	1·00	1·06	1·37
Wasdale Head via Sty Head		2800	3·25	2·48	3·17
Seathwaite via Sty Head		2650	3·25	2·41	3·07
Wasdale Head via Corridor Route		2750	4·00	2·71	3·43
Seatoller		2650	5·00	2·99	3·77
Dungeon Ghyll Old Hotel		2900	5·00	3·12	3·93
27 GREEN CRAG	1602				
Woolpack Inn via Crook Crag		1450	2·50	1·56	1·97
Woolpack Inn via Low Birker Tarn		1450	2·50	1·56	1·97
15 GREY FRIAR	2536				
Seathwaite (Duddon Valley)		2200	4·00	2·43	3·07
Troutal		2000	2·25	1·75	2·23
Wrynose Pass		1350	2·25	1·43	1·80
Wrynose Bottom *		1750	1·25	1·29	1·67
25 HARD KNOTT	1803				
Hardknott Pass		550	0·75	0·53	0·67

FELL NUMBER & FELL NAME STARTING POINT & ROUTE	HEIGHT ABOVE SEA LEVEL (feet)	HEIGHT OF ASCENT (feet)	DISTANCE OF ASCENT (miles)	ASCENT TIME FASTER (hours)	ASCENT TIME SLOWER (hours)
20 HARTER FELL	2140				
Boot		2000	3·50	2·17	2·73
Hardknott Pass		900	1·50	0·95	1·20
30 HOLME FELL	1040				
Yew Tree House *		750	1·00	0·71	0·90
22 ILLGILL HEAD	1983				
Wasdale Head		1750	4·00	2·21	2·77
Boot via old corpse-road *		1700	4·75	2·43	3·03
Eskdale Green via WHIN RIGG		2100	4·83	2·66	3·33
7 LINGMELL	2649				
Wasdale Head via The Shoulder		2450	2·50	2·06	2·63
Wasdale Head via Brown Tongue		2450	3·00	2·23	2·83
Wasdale Head via Piers Gill		2450	3·50	2·39	3·03
28 LINGMOOR FELL	1530				
Dungeon Ghyll Old Hotel direct		1250	2·00	1·29	1·63
Dungeon Ghyll Old Hotel via Side Pike		1500	2·50	1·58	2·00
Dungeon Ghyll Old Hotel via Bleatarn House		1250	2·00	1·29	1·63
Elterwater		1350	2·50	1·51	1·90
Chapel Stile		1350	2·50	1·51	1·90
Dale End		1100	1·50	1·05	1·33
18 PIKE O'BLISCO	2304				
Dungeon Ghyll Old Hotel via Wall End		2100	2·25	1·80	2·30
Dungeon Ghyll Old Hotel via Stool End		2100	2·50	1·88	2·40
Fell Foot via Little Langdale		1800	2·50	1·73	2·20
Wrynose Pass		1100	1·25	0·97	1·23
21 ROSSETT PIKE	2106				
Mickleden sheepfold via Rossett Gill		1600	1·50	1·30	1·67
Mickleden sheepfold via Littlegill Head		1600	1·50	1·30	1·67
24 ROSTHWAITE FELL	1807				
Stonethwaite		1500	1·50	1·25	1·60
2 SCAFELL	3162				
Wasdale Head via Brown Tongue		3000	3·00	2·50	3·20
Wasdale Head via Green How		2950	3·75	2·73	3·47
Boot direct		3100	6·00	3·55	4·47
Boot via Cam Spout Crag		3050	7·25	3·94	4·93
Boot via Cam Spout and Foxes Tarn		3050	7·25	3·94	4·93
1 SCAFELL PIKE	3210				
Wasdale Head via Brown Tongue and Lingmell col		3000	3·50	2·67	3·40
Wasdale Head via Brown Tongue and Mickledore		3000	3·50	2·67	3·40

FELL NUMBER & FELL NAME STARTING POINT & ROUTE	HEIGHT ABOVE SEA LEVEL (feet)	HEIGHT OF ASCENT (feet)	DISTANCE OF ASCENT (miles)	ASCENT TIME FASTER (hours)	SLOWER (hours)
1 SCAFELL PIKE *(continued)*	3210				
Wasdale Head via Piers Gill and Lingmell col		3000	3·75	2·75	3·50
Wasdale Head via Piers Gill and Broad Crag col		3000	3·75	2·75	3·50
Seatoller via Sty Head		3000	6·00	3·50	4·40
Seatoller via Esk Hause		3200	5·50	3·43	4·33
Dungeon Ghyll Old Hotel via Esk Hause		3400	5·50	3·53	4·47
Boot via Mickledore		3100	7·50	4·05	5·07
Boot via Broad Crag col		3100	7·50	4·05	5·07
23 SEATHWAITE FELL	1970				
Seathwaite via Black Waugh		1550	1·75	1·36	1·73
Seathwaite via Styhead Gill		1550	1·75	1·36	1·73
17 SLIGHT SIDE	2499				
Boot		2350	4·75	2·76	3·47
9 SWIRL HOW	2630				
Coniston via Levers Hause		2450	3·50	2·39	3·03
Coniston via Swirl Hause		2450	3·50	2·39	3·03
Little Langdale via Greenburn Tarn		2400	4·00	2·53	3·20
Little Langdale via Long Crag levels		2400	4·00	2·53	3·20
16 WETHERLAM	2502				
Little Langdale via High Fellside Quarry		2250	3·00	2·13	2·70
Little Langdale via Greenburn Copper Works		2250	3·00	2·13	2·70
Tilberthwaite		2100	2·00	1·72	2·20
Coniston via Red Dell Copper Works		2350	3·50	2·34	2·97
Coniston via Lad Stones		2350	3·50	2·34	2·97
26 WHIN RIGG	1755				
Woodhow Farm		1600	2·00	1·47	1·87
Eskdale Green		1650	3·50	1·99	2·50

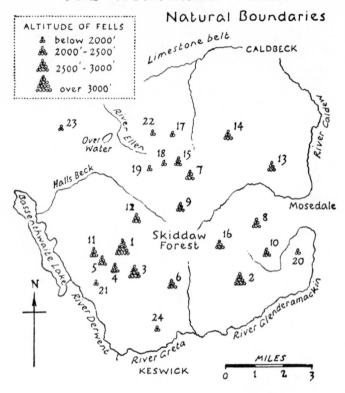

THE NORTHERN FELLS
Natural Boundaries

ALTITUDE OF FELLS
🔺 below 2000'
🔺 2000' - 2500'
🔺 2500' - 3000'
🔺 over 3000'

Limestone belt CALDBECK

River Ellen

23

Over Water

22 17 14

18 15 13

19 7

Halls Beck

12 9 Mosedale

11 1 8

5 3 16 10

4 21 2 20

6

24

N

Bassenthwaite Lake

River Derwent

River Greta

River Glenderamackin

River Caldew

Skiddaw Forest

MILES
0 1 2 3

KESWICK

1 : SKIDDAW
2 : BLENCATHRA
3 : SKIDDAW LITTLE MAN
4 : CARL SIDE
5 : LONG SIDE
6 : LONSCALE FELL
7 : KNOTT
8 : BOWSCALE FELL

9 : GREAT CALVA
10 : BANNERDALE CRAGS
11 : ULLOCK PIKE
12 : BAKESTALL
13 : CARROCK FELL
14 : HIGH PIKE
15 : GREAT SCA FELL
16 : MUNGRISDALE COMMON

17 : BRAE FELL
18 : MEAL FELL
19 : GREAT COCKUP
20 : SOUTHER FELL
21 : DODD
22 : LONGLANDS FELL
23 : BINSEY
24 : LATRIGG

THE NORTHERN FELLS

in the order of their appearance in this book

Reference to map opposite						
over 3000	2500-3000	2000-2500	below 2000			Altitude in feet
		12		..	BAKESTALL ..	2189
		10		..	BANNERDALE CRAGS ..	2230
			23	..	BINSEY ..	1466
	2			..	BLENCATHRA ..	2847
		8		..	BOWSCALE FELL ..	2306
			17	..	BRAE FELL ..	1920
		4		..	CARL SIDE ..	2420
		13		..	CARROCK FELL ..	2174
			21	..	DODD ..	1612
		9		..	GREAT CALVA ..	2265
			19	..	GREAT COCKUP ..	1720
		15		..	GREAT SCA FELL ..	2131
		14		..	HIGH PIKE ..	2157
		7		..	KNOTT ..	2329
			24	..	LATRIGG ..	1203
			22	..	LONGLANDS FELL ..	1580
		5		..	LONG SIDE ..	2405
		6		..	LONSCALE FELL ..	2344
			18	..	MEAL FELL ..	1770
		16		..	MUNGRISDALE COMMON	2068
1					SKIDDAW	3053
	3				SKIDDAW LITTLE MAN	2837
			20	..	SOUTHER FELL ..	1680
			11	..	ULLOCK PIKE ..	2230
1	2	13	8			
		24				

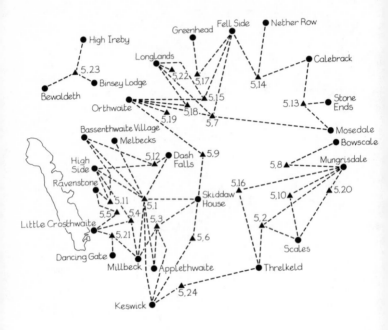

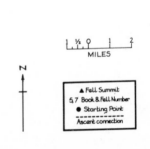

High Ireby

LongLands

Greenhead

Fell Side

Nether Row

Calebrack

5,23

Binsey Lodge

5,22

5,17

5,14

Bewaldeth

5,15

Stone Ends

Orthwaite

5,18

5,13

5,19

5,7

Mosedale

Bassenthwaite Village

Melbecks

Bowscale

5,12

Dash Falls

5,9

Mungrisdale

High Side

5,8

Ravenstone

Skiddaw House

5,16

5,20

5,11

5,1

5,10

5,5

5,4

5,2

Little Crosthwaite

5,21

5,3

Scales

Dancing Gate

5,6

Millbeck

Applethwaite

Threlkeld

Keswick

5,24

MILES

N

FELL NUMBER & FELL NAME STARTING POINT & ROUTE	HEIGHT ABOVE SEA LEVEL (feet)	HEIGHT OF ASCENT (feet)	DISTANCE OF ASCENT (miles)	ASCENT TIME	
				FASTER (hours)	SLOWER (hours)
2 BAKESTALL	2189				
Dash Falls via Birkett Edge		900	0·67	0·67	0·87
High Side		1750	4·67	2·43	3·03
Bassenthwaite village		1750	4·67	2·43	3·03
0 BANNERDALE CRAGS	2230				
Mungrisdale via east ridge		1500	2·00	1·42	1·80
Mungrisdale via The Tongue		1500	3·00	1·75	2·20
Scales direct		1550	2·50	1·61	2·03
Scales via Glendermackin col		1550	2·50	1·61	2·03
23 BINSEY	1466				
Bewaldeth		950	1·75	1·06	1·33
Binsey Lodge		620	1·00	0·64	0·81
High Ireby		700	1·50	0·85	1·07
2 BLENCATHRA	2847				
Threlkeld via Roughten Gill		2400	5·00	2·87	3·60
Threlkeld via Blease Fell		2450	2·50	2·06	2·63
Threlkeld via Blease Gill		2400	2·00	1·87	2·40
Threlkeld via Gategill Fell		2450	2·00	1·89	2·43
Threlkeld via Middle Tongue		2400	2·00	1·87	2·40
Threlkeld via Hall's Fell		2400	2·00	1·87	2·40
Threlkeld via Doddick Gill		2150	2·75	1·99	2·53
Scales via Doddick Fell		2150	1·75	1·66	2·13
Scales via Scaley Beck		2150	2·00	1·74	2·23
Scales via Sharp Edge		2250	2·75	2·04	2·60
Scales via Scales Fell		2150	2·25	1·82	2·33
Mungrisdale		2250	4·00	2·46	3·10
8 BOWSCALE FELL	2306				
Mungrisdale via old bridle path		1450	2·25	1·48	1·87
Mungrisdale via The Tongue		1470	2·25	1·48	1·88
Mungrisdale via Bullfell Beck		1450	2·25	1·48	1·87
Mungrisdale via east ridge		1550	2·50	1·61	2·03
Bowscale		1550	2·50	1·61	2·03
7 BRAE FELL	1920				
Greenhead		1100	2·00	1·22	1·53
Fell Side		1150	2·50	1·41	1·77
4 CARL SIDE	2420				
Little Crosthwaite		2070	2·25	1·78	2·28
Millbeck via White Stones		2100	1·75	1·63	2·10
Millbeck via cliffs of Doups		2100	1·75	1·63	2·10
Millbeck via Carsleddam		2100	1·75	1·63	2·10
Millbeck via Slades Beck		2100	1·75	1·63	2·10
High Side		2050	3·00	2·02	2·57

All ascents shown with an * following the Starting Points were not evaluated explicitly by Wainwright in his guidebooks but have been computed for the Gazetteer from data given therein.

| FELL NUMBER & FELL NAME | | | | ASCENT TIME | |
STARTING POINT & ROUTE	HEIGHT ABOVE SEA LEVEL (feet)	HEIGHT OF ASCENT (feet)	DISTANCE OF ASCENT (miles)	FASTER (hours)	SLOWER (hours)
13 CARROCK FELL	2174				
Mosedale direct		1450	2·00	1·39	1·77
Mosedale via east peak		1450	2·00	1·39	1·77
Stone Ends		1400	1·25	1·12	1·43
Calebrack		1300	3·50	1·82	2·27
21 DODD	1612				
Little Crosthwaite		1300	2·50	1·48	1·87
Dancing Gate		1320	1·50	1·16	1·48
Millbeck		1250	1·50	1·13	1·43
9 GREAT CALVA	2265				
Orthwaite direct		1500	3·75	2·00	2·50
Orthwaite via Brockle Crag		1500	3·75	2·00	2·50
Skiddaw House direct		900	2·00	1·12	1·40
Skiddaw House via Dead Beck		900	2·00	1·12	1·40
19 GREAT COCKUP	1720				
Orthwaite		950	2·00	1·14	1·43
15 GREAT SCA FELL	2131				
Fell Side via Roughton Gill		1300	3·00	1·65	2·07
Fell Side via Ward Steel		1300	3·00	1·65	2·07
Orthwaite direct		1400	3·50	1·87	2·33
Orthwaite via Brockle Crag		1400	3·50	1·87	2·33
Longlands direct		1550	2·50	1·61	2·03
Longlands via the bridle road		1550	3·00	1·77	2·23
14 HIGH PIKE	2157				
Fell Side		1350	2·50	1·51	1·90
Nether Row via Sandbed Mine		1300	2·50	1·48	1·87
Nether Row via Potts Gill Mine		1300	2·50	1·48	1·87
Calebrack		1300	2·75	1·57	1·97
7 KNOTT	2329				
Orthwaite direct		1500	3·75	2·00	2·50
Orthwaite via Brockle Crag		1500	3·75	2·00	2·50
Longlands		1700	3·50	2·02	2·53
Fell Side		1500	3·50	1·92	2·40
Mosedale		1650	4·50	2·33	2·90
24 LATRIGG	1203				
Keswick		950	2·50	1·31	1·63
Threlkeld		900	3·00	1·45	1·80
22 LONGLANDS FELL	1580				
Longlands		900	1·25	0·87	1·10
5 LONG SIDE	2405				
Little Crosthwaite via Longside Edge		2050	2·50	1·86	2·37
Little Crosthwaite via Gable Gill		2050	2·50	1·86	2·37
Ravenstone		2150	2·25	1·82	2·33

| FELL NUMBER & FELL NAME | | | | ASCENT TIME | |
STARTING POINT & ROUTE	HEIGHT ABOVE SEA LEVEL (feet)	HEIGHT OF ASCENT (feet)	DISTANCE OF ASCENT (miles)	FASTER (hours)	SLOWER (hours)
6 LONSCALE FELL	2344				
Keswick via Whit Beck		2150	3·75	2·33	2·93
Keswick via the central approach		2150	3·75	2·33	2·93
Keswick via shepherd's tracks		2150	4·25	2·49	3·13
Keswick via Lonscale Crags		2150	4·25	2·49	3·13
Skiddaw House to East Peak *		1000	1·75	1·08	1·37
Skiddaw House via Burnt Horse Ridge *		1000	1·75	1·08	1·37
18 MEAL FELL	1770				
Orthwaite direct		1050	3·00	1·52	1·90
Orthwaite via Brockle Crag		1050	3·00	1·52	1·90
Longlands via Lowthwaite Fell		1100	2·25	1·30	1·63
Longlands via Trusmadoor		1100	2·25	1·30	1·63
16 MUNGRISDALE COMMON	2068				
Mungrisdale via Glendermackin col *		1300	4·25	2·07	2·57
Threlkeld via Sinen Gill *		1500	4·25	2·17	2·70
Threlkeld via The Stake and Cloven Stone *		1500	4·50	2·25	2·80

Great Cockup

THE SUMMIT

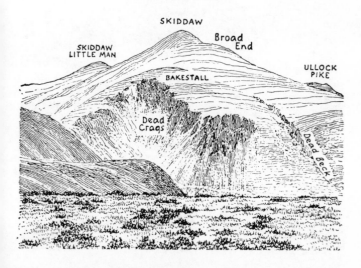

Skiddaw Little Man

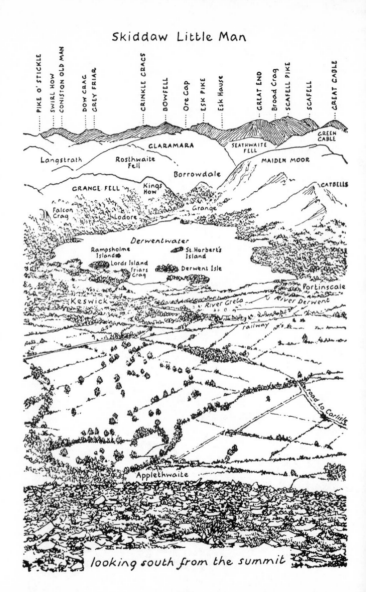

looking south from the summit

FELL NUMBER & FELL NAME STARTING POINT & ROUTE	HEIGHT ABOVE SEA LEVEL (feet)	HEIGHT OF ASCENT (feet)	DISTANCE OF ASCENT (miles)	ASCENT TIME	
				FASTER (hours)	SLOWER (hours)
1 SKIDDAW	3053				
Keswick		2850	5·50	3·26	4·10
Millbeck		2750	2·75	2·29	2·93
Applethwaite direct		2700	3·00	2·35	3·00
Applethwaite via Howgill Tongue		2700	3·00	2·35	3·00
Bassenthwaite village via north-west ridge		2800	4·00	2·73	3·47
Bassenthwaite village via Southerndale		2800	4·50	2·90	3·67
High Side via north-west ridge		2700	3·25	2·43	3·10
High Side via Southerndale		2700	3·75	2·60	3·30
Bassenthwaite village via Barkbethdale		2800	5·00	3·07	3·87
High Side via Barkbethdale		2700	4·25	2·77	3·50
Melbecks		2500	3·00	2·25	2·87
Dash Falls via the Skiddaw House road		1800	2·00	1·57	2·00
Skiddaw House via Sale How		1600	2·50	1·63	2·07
Skiddaw House via Hare Crag		1700	3·00	1·85	2·33
3 SKIDDAW LITTLE MAN	2837				
Millbeck via the two boulders		2500	1·75	1·83	2·37
Millbeck via south-west arete		2500	1·75	1·83	2·37
Applethwaite direct		2450	1·75	1·81	2·33
Applethwaite via Howgill Tongue		2450	2·00	1·89	2·43
Skiddaw House		1350	2·25	1·43	1·80
Keswick		2630	4·50	2·81	3·55
20 SOUTHER FELL	1680				
Mungrisdale		950	1·25	0·89	1·13
Scales		1000	2·00	1·17	1·47
11 ULLOCK PIKE	2230				
Bassenthwaite village		2000	3·25	2·08	2·63
High Side		1900	2·50	1·78	2·27
Ravenstone		1850	1·75	1·51	1·93

THE NORTH WESTERN FELLS

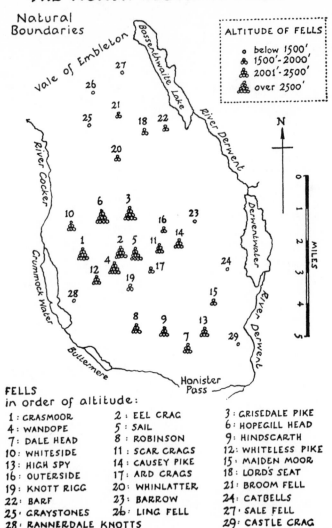

Natural Boundaries

Vale of Embleton

Bassenthwaite Lake

River Derwent

Derwentwater

River Cocker

Crummock Water

River Derwent

Buttermere

Honister Pass

ALTITUDE OF FELLS:

- ○ below 1500'
- 1500'- 2000'
- 2001'- 2500'
- over 2500'

N

MILES
0
1
2
3
4
5

FELLS
in order of altitude:

1: CRASMOOR	2: EEL CRAG	3: GRISEDALE PIKE
4: WANDOPE	5: SAIL	6: HOPEGILL HEAD
7: DALE HEAD	8: ROBINSON	9: HINDSCARTH
10: WHITESIDE	11: SCAR CRAGS	12: WHITELESS PIKE
13: HIGH SPY	14: CAUSEY PIKE	15: MAIDEN MOOR
16: OUTERSIDE	17: ARD CRAGS	18: LORD'S SEAT
19: KNOTT RIGG	20: WHINLATTER	21: BROOM FELL
22: BARF	23: BARROW	24: CATBELLS
25: GRAYSTONES	26: LING FELL	27: SALE FELL
28: RANNERDALE KNOTTS		29: CASTLE CRAG

THE NORTH WESTERN FELLS

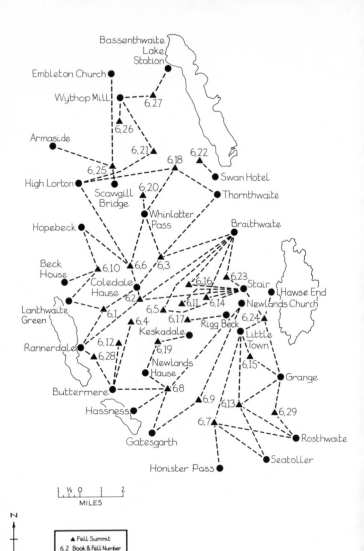

Bassenthwaite
Lake
Station

Embleton Church

Wythop Mill

6,27

6,26

Armaside

6,21

6,25

High Lorton

Scawgill
Bridge

6,20

6,18

6,22

Swan Hotel

Thornthwaite

Whinlatter
Pass

Braithwaite

Hopebeck

Beck
House

6,10

6,6

6,3

Coledale
Hause

6,2

6,16

6,23

Stair

Hawse End

Lanthwaite
Green

6,1

6,5

6,11

6,14

Newlands Church

6,17

6,4

Keskadale

Rigg Beck

6,24

Little
Town

Rannerdale

6,12

6,19

Newlands
Hause

6,15

Grange

6,28

Buttermere

6,8

6,9

6,13

Hassness

6,29

Gatesgarth

6,7

Rosthwaite

Seatoller

Honister Pass

½   0   1   2
MILES

N

▲ Fell Summit
6,2 Book & Fell Number
● Starting Point
- - - - Ascent connection

FELL NUMBER & FELL NAME

STARTING POINT & ROUTE	HEIGHT ABOVE SEA LEVEL (feet)	HEIGHT OF ASCENT (feet)	DISTANCE OF ASCENT (miles)	ASCENT TIME FASTER (hours)	ASCENT TIME SLOWER (hours)
17 ARD CRAGS	1860				
Rigg Beck		1350	1·50	1·18	1·50
22 BARF	1536				
Thornthwaite, Swan Hotel via Beckstones Plantation		1220	1·00	0·94	1·21
Thornthwaite, Swan Hotel via The Bishop		1200	0·75	0·85	1·10
23 BARROW	1494				
Braithwaite direct		1250	1·50	1·13	1·43
Braithwaite via Barrow door *		1250	2·00	1·29	1·63
Stair		1200	2·25	1·35	1·70
21 BROOM FELL	1670				
Wythop Mill		1450	4·00	2·06	2·57
High Lorton		1400	3·00	1·70	2·13
29 CASTLE CRAG	985				
Grange		700	1·50	0·85	1·07
Rosthwaite		700	1·50	0·85	1·07
24 CATBELLS	1481				
Hawse End		1250	1·50	1·13	1·43
Grange		1250	2·00	1·29	1·63
Stair via Skelgill		1200	1·33	1·04	1·33
Little Town		950	1·33	0·92	1·17
14 CAUSEY PIKE	2035				
Stair direct		1750	1·50	1·38	1·77
Stair via Rowling End		1750	1·50	1·38	1·77
Braithwaite via Sail Pass		2150	4·50	2·58	3·23
Braithwaite direct		2150	4·50	2·58	3·23
7 DALE HEAD	2473				
Little Town via Dalehead Tarn		2000	4·00	2·33	2·93
Little Town via Copper Mine		2000	3·50	2·17	2·73
Honister Pass		1300	1·25	1·07	1·37
Seatoller		2150	3·25	2·16	2·73
Rosthwaite		2250	3·75	2·38	3·00
2 EEL CRAG	2749				
Rannerdale		2400	2·50	2·03	2·60
Stair via Causey Pike		2850	3·40	2·56	3·26
Stair via the mine road		2700	3·50	2·52	3·20
Braithwaite via Tower Ridge		2500	3·75	2·50	3·17
Braithwaite via Shelf Route		2500	4·00	2·58	3·27
Coledale Hause direct		850	1·00	0·76	0·97
Coledale Hause via the pools		850	1·00	0·76	0·97

All ascents shown with an * following the Starting Points were not evaluated explicitly by Wainwright in his guidebooks but have been computed for the Gazetteer from data given therein.

FELL NUMBER & FELL NAME STARTING POINT & ROUTE	HEIGHT ABOVE SEA LEVEL (feet)	HEIGHT OF ASCENT (feet)	DISTANCE OF ASCENT (miles)	ASCENT TIME FASTER (hours)	ASCENT TIME SLOWER (hours)
1 GRASMOOR	2791				
Lanthwaite Green via Dove Crags		2300	2·00	1·82	2·33
Lanthwaite Green direct		2300	1·50	1·65	2·13
Rannerdale via Red Gill		2430	1·25	1·63	2·12
Rannerdale via Lad Hows		2450	1·75	1·81	2·33
Coledale Hause		850	1·25	0·84	1·07
25 GRAYSTONES	1476				
Embleton Church		1200	2·50	1·43	1·80
Armaside direct		1200	2·75	1·52	1·90
Armaside via Kirk Fell		1200	2·75	1·52	1·90
Scawgill Bridge		900	0·75	0·70	0·90
3 GRISEDALE PIKE	2593				
Braithwaite		2400	3·00	2·20	2·80
Thornthwaite via north-east ridge		2350	3·25	2·26	2·87
Thornthwaite via north ridge		2400	3·75	2·45	3·10
Whinlatter Pass		1600	2·25	1·55	1·97
Coledale Hause		700	1·25	0·77	0·97
13 HIGH SPY	2143				
Grange via High White Rake		1950	2·00	1·64	2·10
Grange via Narrow Moor		1950	2·50	1·81	2·30
Seatoller		1800	2·50	1·73	2·20
Rosthwaite		1900	2·50	1·78	2·27
Little Town		1650	4·00	2·16	2·70
9 HINDSCARTH	2385				
Newlands Church		2000	2·50	1·83	2·33
Gatesgarth via Littledale Edge		2050	3·00	2·02	2·57
Gatesgarth via Hindscarth Edge		2050	3·00	2·02	2·57
6 HOPEGILL HEAD	2525				
Coledale Hause via Sand Hill		600	0·75	0·55	0·70
Coledale Hause via Hobcarton Crag		600	0·75	0·55	0·70
Whinlatter Pass		1850	2·50	1·76	2·23
High Lorton		2450	3·75	2·48	3·13
Hopebeck		2150	2·50	1·91	2·43
19 KNOTT RIGG	1790				
Newlands Hause		720	1·00	0·69	0·88
Keskadale direct		1000	1·25	0·92	1·17
Keskadale via the ridge		1000	1·25	0·92	1·17
Keskadale via Ill Gill		1000	1·25	0·92	1·17
26 LING FELL	1224				
Wythop Mill		850	1·50	0·93	1·17
18 LORD'S SEAT	1811				
Thornthwaite		1550	2·50	1·61	2·03
High Lorton		1550	4·00	2·11	2·63
Whinlatter Pass		800	2·00	1·07	1·33

FELL NUMBER & FELL NAME					
STARTING POINT & ROUTE	HEIGHT ABOVE SEA LEVEL (feet)	HEIGHT OF ASCENT (feet)	DISTANCE OF ASCENT (miles)	ASCENT TIME FASTER (hours)	SLOWER (hours)
15 MAIDEN MOOR	1887				
Grange via Manesty		1600	2·50	1·63	2·07
Grange via Peace How		1600	2·00	1·47	1·87
Little Town direct		1250	1·50	1·13	1·43
Little Town via Hause Gate		1250	2·00	1·29	1·63
16 OUTERSIDE	1863				
Stair		1550	2·25	1·52	1·93
Braithwaite		1650	2·50	1·66	2·10
28 RANNERDALE KNOTTS	1160				
Rannerdale		800	0·75	0·65	0·83
Buttermere		850	1·50	0·93	1·17
8 ROBINSON	2417				
Newlands Church via Scope Beck		2000	3·00	2·00	2·53
Newlands Church via High Snab Bank		2000	3·00	2·00	2·53
Newlands Hause		1400	1·25	1·12	1·43
Buttermere		2100	2·50	1·88	2·40
Hassness		1900	1·50	1·45	1·87
Gatesgarth		2050	3·00	2·02	2·57
5 SAIL	2530				
Stair		2200	3·00	2·10	2·67
Braithwaite		2350	3·50	2·34	2·97
27 SALE FELL	1170				
Bassenthwaite Lake Station direct		930	2·00	1·13	1·42
Bassenthwaite Lake Station via Dodd Crag		930	2·00	1·13	1·42
Wythop Mill		750	1·50	0·88	1·10
11 SCAR CRAGS	2205				
Stair		1950	3·00	1·98	2·50
4 WANDOPE	2533				
Buttermere via Third Gill		2250	2·75	2·04	2·60
Buttermere via the Addacomb Ridge		2250	3·50	2·29	2·90
Buttermere direct		2300	2·50	1·98	2·53
20 WHINLATTER	1696				
Whinlatter Pass		750	1·75	0·96	1·20
12 WHITELESS PIKE	2159				
Buttermere		1800	1·75	1·48	1·90
10 WHITESIDE	2317				
Hopebeck via Dodd		1950	2·25	1·73	2·20
Hopebeck via Cold Gill		1950	2·25	1·73	2·20
Hopebeck via Penn		1950	2·25	1·73	2·20
Beck House		1950	1·25	1·39	1·80
Lanthwaite Green		1850	1·50	1·43	1·83

THE WESTERN FELLS
Natural Boundaries

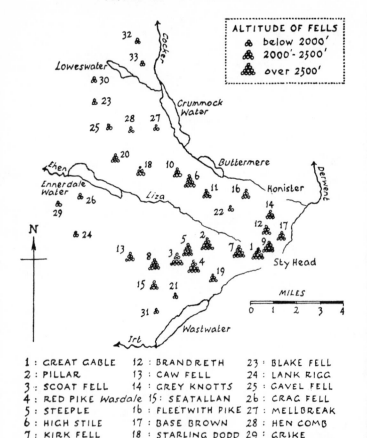

ALTITUDE OF FELLS
- below 2000'
- 2000'-2500'
- over 2500'

1 : GREAT GABLE	12 : BRANDRETH	23 : BLAKE FELL
2 : PILLAR	13 : CAW FELL	24 : LANK RIGG
3 : SCOAT FELL	14 : GREY KNOTTS	25 : GAVEL FELL
4 : RED PIKE *Wasdale*	15 : SEATALLAN	26 : CRAG FELL
5 : STEEPLE	16 : FLEETWITH PIKE	27 : MELLBREAK
6 : HIGH STILE	17 : BASE BROWN	28 : HEN COMB
7 : KIRK FELL	18 : STARLING DODD	29 : GRIKE
8 : HAYCOCK	19 : YEWBARROW	30 : BURNBANK FELL
9 : GREEN GABLE	20 : GREAT BORNE	31 : BUCKBARROW
10 : RED PIKE *Buttermere*	21 : MIDDLE FELL	32 : FELLBARROW
11 : HIGH CRAG	22 : HAYSTACKS	33 : LOW FELL

THE WESTERN FELLS

in the order of
their appearance
in this book

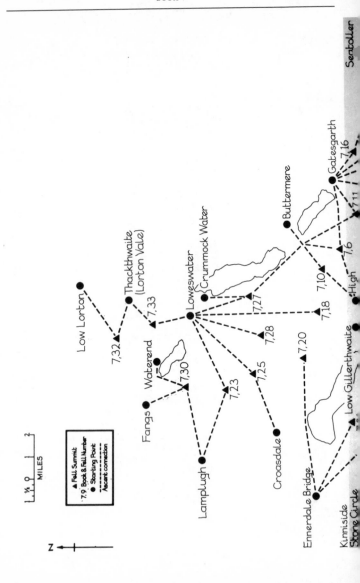

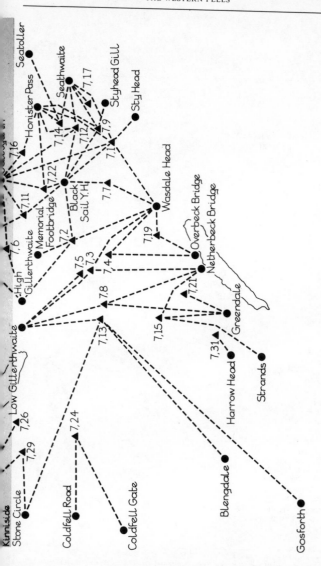

THE WESTERN FELLS

FELL NUMBER & FELL NAME STARTING POINT & ROUTE	HEIGHT ABOVE SEA LEVEL (feet)	HEIGHT OF ASCENT (feet)	DISTANCE OF ASCENT (miles)	ASCENT TIME	
				FASTER (hours)	SLOWER (hours)
17 BASE BROWN	2120				
Seathwaite		1750	1·50	1·38	1·77
23 BLAKE FELL	1878				
Loweswater via High Nook Tarn		1550	3·00	1·77	2·23
Loweswater via Carling Knott		1550	3·00	1·77	2·23
Lamplugh		1400	3·25	1·78	2·23
12 BRANDRETH	2344				
Honister Pass		1150	2·00	1·24	1·57
Gatesgarth via Dubbs Quarry		2000	3·00	2·00	2·53
Gatesgarth via Warnscale Bottom		2000	3·00	2·00	2·53
Black Sail Youth Hostel via Loft Beck		1400	1·75	1·28	1·63
Black Sail Youth Hostel via The Tongue		1400	1·75	1·28	1·63
Seathwaite		2000	2·00	1·67	2·13
31 BUCKBARROW	1410				
Harrow Head		1100	1·00	0·88	1·13
30 BURNBANK FELL	1580				
Waterend		1250	2·75	1·54	1·93
Fangs *		1100	2·75	1·47	1·83
Lamplugh		1000	1·75	1·08	1·37
13 CAW FELL	2288				
Blengdale		2100	5·50	2·88	3·60
Gosforth		2100	7·50	3·55	4·40
Kinniside Stone Circle		1850	6·00	2·92	3·63
Low Gillerthwaite		1950	2·75	1·89	2·40
26 CRAG FELL	1710				
Ennerdale Bridge via Anglers' Crag		1350	2·50	1·51	1·90
Ennerdale Bridge direct		1350	2·50	1·51	1·90
32 FELLBARROW	1363				
Low Lorton		1200	3·00	1·60	2·00
Thackthwaite (Lorton Vale) direct		1000	1·25	0·92	1·17
Thackthwaite (Lorton Vale) via Watching Crag		1150	2·00	1·24	1·57
16 FLEETWITH PIKE	2126				
Honister Pass via the old Drum House		1000	1·75	1·08	1·37
Honister Pass via the old tramway		1000	1·75	1·08	1·37
Gatesgarth		1750	1·13	1·25	1·62

All ascents shown with an * following the Starting Points were not evaluated explicitly by Wainwright in his guidebooks but have been computed for the Gazetteer from data given therein

FELL NUMBER & FELL NAME					
STARTING POINT & ROUTE	HEIGHT ABOVE SEA LEVEL (feet)	HEIGHT OF ASCENT (feet)	DISTANCE OF ASCENT (miles)	ASCENT TIME	
				FASTER (hours)	SLOWER (hours)
25 GAVEL FELL	1720				
Loweswater via the drove road		1400	3·00	1·70	2·13
Loweswater via Highnook Beck		1400	3·00	1·70	2·13
Croasdale direct		1250	2·00	1·29	1·63
Croasdale via Banna Fell		1250	2·00	1·29	1·63
20 GREAT BORNE	2019				
Ennerdale Bridge via Floutern Pass		1600	4·00	2·13	2·67
Ennerdale Bridge direct		1600	4·00	2·13	2·67
1 GREAT GABLE	2949				
Seathwaite direct		2700	2·75	2·27	2·90
Sty Head		1350	1·00	1·01	1·30
Wasdale Head via Sty Head		2750	3·25	2·46	3·13
Seathwaite via Sty Head and the Breast Route		2600	3·25	2·38	3·03
Seathwaite via Aaron Slack and Windy Gap		2600	3·25	2·38	3·03
Honister Pass via GREEN GABLE		1950	3·00	1·98	2·50
Honister Pass via Beck Head		1950	3·00	1·98	2·50
Gatesgarth via GREEN GABLE		2800	4·00	2·73	3·47
Gatesgarth via Beck Head		2800	4·00	2·73	3·47
Black Sail Youth Hostel via Windy Gap		2000	2·25	1·75	2·23
Black Sail Youth Hostel via Beck Head		2000	2·25	1·75	2·23
Wasdale Head via Gavel Neese and Beck Head		2700	2·50	2·18	2·80
Wasdale Head via Gavel Neese and Moses' Finger		2700	2·50	2·18	2·80
9 GREEN GABLE	2603				
Honister Pass		1550	2·50	1·61	2·03
Seathwaite		2250	2·25	1·88	2·40
Styhead Gill via Aaron Slack		1200	0·75	0·85	1·10
Styhead Gill via Mitchell Cove		1200	0·75	0·85	1·10
Black Sail Youth Hostel via The Tongue		1650	2·25	1·57	2·00
Black Sail Youth Hostel via River Liza		1650	2·25	1·57	2·00
14 GREY KNOTTS	2287				
Seathwaite		1900	1·50	1·45	1·87
Seatoller		1950	2·50	1·81	2·30
Honister Pass direct		1150	1·00	0·91	1·17
Honister Pass via the old Drum House *		1150	1·25	0·99	1·27
29 GRIKE	1596				
Kinniside Stone Circle		850	2·00	1·09	1·37
Ennerdale Bridge		1250	2·50	1·46	1·83
8 HAYCOCK	2618				
Greendale		2500	4·25	2·67	3·37
Netherbeck Bridge via Little Lad Crag		2400	4·00	2·53	3·20
Netherbeck Bridge via Ladcrag Beck		2400	4·00	2·53	3·20
Low Gillerthwaite		2300	3·00	2·15	2·73

FELL NUMBER & FELL NAME STARTING POINT & ROUTE	HEIGHT ABOVE SEA LEVEL (feet)	HEIGHT OF ASCENT (feet)	DISTANCE OF ASCENT (miles)	ASCENT TIME FASTER (hours)	SLOWER (hours)
22 HAYSTACKS	1900				
Gatesgarth via Scarth Gap		1550	1·75	1·36	1·73
Gatesgarth via Warnscale		1600	2·75	1·72	2·17
Honister Pass		1050	2·25	1·27	1·60
Black Sail Youth Hostel		970	1·25	0·90	1·15
28 HEN COMB	1661				
Loweswater direct		1300	2·50	1·48	1·87
Loweswater via Little Dodd		1300	2·50	1·48	1·87
11 HIGH CRAG	2443				
Black Sail Youth Hostel		1500	1·75	1·33	1·70
Gatesgarth via Scarth Gap		2100	1·75	1·63	2·10
Gatesgarth direct		2100	1·75	1·63	2·10
Buttermere		2100	2·50	1·88	2·40
6 HIGH STILE	2644				
Buttermere direct		2350	2·25	1·93	2·47
Buttermere via north-east ridge		2350	2·25	1·93	2·47
Gatesgarth		2300	2·00	1·82	2·33
High Gillerthwaite		2200	2·50	1·93	2·47
7 KIRK FELL	2630				
Wasdale Head		2330	1·25	1·58	2·05
Black Sail Youth Hostel		1700	1·50	1·35	1·73
24 LANK RIGG	1775				
Coldfell road		1400	2·50	1·53	1·93
Coldfell Gate		1100	4·00	1·88	2·33
33 LOW FELL	1360				
Loweswater direct		1050	2·00	1·19	1·50
Loweswater via Darling Fell		1350	3·00	1·68	2·10
Thackthwaite (Lorton Vale) via the drove road		1250	2·00	1·29	1·63
Thackthwaite (Lorton Vale) via Watching Gill *		1250	1·50	1·13	1·43
27 MELLBREAK	1676				
Loweswater to the north top direct		1300	1·25	1·07	1·37
Loweswater to the north top via the scree *		1300	2·25	1·40	1·77
Loweswater to the north top via the valley path *		1300	2·25	1·40	1·77
Crummock Water to the north top		1350	0·75	0·93	1·20
Crummock Water to the south top		1450	1·00	1·06	1·37
Buttermere to the south top		1300	2·50	1·48	1·87
21 MIDDLE FELL	1908				
Greendale		1650	1·50	1·32	1·70

FELL NUMBER & FELL NAME					
STARTING POINT & ROUTE	HEIGHT ABOVE SEA LEVEL (feet)	HEIGHT OF ASCENT (feet)	DISTANCE OF ASCENT (miles)	ASCENT TIME	
				FASTER (hours)	SLOWER (hours)
2 PILLAR	2927				
Wasdale Head via Black Sail Pass		2700	4·50	2·85	3·60
Wasdale Head via Wind Gap		2700	3·25	2·43	3·10
Black Sail Youth Hostel via High Level Route		2100	3·00	2·05	2·60
Black Sail Youth Hostel direct		2000	2·75	1·92	2·43
High Gillerthwaite via Wind Gap		2500	3·25	2·33	2·97
High Gillerthwaite via the north-west ridge		2500	2·75	2·17	2·77
Memorial Footbridge		2250	1·25	1·54	2·00
10 RED PIKE (Buttermere)	2479				
Buttermere via Bleaberry Tarn		2150	1·75	1·66	2·13
Buttermere via Far Ruddy Beck		2150	2·25	1·82	2·33
Buttermere via Lingcomb Edge		2150	2·75	1·99	2·53
Buttermere via Scale Force		2200	4·00	2·43	3·07
High Gillerthwaite		2000	1·75	1·58	2·03
4 RED PIKE (Wasdale)	2707				
Overbeck Bridge via Dore Head		2500	3·00	2·25	2·87
Overbeck Bridge via Low Tarn		2500	3·00	2·25	2·87
Wasdale Head		2450	2·50	2·06	2·63
3 SCOAT FELL	2760				
Netherbeck Bridge direct		2550	4·25	2·69	3·40
Netherbeck Bridge via Scoat Tarn		2550	4·25	2·69	3·40
Wasdale Head		2500	3·00	2·25	2·87
Low Gillerthwaite direct		2400	3·00	2·20	2·80
Low Gillerthwaite via Deep Gill		2400	3·50	2·37	3·00
15 SEATALLAN	2266				
Strands		2150	4·00	2·41	3·03
Strands via BUCKBARROW		2150	4·50	2·58	3·23
Greendale		2050	2·00	1·69	2·17
Netherbeck Bridge		2100	3·00	2·05	2·60
18 STARLING DODD	2085				
Loweswater		1700	4·50	2·35	2·93
5 STEEPLE	2687				
Low Gillerthwaite		2350	3·00	2·17	2·77
19 YEWBARROW	2058				
Overbeck Bridge		1900	1·50	1·45	1·87
Wasdale Head		1900	2·50	1·78	2·27

CHAPTER 2

THE HIGHEST TO
THE LOWEST

Many walkers, when being strictly honest, will admit to being interested in the height above sea level of the hill or mountain being climbed. This is often irrespective of the height of ascent which, of course, is a much more significant indicator of the 'work done'. I know one person who is only interested in climbing the highest mountain of any country which he visits; as yet, he has not visited the Himalaya.

Some walkers who are conscious of the height above sea level will attempt only fells over 3000 feet, 2000 feet etc, and in Scotland this philosophy has led to the phenomenon known as 'Munro Bagging' which entails the systematic climbing of the 277 mountains which are over 3000 feet, and then ticking them off the list compiled by Sir Hugo T. Munro in 1891. The Lake District sports only four mountains over this height but has 127 over 2000 feet. Whether the reader is gripped with this desire to conquer the highest or not, there is usually some interest in knowing where the hill being climbed fits into the distribution of the 214 listed fells.

This chapter describes the ascents in descending height of fell order, starting with Scafell Pike (3210 feet) and ending with Castle Crag (985 feet). Within each fell, the starting points and routes appear in the descending order of height of ascent, and where two are the same the order will be further determined by the distance of ascent in descending order. The two selected assessments of ascent time also appear.

As has been shown in chapter one, each of the Pictorial Guides gives, on the double-page spread preceding the description of the first individual fell, a map of the area covered by the book and a small table named 'Altitude of Fells', *see* page 21. This table shows the number of fells which fall into each of five height bands although some of the height bands do not always apply and these are, naturally, excluded. The lowest band includes all fells under 1500 feet above sea level but only Castle Crag is lower than 1000 feet.

The bands defined by AW are used in the tables which follow, and of the 214 fells listed in the seven guide books:

27	are below 1500 feet
60	are 1500 to 2000 feet
71	are 2001 to 2500 feet
52	are 2501 to 3000 feet
4	are over 3000 feet above sea level

The distribution of the fell heights over the seven guide books is given in Table 7.

TABLE 7: **Distribution of Heights of Fells above Sea Level – by Book**

GUIDE BOOK NUMBER

FEET ABOVE SEA LEVEL	1	2	3	4	5	6	7	ALL
Below 1500	3	3	7	2	2	7	3	27
1500–2000	7	10	12	7	6	8	10	60
2001–2500	10	16	8	5	13	8	11	71
2501–3000	14	7	0	14	2	6	9	52
Over 3000	1	0	0	2	1	0	0	4
ALL FELLS	**35**	**36**	**27**	**30**	**24**	**29**	**33**	**214**

A more detailed analysis of the heights of the fells is given by looking at the 759 ascents of those fells and distributing them by their heights above sea level and between the seven guide books.

TABLE 8: **Distribution of Numbers of Ascents by their Height above Sea Level**

GUIDE BOOK NUMBER

FEET ABOVE SEA LEVEL	1	2	3	4	5	6	7	ALL
Below 1500	5	6	25	2	5	19	8	70
1500–2000	12	24	40	17	13	19	29	154
2001–2500	26	59	33	11	56	30	36	251
2501–3000	49	35	0	67	18	27	45	241
Over 3000	15	0	0	14	14	0	0	43
ALL FELLS	**107**	**124**	**98**	**111**	**106**	**95**	**118**	**759**

As I have noted earlier, 'quantity should not be confused with quality', and I am sure that many readers will share similar occasions to my happy returns to old but low favourites such as Loughrigg Fell (1101 feet) or Castle Crag (985 feet), and memories of a particularly exciting ascent of Blea Rigg (1776 feet) in snow and temperatures minus 8° Celsius. Equally thrilling, however, was the delight of the day when we missed Great End in the cloud and found ourselves almost at Scafell Pike which we decided to climb despite the lack of visibility on this dull October day. We were then rewarded with the joyful experience of the cloud clearing from the summit to reveal a stunning autumnal panorama. Indeed, so good was the view that we overlooked the time which had crept to almost 5 pm before we turned back; we reached Sty Head in the near dark and had to pick our way to Stonethwaite which we reached in the pitch black.

THE HIGHEST TO THE LOWEST
the fells listed in order of height above sea level

FELLS OVER 3000 FEET ABOVE SEA LEVEL

FELL NUMBER & FELL NAME

STARTING POINT & ROUTE	HEIGHT ABOVE SEA LEVEL (feet)	HEIGHT OF ASCENT (feet)	DISTANCE OF ASCENT (miles)	ASCENT TIME FASTER (hours)	ASCENT TIME SLOWER (hours)
4·1 SCAFELL PIKE	3210				
Dungeon Ghyll Old Hotel via Esk Hause		3400	5·50	3·53	4·47
Seatoller via Esk Hause		3200	5·50	3·43	4·33
Boot via Mickledore		3100	7·50	4·05	5·07
Boot via Broad Crag col		3100	7·50	4·05	5·07
Seatoller via Sty Head		3000	6·00	3·50	4·40
Wasdale Head via Piers Gill and Lingmell col		3000	3·75	2·75	3·50
Wasdale Head via Piers Gill and Broad Crag col		3000	3·75	2·75	3·50
Wasdale Head via Brown Tongue and Lingmell col		3000	3·50	2·67	3·40
Wasdale Head via Brown Tongue and Mickledore		3000	3·50	2·67	3·40
4·2 SCAFELL	3162				
Boot direct		3100	6·00	3·55	4·47
Boot via Cam Spout Crag		3050	7·25	3·94	4·93
Boot via Cam Spout and Foxes Tarn		3050	7·25	3·94	4·93
Wasdale Head via Brown Tongue		3000	3·00	2·50	3·20
Wasdale Head via Green How		2950	3·75	2·73	3·47
1·1 HELVELLYN	3118				
Grasmere		3050	6·50	3·69	4·63
Glenridding via the old pony-route and Keppel Cove		2750	5·50	3·21	4·03
Glenridding via Red Tarn and Swirral Edge		2750	4·50	2·88	3·63
Patterdale via Grisedale Tarn		2700	7·25	3·77	4·70
Patterdale via Ruthwaite cove and DOLLYWAGGON PIKE		2700	6·25	3·43	4·30
Patterdale via Red Tarn and Swirral Edge		2700	5·50	3·18	4·00
Patterdale via Striding Edge		2700	5·25	3·10	3·90
Patterdale via Nethermost Cove and NETHERMOST PIKE		2700	5·00	3·02	3·80
Thirlspot via the old pony-route		2600	4·00	2·63	3·33
Thirlspot via the 'White Stones' Route		2600	3·50	2·47	3·13
Thirlspot via Helvellyn Gill		2600	3·50	2·47	3·13
Wythburn via Birk Side		2550	2·75	2·19	2·80
Wythburn via old lead mine		2550	2·50	2·11	2·70
Wythburn via Whelpside Gill		2550	2·25	2·02	2·60
Wythburn via Comb Gill		2550	2·25	2·02	2·60

FELL NUMBER & FELL NAME STARTING POINT & ROUTE	HEIGHT ABOVE SEA LEVEL (feet)	HEIGHT OF ASCENT (feet)	DISTANCE OF ASCENT (miles)	ASCENT TIME FASTER (hours)	ASCENT TIME SLOWER (hours)
5·1 SKIDDAW	3053				
Keswick		2850	5·50	3·26	4·10
Bassenthwaite village via Barkbethdale		2800	5·00	3·07	3·87
Bassenthwaite village via Southerndale		2800	4·50	2·90	3·67
Bassenthwaite village via north-west ridge		2800	4·00	2·73	3·47
Millbeck		2750	2·75	2·29	2·93
High Side via Barkbethdale		2700	4·25	2·77	3·50
High Side via Southerndale		2700	3·75	2·60	3·30
High Side via north-west ridge		2700	3·25	2·43	3·10
Applethwaite direct		2700	3·00	2·35	3·00
Applethwaite via Howgill Tongue		2700	3·00	2·35	3·00
Melbecks		2500	3·00	2·25	2·87
Dash Falls via the Skiddaw House road		1800	2·00	1·57	2·00
Skiddaw House via Hare Crag		1700	3·00	1·85	2·33
Skiddaw House via Sale How		1600	2·50	1·63	2·07

FELLS 3000–2501 FEET ABOVE SEA LEVEL

4·3 GREAT END	2984				
Dungeon Ghyll Old Hotel		2900	5·00	3·12	3·93
Wasdale Head via Sty Head		2800	3·25	2·48	3·17
Wasdale Head via Corridor Route		2750	4·00	2·71	3·43
Seatoller		2650	5·00	2·99	3·77
Seathwaite via Sty Head		2650	3·25	2·41	3·07
Sty Head		1450	1·00	1·06	1·37
4·4 BOWFELL	2960				
Wasdale Head via ESK PIKE		3100	5·25	3·30	4·17
Boot via Ore Gap		2900	8·00	4·12	5·13
Boot via Three Tarns		2900	7·50	3·95	4·93
Dungeon Ghyll Old Hotel via Three Tarns		2700	3·25	2·43	3·10
Dungeon Ghyll Old Hotel direct		2700	3·00	2·35	3·00
Stonethwaite via Stake Beck		2650	6·50	3·49	4·37
Stonethwaite via Angletarn Gill		2650	6·50	3·49	4·37
Mickleden sheepfold		2500	1·75	1·83	2·37
7·1 GREAT GABLE	2949				
Gatesgarth via GREEN GABLE		2800	4·00	2·73	3·47
Gatesgarth via Beck Head		2800	4·00	2·73	3·47
Wasdale Head via Sty Head		2750	3·25	2·46	3·13
Seathwaite direct		2700	2·75	2·27	2·90
Wasdale Head via Gavel Neese and Beck Head		2700	2·50	2·18	2·80
Wasdale Head via Gavel Neese and Moses' Finger		2700	2·50	2·18	2·80
Seathwaite via Sty Head and the Breast Route		2600	3·25	2·38	3·03
Seathwaite via Aaron Slack and Windy Gap		2600	3·25	2·38	3·03

FELL NUMBER & FELL NAME					
STARTING POINT & ROUTE	HEIGHT ABOVE SEA LEVEL (feet)	HEIGHT OF ASCENT (feet)	DISTANCE OF ASCENT (miles)	ASCENT TIME	
				FASTER (hours)	SLOWER (hours)
7·1 GREAT GABLE *(continued)*	2949				
Black Sail Youth Hostel via Windy Gap		2000	2·25	1·75	2·23
Black Sail Youth Hostel via Beck Head		2000	2·25	1·75	2·23
Honister Pass via GREEN GABLE		1950	3·00	1·98	2·50
Honister Pass via Beck Head		1950	3·00	1·98	2·50
Sty Head		1350	1·00	1·01	1·30
7·2 PILLAR	2927				
Wasdale Head via Black Sail Pass		2700	4·50	2·85	3·60
Wasdale Head via Wind Gap		2700	3·25	2·43	3·10
High Gillerthwaite via Wind Gap		2500	3·25	2·33	2·97
High Gillerthwaite via the north-west ridge		2500	2·75	2·17	2·77
Memorial Footbridge		2250	1·25	1·54	2·00
Black Sail Youth Hostel via High Level Route		2100	3·00	2·05	2·60
Black Sail Youth Hostel direct		2000	2·75	1·92	2·43
1·2 NETHERMOST PIKE	2920				
Patterdale via Grisedale		2500	5·00	2·92	3·67
Wythburn		2400	2·00	1·87	2·40
1·3 CATSTYCAM	2917				
Glenridding via Redtarn Beck		2500	4·00	2·58	3·27
Glenridding via north-west ridge		2500	4·00	2·58	3·27
4·5 ESK PIKE	2903				
Boot via Cam Spout		2800	9·50	4·57	5·67
Boot via Lingcove Bridge		2800	8·50	4·23	5·27
Dungeon Ghyll Old Hotel via Ore Gap		2800	4·25	2·82	3·57
Dungeon Ghyll Old Hotel via Esk Hause		2800	4·25	2·82	3·57
Wasdale Head		2700	4·25	2·77	3·50
Seatoller		2550	4·75	2·86	3·60
1·4 RAISE	2889				
Glenridding direct		2500	4·00	2·58	3·27
Glenridding via Sticks Pass		2500	4·00	2·58	3·27
Stanah		2400	2·50	2·03	2·60
Thirlspot direct		2400	2·50	2·03	2·60
Thirlspot via Brund Gill		2400	2·50	2·03	2·60
1·5 FAIRFIELD	2863				
Grasmere via Little Tongue Gill		2650	4·25	2·74	3·47
Grasmere via Tongue Gill		2650	4·25	2·74	3·47
Patterdale via Greenhow End		2400	5·50	3·03	3·80
Patterdale via Deepdale Hause		2400	5·50	3·03	3·80
5·2 BLENCATHRA	2847				
Threlkeld via Blease Fell		2450	2·50	2·06	2·63
Threlkeld via Gategill Fell		2450	2·00	1·89	2·43

FELL NUMBER & FELL NAME STARTING POINT & ROUTE	HEIGHT ABOVE SEA LEVEL (feet)	HEIGHT OF ASCENT (feet)	DISTANCE OF ASCENT (miles)	ASCENT TIME FASTER (hours)	SLOWER (hours)
5·2 BLENCATHRA *(continued)*	2847				
Threlkeld via Roughten Gill		2400	5·00	2·87	3·60
Threlkeld via Blease Gill		2400	2·00	1·87	2·40
Threlkeld via Middle Tongue		2400	2·00	1·87	2·40
Threlkeld via Hall's Fell		2400	2·00	1·87	2·40
Mungrisdale		2250	4·00	2·46	3·10
Scales via Sharp Edge		2250	2·75	2·04	2·60
Threlkeld via Doddick Gill		2150	2·75	1·99	2·53
Scales via Scaley Beck		2150	2·00	1·74	2·23
Scales via Doddick Fell		2150	1·75	1·66	2·13
5·3 SKIDDAW LITTLE MAN	2837				
Keswick		2630	4·50	2·81	3·55
Millbeck via the two boulders		2500	1·75	1·83	2·37
Millbeck via south-west arete		2500	1·75	1·83	2·37
Applethwaite via Howgill Tongue		2450	2·00	1·89	2·43
Applethwaite direct		2450	1·75	1·81	2·33
Skiddaw House		1350	2·25	1·43	1·80
1·6 WHITE SIDE	2832				
Glenridding		2400	4·00	2·53	3·20
Thirlspot		2300	2·50	1·98	2·53
4·6 CRINKLE CRAGS	2816				
Boot via Three Tarns		2650	8·00	3·99	4·97
Boot via Rest Gill		2650	7·50	3·83	4·77
Boot via Swinsty Gill		2650	7·50	3·83	4·77
Dungeon Ghyll Old Hotel via Hell Gill and Three Tarns		2650	4·00	2·66	3·37
Dungeon Ghyll Old Hotel via The Band and Three Tarns		2650	4·00	2·66	3·37
Dungeon Ghyll Old Hotel via Red Tarn direct		2600	4·00	2·63	3·33
Dungeon Ghyll Old Hotel via Red Tarn and Isaac Gill		2600	4·00	2·63	3·33
Dungeon Ghyll Old Hotel via Oxendale		2550	3·50	2·44	3·10
Cockley Beck Bridge		2350	3·00	2·17	2·77
Wrynose Pass		1650	2·75	1·74	2·20
1·7 DOLLYWAGGON PIKE	2810				
Grasmere via Little Tongue Gill		2700	5·00	3·02	3·80
Grasmere via Tongue Gill		2700	5·00	3·02	3·80
Patterdale via Grisedale		2400	5·00	2·87	3·60
Dunmail Raise via Birkside Gill		2100	2·00	1·72	2·20
Dunmail Raise via Reggle Knott		2100	2·00	1·72	2·20
Dunmail Raise via Raise Beck		2100	2·00	1·72	2·20
1·8 GREAT DODD	2807				
Fornside		2300	2·50	1·98	2·53
Legburthwaite		2300	2·25	1·90	2·43
Dockray direct		2000	4·75	2·58	3·23
Dockray via Groove Beck		2000	4·75	2·58	3·23

FELL NUMBER & FELL NAME					
STARTING POINT & ROUTE	HEIGHT ABOVE SEA LEVEL (feet)	HEIGHT OF ASCENT (feet)	DISTANCE OF ASCENT (miles)	ASCENT TIME	
				FASTER (hours)	SLOWER (hours)
6·1 GRASMOOR	2791				
Rannerdale via Lad Hows		2450	1·75	1·81	2·33
Rannerdale via Red Gill		2430	1·25	1·63	2·12
Lanthwaite Green via Dove Crags		2300	2·00	1·82	2·33
Lanthwaite Green direct		2300	1·50	1·65	2·13
Coledale Hause		850	1·25	0·84	1·07
1·9 STYBARROW DODD	2770				
Stanah via Stanah Gill		2300	2·50	1·98	2·53
Stanah via Sticks Pass		2300	2·50	1·98	2·53
Dockray via Green Side		1900	5·50	2·78	3·47
Dockray via Deep Dale		1900	5·50	2·78	3·47
7·3 SCOAT FELL	2760				
Netherbeck Bridge direct		2550	4·25	2·69	3·40
Netherbeck Bridge via Scoat Tarn		2550	4·25	2·69	3·40
Wasdale Head		2500	3·00	2·25	2·87
Low Gillerthwaite via Deep Gill		2400	3·50	2·37	3·00
Low Gillerthwaite direct		2400	3·00	2·20	2·80
1·10 SAINT SUNDAY CRAG	2756				
Patterdale via east ridge		2300	4·00	2·48	3·13
Patterdale via Trough Head		2300	3·00	2·15	2·73
Patterdale via Thornhow End		2300	3·00	2·15	2·73
Grisedale Tarn		1000	1·75	1·08	1·37
6·2 EEL CRAG	2749				
Stair via Causey Pike		2850	3·40	2·56	3·26
Stair via the mine road		2700	3·50	2·52	3·20
Braithwaite via Shelf Route		2500	4·00	2·58	3·27
Braithwaite via Tower Ridge		2500	3·75	2·50	3·17
Rannerdale		2400	2·50	2·03	2·60
Coledale Hause direct		850	1·00	0·76	0·97
Coledale Hause via the pools		850	1·00	0·76	0·97
2·1 HIGH STREET	2718				
Patterdale		2450	5·50	3·06	3·83
Troutbeck		2350	6·00	3·17	3·97
Kentmere via Nan Bield Pass		2300	6·00	3·15	3·93
Kentmere via Hall Cove		2300	5·50	2·98	3·73
Kentmere via Lingmell End		2300	5·50	2·98	3·73
Hartsop		2300	3·75	2·40	3·03
Mardale Head via Rough Crag		2050	3·75	2·27	2·87
Mardale Head via Blea Water		2050	3·00	2·02	2·57
7·4 RED PIKE (Wasdale)	2707				
Overbeck Bridge via Dore Head		2500	3·00	2·25	2·87
Overbeck Bridge via Low Tarn		2500	3·00	2·25	2·87
Wasdale Head		2450	2·50	2·06	2·63

FELL NUMBER & FELL NAME STARTING POINT & ROUTE	HEIGHT ABOVE SEA LEVEL (feet)	HEIGHT OF ASCENT (feet)	DISTANCE OF ASCENT (miles)	ASCENT TIME FASTER (hours)	ASCENT TIME SLOWER (hours)
1·11 HART CRAG	2698				
Rydal via Rydal Head		2600	4·50	2·80	3·53
Rydal direct		2600	4·50	2·80	3·53
Patterdale via Wallend		2300	4·50	2·65	3·33
Patterdale via HARTSOP ABOVE HOW		2300	4·50	2·65	3·33
7·5 STEEPLE	2687				
Low Gillerthwaite		2350	3·00	2·17	2·77
4·7 LINGMELL	2649				
Wasdale Head via Piers Gill		2450	3·50	2·39	3·03
Wasdale Head via Brown Tongue		2450	3·00	2·23	2·83
Wasdale Head via The Shoulder		2450	2·50	2·06	2·63
7·6 HIGH STILE	2644				
Buttermere direct		2350	2·25	1·93	2·47
Buttermere via north-east ridge		2350	2·25	1·93	2·47
Gatesgarth		2300	2·00	1·82	2·33
High Gillerthwaite		2200	2·50	1·93	2·47
2·2 HIGH RAISE	2634				
Patterdale		2400	5·25	2·95	3·70
Hartsop		2250	3·50	2·29	2·90
Martindale		2100	5·00	2·72	3·40
Measand via Long Grain		1900	3·50	2·12	2·67
Riggindale via Mardale		1900	2·50	1·78	2·27
4·8 CONISTON OLD MAN	2633				
Coniston direct		2450	3·00	2·23	2·83
Coniston via Church Beck		2450	2·50	2·06	2·63
Coniston via Boo Tarn		2400	3·00	2·20	2·80
Torver via Goat's Hause		2350	3·75	2·42	3·07
Torver direct		2350	3·25	2·26	2·87
7·7 KIRK FELL	2630				
Wasdale Head		2330	1·25	1·58	2·05
Black Sail Youth Hostel		1700	1·50	1·35	1·73
4·9 SWIRL HOW	2630				
Coniston via Levers Hause		2450	3·50	2·39	3·03
Coniston via Swirl Hause		2450	3·50	2·39	3·03
Little Langdale via Greenburn Tarn		2400	4·00	2·53	3·20
Little Langdale via Long Crag levels		2400	4·00	2·53	3·20
7·8 HAYCOCK	2618				
Greendale		2500	4·25	2·67	3·37
Netherbeck Bridge via Little Lad Crag		2400	4·00	2·53	3·20
Netherbeck Bridge via Ladcrag Beck		2400	4·00	2·53	3·20
Low Gillerthwaite		2300	3·00	2·15	2·73

LL NUMBER & FELL NAME STARTING POINT & ROUTE	HEIGHT ABOVE SEA LEVEL (feet)	HEIGHT OF ASCENT (feet)	DISTANCE OF ASCENT (miles)	ASCENT TIME FASTER (hours)	ASCENT TIME SLOWER (hours)
10 BRIM FELL	2611				
Coniston via Gill Cove		2450	3·50	2·39	3·03
Coniston direct		2450	3·00	2·23	2·83
9 GREEN GABLE	2603				
Seathwaite		2250	2·25	1·88	2·40
Black Sail Youth Hostel via The Tongue		1650	2·25	1·57	2·00
Black Sail Youth Hostel via River Liza		1650	2·25	1·57	2·00
Honister Pass		1550	2·50	1·61	2·03
Styhead Gill via Aaron Slack		1200	0·75	0·85	1·10
Styhead Gill via Mitchell Cove		1200	0·75	0·85	1·10
12 DOVE CRAG	2603				
Ambleside via HIGH PIKE		2500	5·00	2·92	3·67
Ambleside via Scandale		2500	5·00	2·92	3·67
Ambleside via Scandale and High Bakestones		2500	4·75	2·83	3·57
Patterdale via Black Brow		2200	5·00	2·77	3·47
Patterdale direct		2200	5·00	2·77	3·47
3 GRISEDALE PIKE	2593				
Thornthwaite via north ridge		2400	3·75	2·45	3·10
Braithwaite		2400	3·00	2·20	2·80
Thornthwaite via north-east ridge		2350	3·25	2·26	2·87
Whinlatter Pass		1600	2·25	1·55	1·97
Coledale Hause		700	1·25	0·77	0·97
13 WATSON'S DODD	2584				
Legburthwaite		2050	1·75	1·61	2·07
3 RAMPSGILL HEAD	2581				
Patterdale		2200	4·50	2·60	3·27
Hartsop		2050	2·75	1·94	2·47
Mardale Head		1950	3·50	2·14	2·70
11 GREAT CARRS	2575				
Little Langdale village via Broad Slack		2350	4·00	2·51	3·17
Little Langdale village via Wet Side Edge		2350	4·00	2·51	3·17
12 ALLEN CRAGS	2572				
Seatoller direct		2250	4·50	2·63	3·30
Seatoller via Allen Gill		2250	4·00	2·46	3·10
4 THORNTHWAITE CRAG	2569				
Troutbeck via Threshthwaite Mouth		2200	5·50	2·93	3·67
Troutbeck via Scot Rake		2200	5·00	2·77	3·47
Hartsop via Hayeswater Gill		2000	3·75	2·25	2·83
Hartsop via GRAY CRAG		2000	3·25	2·08	2·63
Hartsop via Threshthwaite Mouth		2000	3·25	2·08	2·63
Kentmere Reservoir via Hall Cove		1650	2·25	1·57	2·00
Kentmere Reservoir via Gavel Crag		1650	2·00	1·49	1·90

FELL NUMBER & FELL NAME STARTING POINT & ROUTE	HEIGHT ABOVE SEA LEVEL (feet)	HEIGHT OF ASCENT (feet)	DISTANCE OF ASCENT (miles)	ASCENT TIME	
				FASTER (hours)	SLOWER (hours)
4·13 GLARAMARA	2560				
Stonethwaite via Langstrath and Tray Dub		2300	4·50	2·65	3·33
Stonethwaite via Langstrath and shepherd's track		2300	4·50	2·65	3·33
Rosthwaite via Comb Gill		2300	3·75	2·40	3·03
Rosthwaite via Thornythwaite Fell		2300	3·75	2·40	3·03
2·5 KIDSTY PIKE	2560				
Mardale Head		1900	3·00	1·95	2·47
4·14 DOW CRAG	2555				
Coniston via Walna Scar Pass		2350	4·25	2·59	3·27
Coniston via Goat's Hause		2350	4·00	2·51	3·17
Seathwaite (Duddon Valley) via Seathwaite Tarn		2300	4·50	2·65	3·33
Seathwaite (Duddon Valley) via Walna Scar Pass		2300	3·75	2·40	3·03
Torver via Goat's Hause		2250	3·75	2·38	3·00
Torver via Walna Scar Pass		2250	3·50	2·29	2·90
1·14 RED SCREES	2541				
Ambleside via Scandale Pass		2400	5·00	2·87	3·60
Ambleside via Kirkstone Pass road		2400	4·00	2·53	3·20
Patterdale		2200	6·50	3·27	4·07
Kirkstone Pass		1050	0·75	0·78	1·00
2·6 HARTER FELL	2539				
Kentmere via Nan Bield Pass		2200	5·25	2·85	3·57
Kentmere via KENTMERE PIKE		2200	4·25	2·52	3·17
Sadgill via Wren Gill		1950	4·25	2·39	3·00
Sadgill via Gatescarth Pass		1950	4·25	2·39	3·00
Mardale Head		1750	2·00	1·54	1·97
4·15 GREY FRIAR	2536				
Seathwaite (Duddon Valley)		2200	4·00	2·43	3·07
Troutal		2000	2·25	1·75	2·23
Wrynose Bottom		1750	1·25	1·29	1·67
Wrynose Pass		1350	2·25	1·43	1·80
6·4 WANDOPE	2533				
Buttermere direct		2300	2·50	1·98	2·53
Buttermere via the Addacomb Ridge		2250	3·50	2·29	2·90
Buttermere via Third Gill		2250	2·75	2·04	2·60
6·5 SAIL	2530				
Braithwaite		2350	3·50	2·34	2·97
Stair		2200	3·00	2·10	2·67
6·6 HOPEGILL HEAD	2525				
High Lorton		2450	3·75	2·48	3·13
Hopebeck		2150	2·50	1·91	2·43

FELL NUMBER & FELL NAME STARTING POINT & ROUTE	HEIGHT ABOVE SEA LEVEL (feet)	HEIGHT OF ASCENT (feet)	DISTANCE OF ASCENT (miles)	ASCENT TIME	
				FASTER (hours)	SLOWER (hours)
6 HOPEGILL HEAD *(continued)*	2525				
Whinlatter Pass		1850	2·50	1·76	2·23
Coledale Hause via Sand Hill		600	0·75	0·55	0·70
Coledale Hause via Hobcarton Crag		600	0·75	0·55	0·70
15 GREAT RIGG	2513				
Grasmere via Greenhead Gill		2300	3·00	2·15	2·73
Grasmere via STONE ARTHUR		2300	3·00	2·15	2·73
16 WETHERLAM	2502				
Coniston via Red Dell Copper Works		2350	3·50	2·34	2·97
Coniston via Lad Stones		2350	3·50	2·34	2·97
Little Langdale via High Fellside Quarry		2250	3·00	2·13	2·70
Little Langdale via Greenburn Copper Works		2250	3·00	2·13	2·70
Tilberthwaite		2100	2·00	1·72	2·20
7 CAUDALE MOOR	2502				
Troutbeck via St Ravens Edge		2350	6·00	3·17	3·97
Troutbeck via Threshthwaite Mouth		2350	6·00	3·17	3·97
Troutbeck via Woundale		2200	5·50	2·93	3·67
Troutbeck via Sad Gill		2200	5·00	2·77	3·47
Brothers Water		2000	2·50	1·83	2·33
Kirkstone Pass		1150	2·50	1·41	1·77

FELLS 2500–2001 FEET ABOVE SEA LEVEL

1 HIGH RAISE	2500				
Grasmere		2350	5·50	3·01	3·77
Dungeon Ghyll New Hotel		2250	2·50	1·96	2·50
Stonethwaite		2200	3·75	2·35	2·97
Wythburn		1950	5·00	2·64	3·30
17 SLIGHT SIDE	2499				
Boot		2350	4·75	2·76	3·47
8 MARDALE ILL BELL	2496				
Kentmere via Lingmell End		2100	4·75	2·63	3·30
Kentmere via Nan Bield Pass		2100	4·75	2·63	3·30
Mardale Head via Blea Water		1700	2·50	1·68	2·13
Mardale Head via Small Water		1700	2·00	1·52	1·93
16 HART SIDE	2481				
Dockray via Brown Hills		1600	4·00	2·13	2·67
Dockray via Dowthwaitehead		1600	4·00	2·13	2·67
10 RED PIKE (Buttermere)	2479				
Buttermere via Scale Force		2200	4·00	2·43	3·07
Buttermere via Lingcomb Edge		2150	2·75	1·99	2·53
Buttermere via Far Ruddy Beck		2150	2·25	1·82	2·33

FELL NUMBER & FELL NAME STARTING POINT & ROUTE	HEIGHT ABOVE SEA LEVEL (feet)	HEIGHT OF ASCENT (feet)	DISTANCE OF ASCENT (miles)	ASCENT TIME FASTER (hours)	SLOWER (hours)
7·10 RED PIKE (Buttermere) *(continued)*	2479				
Buttermere via Bleaberry Tarn		2150	1·75	1·66	2·1
High Gillerthwaite		2000	1·75	1·58	2·0
2·9 ILL BELL	2476				
Troutbeck via Hagg Gill		1700	3·75	2·10	2·6
Kentmere Reservoir		1500	0·75	1·00	1·3
Garburn Pass		1050	2·50	1·36	1·7
6·7 DALE HEAD	2473				
Rosthwaite		2250	3·75	2·38	3·0
Seatoller		2150	3·25	2·16	2·7
Little Town via Dalehead Tarn		2000	4·00	2·33	2·9
Little Town via Copper Mine		2000	3·50	2·17	2·7
Honister Pass		1300	1·25	1·07	1·3
7·11 HIGH CRAG	2443				
Buttermere		2100	2·50	1·88	2·4
Gatesgarth via Scarth Gap		2100	1·75	1·63	2·1
Gatesgarth direct		2100	1·75	1·63	2·1
Black Sail Youth Hostel		1500	1·75	1·33	1·7
2·10 THE KNOTT	2423				
Patterdale		1850	4·00	2·26	2·8
Hartsop		1850	2·00	1·59	2·0
5·4 CARL SIDE	2420				
Millbeck via White Stones		2100	1·75	1·63	2·1
Millbeck via cliffs of Doups		2100	1·75	1·63	2·1
Millbeck via Carsleddam		2100	1·75	1·63	2·1
Millbeck via Slades Beck		2100	1·75	1·63	2·1
Little Crosthwaite		2070	2·25	1·78	2·2
High Side		2050	3·00	2·02	2·5
6·8 ROBINSON	2417				
Buttermere		2100	2·50	1·88	2·4
Gatesgarth		2050	3·00	2·02	2·5
Newlands Church via Scope Beck		2000	3·00	2·00	2·5
Newlands Church via High Snab Bank		2000	3·00	2·00	2·5
Hassness		1900	1·50	1·45	1·8
Newlands Hause		1400	1·25	1·12	1·4
1·17 SEAT SANDAL	2415				
Grasmere via Little Tongue Gill		2200	3·50	2·27	2·8
Grasmere via Tongue Gill		2200	3·50	2·27	2·8
Grasmere via south ridge		2200	2·75	2·02	2·5
Dunmail Raise		1700	1·50	1·35	1·7

FELL NUMBER & FELL NAME					
STARTING POINT & ROUTE	HEIGHT ABOVE SEA LEVEL (feet)	HEIGHT OF ASCENT (feet)	DISTANCE OF ASCENT (miles)	ASCENT TIME	
				FASTER (hours)	SLOWER (hours)
3·2 SERGEANT MAN	2414				
Grasmere via Far Easedale		2200	5·50	2·93	3·67
Grasmere by Codale Tarn		2200	4·25	2·52	3·17
Grasmere via Easedale Tarn		2200	4·00	2·43	3·07
Dungeon Ghyll New Hotel direct		2200	2·25	1·85	2·37
Dungeon Ghyll New Hotel via Stickle Tarn		2200	2·00	1·77	2·27
Wythburn via Far Easedale		1850	5·00	2·59	3·23
5·5 LONG SIDE	2405				
Ravenstone		2150	2·25	1·82	2·33
Little Crosthwaite via Longside Edge		2050	2·50	1·86	2·37
Little Crosthwaite via Gable Gill		2050	2·50	1·86	2·37
3·3 HARRISON STICKLE	2403				
Grasmere via SERGEANT MAN and THUNACAR KNOTT		2450	5·50	3·06	3·83
Grasmere via BLEA RIGG and Stickle Tarn		2450	5·16	2·95	3·70
Stonethwaite via HIGH RAISE and THUNACAR KNOTT		2410	4·75	2·79	3·51
Stonethwaite via Langstrath, Stake Pass and PIKE O'STICKLE		2360	5·83	3·12	3·91
Dungeon Ghyll Old Hotel via Thorn Crag		2150	2·00	1·74	2·23
Dungeon Ghyll Old Hotel via The Ravines		2150	1·75	1·66	2·13
Dungeon Ghyll Old Hotel via Stickle Tarn		2100	2·25	1·80	2·30
Dungeon Ghyll New Hotel via Stickle Tarn		2100	1·75	1·63	2·10
Dungeon Ghyll New Hotel via Pike How		2100	1·50	1·55	2·00
·11 KENTMERE PIKE	2397				
Kentmere		1900	3·00	1·95	2·47
Sadgill		1850	3·00	1·93	2·43
·9 HINDSCARTH	2385				
Gatesgarth via Littledale Edge		2050	3·00	2·02	2·57
Gatesgarth via Hindscarth Edge		2050	3·00	2·02	2·57
Newlands Church		2000	2·50	1·83	2·33
·18 CLOUGH HEAD	2381				
Wanthwaite via Hause Well		1900	3·00	1·95	2·47
Wanthwaite direct		1900	2·00	1·62	2·07
·4 ULLSCARF	2370				
Stonethwaite via Coldbarrow Fell		2100	3·25	2·13	2·70
Stonethwaite via Lining Crag		2100	3·25	2·13	2·70
Wythburn via West Head		1800	3·50	2·07	2·60
Watendlath		1600	3·50	1·97	2·47

| FELL NUMBER & FELL NAME | HEIGHT ABOVE | HEIGHT | DISTANCE | ASCENT TIME | |
STARTING POINT & ROUTE	SEA LEVEL (feet)	OF ASCENT (feet)	OF ASCENT (miles)	FASTER (hours)	SLOWER (hours)
2·12 FROSWICK	2359				
Kentmere via the reservoir		1850	5·00	2·59	3·23
Troutbeck via Blue Gill		1850	3·75	2·17	2·73
3·5 THUNACAR KNOTT	2351				
Dungeon Ghyll New Hotel		2100	2·00	1·72	2·20
1·19 BIRKHOUSE MOOR	2350				
Patterdale via Grisedale		1900	3·50	2·12	2·67
Glenridding via Mires Beck		1900	2·00	1·62	2·07
Glenridding via north-east ridge		1900	1·50	1·45	1·87
7·12 BRANDRETH	2344				
Gatesgarth via Dubbs Quarry		2000	3·00	2·00	2·53
Gatesgarth via Warnscale Bottom		2000	3·00	2·00	2·53
Seathwaite		2000	2·00	1·67	2·13
Black Sail Youth Hostel via Loft Beck		1400	1·75	1·28	1·63
Black Sail Youth Hostel via The Tongue		1400	1·75	1·28	1·63
Honister Pass		1150	2·00	1·24	1·57
5·6 LONSCALE FELL	2344				
Keswick via shepherd's tracks		2150	4·25	2·49	3·13
Keswick via Lonscale Crags		2150	4·25	2·49	3·13
Keswick via Whit Beck		2150	3·75	2·33	2·93
Keswick via the central approach		2150	3·75	2·33	2·93
Skiddaw House to East Peak		1000	1·75	1·08	1·37
Skiddaw House via Burnt Horse Ridge		1000	1·75	1·08	1·37
2·13 BRANSTREE	2333				
Sadgill		1750	3·50	2·04	2·57
Haweswater Hotel		1500	3·00	1·75	2·20
Mardale Head		1500	1·50	1·25	1·60
Mardale road		1500	1·50	1·25	1·60
5·7 KNOTT	2329				
Longlands		1700	3·50	2·02	2·53
Mosedale		1650	4·50	2·33	2·90
Orthwaite direct		1500	3·75	2·00	2·50
Orthwaite via Brockle Crag		1500	3·75	2·00	2·50
Fell Side		1500	3·50	1·92	2·40
3·6 PIKE O'STICKLE	2323				
Mickleden via Troughton Beck		2000	3·25	2·08	2·63
Dungeon Ghyll Old Hotel via Mickleden		2000	1·75	1·58	2·03
Stake Pass		800	1·33	0·84	1·07
6·10 WHITESIDE	2317				
Hopebeck via Dodd		1950	2·25	1·73	2·20
Hopebeck via Cold Gill		1950	2·25	1·73	2·20
Hopebeck via Penn		1950	2·25	1·73	2·20
Beck House		1950	1·25	1·39	1·80
Lanthwaite Green		1850	1·50	1·43	1·83

FELL NUMBER & FELL NAME STARTING POINT & ROUTE	HEIGHT ABOVE SEA LEVEL (feet)	HEIGHT OF ASCENT (feet)	DISTANCE OF ASCENT (miles)	ASCENT TIME FASTER (hours)	SLOWER (hours)
·14 YOKE	2309				
Kentmere via Garburn Pass		1800	3·00	1·90	2·4
Kentmere direct		1800	2·50	1·73	2·20
Garburn Pass		850	1·75	1·01	1·27
·8 BOWSCALE FELL	2306				
Bowscale		1550	2·50	1·61	2·03
Mungrisdale via east ridge		1550	2·50	1·61	2·03
Mungrisdale via The Tongue		1470	2·25	1·48	1·88
Mungrisdale via old bridle path		1450	2·25	1·48	1·87
Mungrisdale via Bullfell Beck		1450	2·25	1·48	1·87
·18 PIKE O'BLISCO	2304				
Dungeon Ghyll Old Hotel via Stool End		2100	2·50	1·88	2·40
Dungeon Ghyll Old Hotel via Wall End		2100	2·25	1·80	2·30
Fell Foot via Little Langdale		1800	2·50	1·73	2·20
Wrynose Pass		1100	1·25	0·97	1·23
·13 CAW FELL	2288				
Gosforth		2100	7·50	3·55	4·40
Blengdale		2100	5·50	2·88	3·60
Low Gillerthwaite		1950	2·75	1·89	2·40
Kinniside Stone Circle		1850	6·00	2·92	3·63
·7 PAVEY ARK	2288				
Dungeon Ghyll New Hotel via south-west ridge		2050	1·75	1·61	2·07
Dungeon Ghyll New Hotel via Easy Gully		2050	1·75	1·61	2·07
Dungeon Ghyll New Hotel via North Rake		2050	1·75	1·61	2·07
Dungeon Ghyll New Hotel via Jack's Rake		2050	1·50	1·52	1·97
·14 GREY KNOTTS	2287				
Seatoller		1950	2·50	1·81	2·30
Seathwaite		1900	1·50	1·45	1·87
Honister Pass via the old Drum House		1150	1·25	0·99	1·27
Honister Pass direct		1150	1·00	0·91	1·17
·15 GRAY CRAG	2286				
Hartsop via Threshthwaite Mouth		1950	4·00	2·31	2·90
Hartsop direct		1800	2·00	1·57	2·00
·16 REST DODD	2278				
Patterdale		1900	3·50	2·12	2·67
Hartsop		1700	2·00	1·52	1·93
·8 LOFT CRAG	2270				
Dungeon Ghyll New Hotel		2000	1·75	1·58	2·03
Dungeon Ghyll Old Hotel		2000	1·25	1·42	1·83

FELL NUMBER & FELL NAME STARTING POINT & ROUTE	HEIGHT ABOVE SEA LEVEL (feet)	HEIGHT OF ASCENT (feet)	DISTANCE OF ASCENT (miles)	ASCENT TIME	
				FASTER (hours)	SLOWER (hours)
7·15 SEATALLAN	2266				
Strands via BUCKBARROW		2150	4·50	2·58	3·23
Strands		2150	4·00	2·41	3·03
Netherbeck Bridge		2100	3·00	2·05	2·60
Greendale		2050	2·00	1·69	2·17
5·9 GREAT CALVA	2265				
Orthwaite direct		1500	3·75	2·00	2·50
Orthwaite via Brockle Crag		1500	3·75	2·00	2·50
Skiddaw House direct		900	2·00	1·12	1·40
Skiddaw House via Dead Beck		900	2·00	1·12	1·40
4·19 COLD PIKE	2259				
Wrynose Bottom		1500	1·25	1·17	1·50
Wrynose Pass		1000	1·25	0·92	1·17
1·20 SHEFFIELD PIKE	2232				
Glenridding via Lead Mine		1800	3·25	1·98	2·50
Glencoyne via HERON PIKE		1800	2·50	1·73	2·20
Glencoyne via Nick Head		1800	2·50	1·73	2·20
Glenridding via south-east ridge		1800	2·00	1·57	2·00
5·10 BANNERDALE CRAGS	2230				
Scales direct		1550	2·50	1·61	2·03
Scales via Glendermackin col		1550	2·50	1·61	2·03
Mungrisdale via The Tongue		1500	3·00	1·75	2·20
Mungrisdale via east ridge		1500	2·00	1·42	1·80
5·11 ULLOCK PIKE	2230				
Bassenthwaite village		2000	3·25	2·08	2·63
High Side		1900	2·50	1·78	2·27
Ravenstone		1850	1·75	1·51	1·93
2·17 WETHER HILL	2210				
Bampton		1750	5·00	2·54	3·17
Howtown		1750	3·00	1·88	2·37
Burn Banks via Measand Beck		1550	5·00	2·44	3·03
Burn Banks direct		1550	4·50	2·27	2·83
Martindale		1550	2·50	1·61	2·03
6·11 SCAR CRAGS	2205				
Stair		1950	3·00	1·98	2·50
2·18 LOADPOT HILL	2201				
Pooley Bridge		1800	6·00	2·90	3·60
Howtown		1750	2·25	1·63	2·07
Helton		1650	5·50	2·66	3·30
Bampton		1650	4·50	2·33	2·90
Askham		1600	6·50	2·97	3·67
Moor Divock		1300	4·50	2·15	2·67

FELL NUMBER & FELL NAME STARTING POINT & ROUTE	HEIGHT ABOVE SEA LEVEL (feet)	HEIGHT OF ASCENT (feet)	DISTANCE OF ASCENT (miles)	ASCENT TIME	
				FASTER (hours)	SLOWER (hours)
5·12 BAKESTALL	2189				
Bassenthwaite village		1750	4·67	2·43	3·03
High Side		1750	4·67	2·43	3·03
Dash Falls via Birkett Edge		900	0·67	0·67	0·87
2·19 TARN CRAG	2176				
Selside via GREY CRAG		1950	7·75	3·56	4·40
Hucks Bridge via GREY CRAG		1950	5·75	2·89	3·60
Jungle Cafe via GREY CRAG		1900	6·75	3·20	3·97
Rosgill via Swindale and Brunt Tongue		1730	7·00	3·20	3·95
Shap via Peat Hill and Brunt Tongue		1680	7·00	3·17	3·92
Sadgill		1600	2·00	1·47	1·87
Kendal-Shap road (summit) via GREY CRAG		1250	5·75	2·54	3·13
5·13 CARROCK FELL	2174				
Mosedale direct		1450	2·00	1·39	1·77
Mosedale via east peak		1450	2·00	1·39	1·77
Stone Ends		1400	1·25	1·12	1·43
Calebrack		1300	3·50	1·82	2·27
6·12 WHITELESS PIKE	2159				
Buttermere		1800	1·75	1·48	1·90
5·14 HIGH PIKE	2157				
Fell Side		1350	2·50	1·51	1·90
Calebrack		1300	2·75	1·57	1·97
Nether Row via Sandbed Mine		1300	2·50	1·48	1·87
Nether Row via Potts Gill Mine		1300	2·50	1·48	1·87
4·21 HIGH PIKE	2155				
Ambleside		2000	4·00	2·33	2·93
2·20 PLACE FELL	2154				
Sandwick via Nettleslack		1700	3·00	1·85	2·33
Sandwick via High Dodd		1700	2·50	1·68	2·13
Sandwick via Sleet Fell		1700	2·50	1·68	2·13
Sandwick via Scalehow Beck		1700	2·50	1·68	2·13
Patterdale via The Knight		1700	2·00	1·52	1·93
Patterdale via Boardale Hause		1700	2·00	1·52	1·93
Patterdale direct		1700	1·75	1·43	1·83
5·13 HIGH SPY	2143				
Grange via Narrow Moor		1950	2·50	1·81	2·30
Grange via High White Rake		1950	2·00	1·64	2·10
Rosthwaite		1900	2·50	1·78	2·27
Seatoller		1800	2·50	1·73	2·20
Little Town		1650	4·00	2·16	2·70
2·21 SELSIDE PIKE	2142				
Swindale Head via Mosedale path		1350	2·25	1·43	1·80
Swindale Head via north-east ridge		1200	1·50	1·10	1·40

FELL NUMBER & FELL NAME STARTING POINT & ROUTE	HEIGHT ABOVE SEA LEVEL (feet)	HEIGHT OF ASCENT (feet)	DISTANCE OF ASCENT (miles)	ASCENT TIME FASTER (hours)	SLOWER (hours)
4·20 HARTER FELL	2140				
Boot		2000	3·50	2·17	2·73
Hardknott Pass		900	1·50	0·95	1·20
5·15 GREAT SCA FELL	2131				
Longlands via the bridle road		1550	3·00	1·77	2·23
Longlands direct		1550	2·50	1·61	2·03
Orthwaite direct		1400	3·50	1·87	2·33
Orthwaite via Brockle Crag		1400	3·50	1·87	2·33
Fell Side via Roughton Gill		1300	3·00	1·65	2·07
Fell Side via Ward Steel		1300	3·00	1·65	2·07
7·16 FLEETWITH PIKE	2126				
Gatesgarth		1750	1·13	1·25	1·62
Honister Pass via the old Drum House		1000	1·75	1·08	1·37
Honister Pass via the old tramway		1000	1·75	1·08	1·37
7·17 BASE BROWN	2120				
Seathwaite		1750	1·50	1·38	1·77
4·21 ROSSETT PIKE	2106				
Mickleden sheepfold via Rossett Gill		1600	1·50	1·30	1·67
Mickleden sheepfold via Littlegill Head		1600	1·50	1·30	1·67
1·22 MIDDLE DODD	2106				
Hartsop Hall		1650	2·00	1·49	1·90
2·22 GREY CRAG	2093				
Selside		1700	7·00	3·18	3·93
Hucks Bridge		1700	5·00	2·52	3·13
Jungle Cafe		1650	6·00	2·83	3·50
Sadgill		1500	1·50	1·25	1·60
Kendal-Shap road (summit)		1000	5·00	2·17	2·67
1·23 LITTLE HART CRAG	2091				
Ambleside		2000	4·25	2·42	3·03
Patterdale via Scandale Pass		1700	5·00	2·52	3·13
Patterdale via HIGH HARTSOP DODD		1700	5·00	2·52	3·13
Patterdale via Hogget Gill		1700	5·00	2·52	3·13
7·18 STARLING DODD	2085				
Loweswater		1700	4·50	2·35	2·93
5·16 MUNGRISDALE COMMON	2068				
Threlkeld via The Stake and Cloven Stone		1500	4·50	2·25	2·80
Threlkeld via Sinen Gill		1500	4·25	2·17	2·70
Mungrisdale via Glendermackin col		1300	4·25	2·07	2·57

FELL NUMBER & FELL NAME STARTING POINT & ROUTE	HEIGHT ABOVE SEA LEVEL (feet)	HEIGHT OF ASCENT (feet)	DISTANCE OF ASCENT (miles)	ASCENT TIME FASTER (hours)	ASCENT TIME SLOWER (hours)
7·19 YEWBARROW	2058				
Wasdale Head		1900	2·50	1·78	2·27
Overbeck Bridge		1900	1·50	1·45	1·87
1·24 BIRKS	2040				
Patterdale via Trough Head		1600	2·50	1·63	2·07
Patterdale via Thornhow End		1600	1·75	1·38	1·77
5·14 CAUSEY PIKE	2035				
Braithwaite via Sail Pass		2150	4·50	2·58	3·23
Braithwaite direct		2150	4·50	2·58	3·23
Stair direct		1750	1·50	1·38	1·77
Stair via Rowling End		1750	1·50	1·38	1·77
7·20 GREAT BORNE	2019				
Ennerdale Bridge via Floutern Pass		1600	4·00	2·13	2·67
Ennerdale Bridge direct		1600	4·00	2·13	2·67
2·23 HARTSOP DODD	2018				
Hartsop		1450	1·25	1·14	1·47
Caudale Bridge via Caudale Beck		1400	1·50	1·20	1·53
Caudale Bridge direct		1400	0·75	0·95	1·23
1·25 HERON PIKE	2003				
Rydal via Blind Cove		1750	2·50	1·71	2·17
Rydal via NAB SCAR		1750	1·67	1·43	1·83
Grasmere, Swan Hotel via Alcock Tarn		1750	1·25	1·29	1·67

3·9 HIGH SEAT	1995				
Keswick via Dale Bottom		1750	6·50	3·04	3·77
Keswick via Ashness Bridge		1750	4·50	2·38	2·97
Dale Bottom via Mere Gill		1600	4·00	2·13	2·67
Dale Bottom via Litt's Memorial		1600	4·00	2·13	2·67
Ashness Bridge via the falls		1500	2·00	1·42	1·80
Ashness Bridge via Dodd		1500	2·00	1·42	1·80
Armboth		1450	2·00	1·39	1·77
Watendlath via HIGH TOVE		1200	2·00	1·27	1·60
Watendlath via Raise Gill		1200	2·00	1·27	1·60
4·22 ILLGILL HEAD	1983				
Eskdale Green via WHIN RIGG		2100	4·83	2·66	3·33
Wasdale Head		1750	4·00	2·21	2·70
Boot via old corpse-road		1700	4·75	2·43	3·03
4·23 SEATHWAITE FELL	1970				
Seathwaite via Black Waugh		1550	1·75	1·36	1·73
Seathwaite via Styhead Gill		1550	1·75	1·36	1·73

FELL NUMBER & FELL NAME STARTING POINT & ROUTE	HEIGHT ABOVE SEA LEVEL (feet)	HEIGHT OF ASCENT (feet)	DISTANCE OF ASCENT (miles)	ASCENT TIME FASTER (hours)	SLOWER (hours)
3·10 BLEABERRY FELL	1932				
Keswick via Dale Bottom		1650	5·50	2·66	3·30
Keswick direct		1650	3·50	1·99	2·50
Keswick via Brown Knotts		1650	3·50	1·99	2·50
Borrowdale road		1650	1·75	1·41	1·80
Dale Bottom		1600	3·00	1·80	2·27
2·24 SHIPMAN KNOTTS	1926				
Kentmere		1400	2·25	1·45	1·83
Sadgill		1300	1·50	1·15	1·47
5·17 BRAE FELL	1920				
Fell Side		1150	2·50	1·41	1·77
Greenhead		1100	2·00	1·22	1·53
7·21 MIDDLE FELL	1908				
Greendale		1650	1·50	1·32	1·70
7·22 HAYSTACKS	1900				
Gatesgarth via Warnscale		1600	2·75	1·72	2·17
Gatesgarth via Scarth Gap		1550	1·75	1·36	1·73
Honister Pass		1050	2·25	1·27	1·60
Black Sail Youth Hostel		970	1·25	0·90	1·15
6·15 MAIDEN MOOR	1887				
Grange via Manesty		1600	2·50	1·63	2·07
Grange via Peace How		1600	2·00	1·47	1·87
Little Town via Hause Gate		1250	2·00	1·29	1·63
Little Town direct		1250	1·50	1·13	1·43
2·25 THE NAB	1887				
Martindale		1300	4·00	1·98	2·47
7·23 BLAKE FELL	1878				
Loweswater via High Nook Tarn		1550	3·00	1·77	2·23
Loweswater via Carling Knott		1550	3·00	1·77	2·23
Lamplugh		1400	3·25	1·78	2·23
3·11 SERGEANT'S CRAG	1873				
Stonethwaite		1600	4·50	2·30	2·87
1·26 HARTSOP ABOVE HOW	1870				
Patterdale		1400	3·00	1·70	2·13
6·16 OUTERSIDE	1863				
Braithwaite		1650	2·50	1·66	2·10
Stair		1550	2·25	1·52	1·93
6·17 ARD CRAGS	1860				
Rigg Beck		1350	1·50	1·18	1·50

FELL NUMBER & FELL NAME STARTING POINT & ROUTE	HEIGHT ABOVE SEA LEVEL (feet)	HEIGHT OF ASCENT (feet)	DISTANCE OF ASCENT (miles)	ASCENT TIME FASTER (hours)	SLOWER (hours)
2·26 ANGLETARN PIKES	1857				
Patterdale via Freeze Beck		1400	1·75	1·28	1·63
Patterdale direct		1400	1·75	1·28	1·63
Martindale via Angle Tarn		1300	3·50	1·82	2·27
Martindale via Bedafell Knott		1300	3·50	1·82	2·27
2·27 BROCK CRAGS	1842				
Hartsop via the filter house		1300	2·00	1·32	1·67
Hartsop direct		1300	1·00	0·98	1·27
6·18 LORD'S SEAT	1811				
High Lorton		1550	4·00	2·11	2·63
Thornthwaite		1550	2·50	1·61	2·03
Whinlatter Pass		800	2·00	1·07	1·33
3·12 STEEL FELL	1811				
Grasmere		1650	3·25	1·91	2·40
Wythburn		1250	2·00	1·29	1·63
Dunmail Raise		1050	1·00	0·86	1·10
4·24 ROSTHWAITE FELL	1807				
Stonethwaite		1500	1·50	1·25	1·60
4·25 HARD KNOTT	1803				
Hardknott Pass		550	0·75	0·53	0·67
3·13 TARN CRAG	1801				
Grasmere via Stythwaite Steps		1650	3·50	1·99	2·50
Grasmere via Deer Bield Crag		1650	3·50	1·99	2·50
Grasmere via Sour Milk Gill		1600	3·00	1·80	2·27
Grasmere via the east ridge		1600	3·00	1·80	2·27
6·19 KNOTT RIGG	1790				
Keskadale direct		1000	1·25	0·92	1·17
Keskadale via the ridge		1000	1·25	0·92	1·17
Keskadale via Ill Gill		1000	1·25	0·92	1·17
Newlands Hause		720	1·00	0·69	0·88
3·14 BLEA RIGG	1776				
Grasmere		1600	3·50	1·97	2·47
Dungeon Ghyll New Hotel via Tarn Crag		1550	2·00	1·44	1·83
Dungeon Ghyll New Hotel via Whitegill Crag		1500	1·50	1·25	1·60
7·24 LANK RIGG	1775				
Coldfell road		1400	2·50	1·53	1·93
Coldfell Gate		1100	4·00	1·88	2·33
5·18 MEAL FELL	1770				
Longlands via Lowthwaite Fell		1100	2·25	1·30	1·63
Longlands via Trusmadoor		1100	2·25	1·30	1·63

FELL NUMBER & FELL NAME STARTING POINT & ROUTE	HEIGHT ABOVE SEA LEVEL (feet)	HEIGHT OF ASCENT (feet)	DISTANCE OF ASCENT (miles)	ASCENT TIME	
				FASTER (hours)	SLOWE (hours
5·18 MEAL FELL *(continued)*	1770				
Orthwaite direct		1050	3·00	1·52	1·90
Orthwaite via Brockle Crag		1050	3·00	1·52	1·90
3·15 CALF CRAG	1762				
Grasmere via Far Easedale		1650	4·50	2·33	2·90
Grasmere via Green Burn		1650	4·50	2·33	2·90
Wythburn		1250	4·00	1·96	2·43
1·27 GREAT MELL FELL	1760				
Troutbeck Old Railway Station		850	1·00	0·76	0·97
4·26 WHIN RIGG	1755				
Eskdale Green		1650	3·50	1·99	2·50
Woodhow Farm		1600	2·00	1·47	1·87
2·28 ARTHUR'S PIKE	1747				
Howtown		1200	3·50	1·77	2·20
7·25 GAVEL FELL	1720				
Loweswater via the drove road		1400	3·00	1·70	2·13
Loweswater via Highnook Beck		1400	3·00	1·70	2·13
Croasdale direct		1250	2·00	1·29	1·63
Croasdale via Banna Fell		1250	2·00	1·29	1·63
5·19 GREAT COCKUP	1720				
Orthwaite		950	2·00	1·14	1·43
2·29 BONSCALE PIKE	1718				
Howtown via the breast		1200	1·25	1·02	1·30
Howtown direct		1200	1·25	1·02	1·30
7·26 CRAG FELL	1710				
Ennerdale Bridge via Anglers' Crag		1350	2·50	1·51	1·90
Ennerdale Bridge direct		1350	2·50	1·51	1·90
1·28 HIGH HARTSOP DODD	1702				
Hartsop Hall		1200	0·75	0·85	1·10
6·20 WHINLATTER	1696				
Whinlatter Pass		750	1·75	0·96	1·20
2·30 SALLOWS	1691				
Kentmere		1100	2·00	1·22	1·53
5·20 SOUTHER FELL	1680				
Scales		1000	2·00	1·17	1·47
Mungrisdale		950	1·25	0·89	1·13
7·27 MELLBREAK	1676				
Crummock Water to the south top		1450	1·00	1·06	1·37
Crummock Water to the north top		1350	0·75	0·93	1·20

FELL NUMBER & FELL NAME					
STARTING POINT & ROUTE	HEIGHT ABOVE SEA LEVEL (feet)	HEIGHT OF ASCENT (feet)	DISTANCE OF ASCENT (miles)	ASCENT TIME	
				FASTER (hours)	SLOWER (hours)
7·27 MELLBREAK *(continued)*	1676				
Buttermere to the south top		1300	2·50	1·48	1·87
Loweswater to the north top via the scree		1300	2·25	1·40	1·77
Loweswater to the north top via the valley path		1300	2·25	1·40	1·77
Loweswater to the north top direct		1300	1·25	1·07	1·37
6·21 BROOM FELL	1670				
Wythop Mill		1450	4·00	2·06	2·57
High Lorton		1400	3·00	1·70	2·13
3·16 HIGH TOVE	1665				
Armboth		1100	1·33	0·99	1·27
Watendlath		800	1·00	0·73	0·93
2·31 BEDA FELL	1664				
Boardale		1100	1·75	1·13	1·43
Martindale		1100	1·75	1·13	1·43
7·28 HEN COMB	1661				
Loweswater direct		1300	2·50	1·48	1·87
Loweswater via Little Dodd		1300	2·50	1·48	1·87
1·30 LOW PIKE	1657				
Ambleside via Low Sweden Bridge		1500	2·25	1·50	1·90
Ambleside via High Sweden Bridge		1500	2·25	1·50	1·90
Rydal		1500	2·00	1·42	1·80
1·29 LITTLE MELL FELL	1657				
Thackthwaite		750	1·00	0·71	0·90
Mellfell House		650	0·50	0·49	0·63
1·31 STONE ARTHUR	1652				
Grasmere, Swan Hotel		1400	1·00	1·03	1·33
3·17 EAGLE CRAG	1650				
Stonethwaite via Greenup path		1300	3·00	1·65	2·07
Stonethwaite direct		1300	2·00	1·32	1·67
5·21 DODD	1612				
Dancing Gate		1320	1·50	1·16	1·48
Little Crosthwaite		1300	2·50	1·48	1·87
Millbeck		1250	1·50	1·13	1·43
4·27 GREEN CRAG	1602				
Woolpack Inn via Crook Crag		1450	2·50	1·56	1·97
Woolpack Inn via Low Birker Tarn		1450	2·50	1·56	1·97
2·32 WANSFELL	1597				
Ambleside via Stock Ghyll Force		1500	2·50	1·58	2·00
Ambleside via Blue Hill road		1500	2·50	1·58	2·00
Troutbeck		1100	1·75	1·13	1·43

FELL NUMBER & FELL NAME STARTING POINT & ROUTE	HEIGHT ABOVE SEA LEVEL (feet)	HEIGHT OF ASCENT (feet)	DISTANCE OF ASCENT (miles)	ASCENT TIME	
				FASTER (hours)	SLOWER (hours)
7·29 GRIKE	1596				
Ennerdale Bridge		1250	2·50	1·46	1·83
Kinniside Stone Circle		850	2·00	1·09	1·37
7·30 BURNBANK FELL	1580				
Waterend		1250	2·75	1·54	1·93
Fangs		1100	2·75	1·47	1·83
Lamplugh		1000	1·75	1·08	1·37
5·22 LONGLANDS FELL	1580				
Longlands		900	1·25	0·87	1·10
1·32 GOWBARROW FELL	1579				
Park Brow Foot via Yew Crag		1000	2·50	1·33	1·67
Park Brow Foot via Aira Force		1000	1·50	1·00	1·27
Dockray direct		650	1·00	0·66	0·83
3·18 ARMBOTH FELL	1570				
Thirlmere via Dob Gill		850	2·50	1·26	1·57
Thirlmere via Brown Rigg		850	1·75	1·01	1·27
Thirlmere via Launchy Gill		850	1·25	0·84	1·07
Thirlmere via Fisher Gill		850	1·25	0·84	1·07
2·33 SOUR HOWES	1568				
Staveley via Browfoot		1250	5·25	2·38	2·93
Windermere		1200	4·25	2·02	2·50
Ings via Grassgarth		1150	3·75	1·82	2·27
Ings via Hugill Hall		1150	3·75	1·82	2·27
High Borrans		850	2·00	1·09	1·37
Garburn Pass		100	1·00	0·38	0·47
6·22 BARF	1536				
Thornthwaite, Swan Hotel via Beckstones Plantation		1220	1·00	0·94	1·21
Thornthwaite, Swan Hotel via The Bishop		1200	0·75	0·85	1·10
4·28 LINGMOOR FELL	1530				
Dungeon Ghyll Old Hotel via Side Pike		1500	2·50	1·58	2·00
Chapel Stile		1350	2·50	1·51	1·90
Elterwater		1350	2·50	1·51	1·90
Dungeon Ghyll Old Hotel direct		1250	2·00	1·29	1·63
Dungeon Ghyll Old Hotel via Bleatarn House		1250	2·00	1·29	1·63
Dale End		1100	1·50	1·05	1·33
3·19 RAVEN CRAG	1520				
Thirlmere Dam		950	1·00	0·81	1·03
3·20 GREAT CRAG	1500				
Stonethwaite via Knotts		1200	1·50	1·10	1·40
Stonethwaite via Dock Tarn		1200	1·50	1·10	1·40
Watendlath		700	1·50	0·85	1·07

FELL NUMBER & FELL NAME STARTING POINT & ROUTE	HEIGHT ABOVE SEA LEVEL (feet)	HEIGHT OF ASCENT (feet)	DISTANCE OF ASCENT (miles)	ASCENT TIME	
				FASTER (hours)	SLOWER (hours)

FELLS LESS THAN 1500 FEET ABOVE SEA LEVEL

	HEIGHT ABOVE SEA LEVEL (feet)	HEIGHT OF ASCENT (feet)	DISTANCE OF ASCENT (miles)	FASTER (hours)	SLOWER (hours)
6·23 BARROW	1494				
Braithwaite via Barrow door		1250	2·00	1·29	1·63
Braithwaite direct		1250	1·50	1·13	1·43
Stair		1200	2·25	1·35	1·70
6·24 CATBELLS	1481				
Grange		1250	2·00	1·29	1·63
Hawse End		1250	1·50	1·13	1·43
Stair via Skelgill		1200	1·33	1·04	1·33
Little Town		950	1·33	0·92	1·17
6·25 GRAYSTONES	1476				
Armaside direct		1200	2·75	1·52	1·90
Armaside via Kirk Fell		1200	2·75	1·52	1·90
Embleton Church		1200	2·50	1·43	1·80
Scawgill Bridge		900	0·75	0·70	0·90
5·23 BINSEY	1466				
Bewaldeth		950	1·75	1·06	1·33
High Ireby		700	1·50	0·85	1·07
Binsey Lodge		620	1·00	0·64	0·81
1·33 NAB SCAR	1450				
Grasmere, Swan Hotel		1200	1·50	1·10	1·40
Rydal		1200	1·00	0·93	1·20
1·34 GLENRIDDING DODD	1425				
Glenridding		1000	1·00	0·83	1·07
1·35 ARNISON CRAG	1424				
Patterdale via Trough Head		900	1·75	1·03	1·30
Patterdale direct		900	0·67	0·67	0·87
2·34 STEEL KNOTTS	1414				
Howtown		900	1·00	0·78	1·00
Lanty Tarn		750	1·00	0·71	0·90
Martindale		750	0·75	0·63	0·80
7·31 BUCKBARROW	1410				
Harrow Head		1100	1·00	0·88	1·13
3·21 GIBSON KNOTT	1379				
Grasmere		1300	4·50	2·15	2·67
7·32 FELLBARROW	1363				
Low Lorton		1200	3·00	1·60	2·00
Thackthwaite (Lorton Vale) via Watching Crag		1150	2·00	1·24	1·57

FELL NUMBER & FELL NAME STARTING POINT & ROUTE	HEIGHT ABOVE SEA LEVEL (feet)	HEIGHT OF ASCENT (feet)	DISTANCE OF ASCENT (miles)	ASCENT TIME	
				FASTER (hours)	SLOWER (hours)
7·32 FELLBARROW *(continued)*	1363				
Thackthwaite (Lorton Vale) direct		1000	1·25	0·92	1·17
3·22 GRANGE FELL	1363				
Grange to Brund Fell via Troutdale and King's How		1300	2·50	1·48	1·87
Grange to Brund Fell via King's How		1300	2·00	1·32	1·67
Rosthwaite to Brund Fell via the bridle path		1100	2·00	1·22	1·53
Rosthwaite to Brund Fell via Hazel Bank		1100	1·50	1·05	1·33
Grange to King's How via Troutdale		1050	2·00	1·19	1·50
Grange to King's How only		1050	1·25	0·94	1·20
Rosthwaite to King's How, direct		1000	1·50	1·00	1·27
Watendlath to Brund Fell		550	1·00	0·61	0·77
7·33 LOW FELL	1360				
Loweswater via Darling Fell		1350	3·00	1·68	2·10
Thackthwaite (Lorton Vale) via the drove road		1250	2·00	1·29	1·63
Thackthwaite (Lorton Vale) via Watching Gill		1250	1·50	1·13	1·43
Loweswater direct		1050	2·00	1·19	1·50
3·23 HELM CRAG	1299				
Grasmere		1100	1·50	1·05	1·33
3·24 SILVER HOW	1292				
Elterwater		1200	2·25	1·35	1·70
Grasmere direct		1100	1·50	1·05	1·33
Grasmere via Wray Gill		1100	1·50	1·05	1·33
Chapel Stile via Spedding Crag		1050	1·75	1·11	1·40
Chapel Stile direct		1050	1·25	0·94	1·20
2·35 HALLIN FELL	1271				
Martindale		600	0·67	0·52	0·67
3·25 WALLA CRAG	1234				
Keswick		1000	2·50	1·33	1·67
Borrowdale road		950	1·00	0·81	1·03
6·26 LING FELL	1224				
Wythop Mill		850	1·50	0·93	1·17
5·24 LATRIGG	1203				
Keswick		950	2·50	1·31	1·63
Threlkeld		900	3·00	1·45	1·80
2·36 TROUTBECK TONGUE	1191				
Troutbeck Park Farm via the Tongue		650	3·00	1·32	1·63
Troutbeck Park Farm		650	0·75	0·57	0·73

FELL NUMBER & FELL NAME STARTING POINT & ROUTE	HEIGHT ABOVE SEA LEVEL (feet)	HEIGHT OF ASCENT (feet)	DISTANCE OF ASCENT (miles)	ASCENT TIME	
				FASTER (hours)	SLOWER (hours)
6·27 SALE FELL	1170				
Bassenthwaite Lake Station direct		930	2·00	1·13	1·42
Bassenthwaite Lake Station via Dodd Crag		930	2·00	1·13	1·42
Wythop Mill		750	1·50	0·88	1·10
3·26 HIGH RIGG	1163				
St John's-in-the-Vale Church		450	0·50	0·39	0·50
6·28 RANNERDALE KNOTTS	1160				
Buttermere		850	1·50	0·93	1·17
Rannerdale		800	0·75	0·65	0·83
3·27 LOUGHRIGG FELL	1101				
Ambleside via Fox Gill		1050	3·00	1·52	1·90
Ambleside via Browhead Farm		1050	2·50	1·36	1·70
Clappersgate		1050	2·50	1·36	1·70
Rydal		1000	2·50	1·33	1·67
Skelwith Bridge		1000	1·75	1·08	1·37
White Moss		925	1·50	0·96	1·22
Grasmere		920	2·25	1·21	1·51
4·29 BLACK FELL	1056				
Borwick Lodge via Iron Keld		600	1·33	0·74	0·93
4·30 HOLME FELL	1040				
Yew Tree House		750	1·00	0·71	0·90
6·29 CASTLE CRAG	985				
Grange		700	1·50	0·85	1·07
Rosthwaite		700	1·50	0·85	1·07

CHAPTER 3

STARTING POINTS

If this gazetteer needs to justify its existence, then I think it is to be found in this chapter which gives the data in order of Starting Point, the lists beginning at Ambleside and ending at Yew Tree House. The times, given in the tables, are in the form of 'round trip' times; shown as usual in hours and decimal parts of an hour. A 'round trip' is, in essence, the addition of an ascent and the return journey to the starting point. To calculate the 'round trip' time, the Naismith calculations are used for the ascents, as in the preceding chapters, to which is added time for the return leg; this is obtained by taking the distance component only and applying the Naismith Rule in respect of that distance.

The chapter will be of great value to the fellwalker who wishes to plan a series of daily excursions from one particular starting point, or from a series of starting points within a close distance of the base chosen for the holiday.

For example, a fellwalker who has made his base in Patterdale and wishes to start all excursions from there (perhaps because he has no means of private transport to reach other starting points easily), could then include the following 20 fells with 36 possible ascents:

Angletarn Pikes	Fairfield	Little Hart Crag
Arnison Crag	Hart Crag	Nethermost Pike
Birkhouse Moor	Hartsop Above How	Place Fell
Birks	Helvellyn	Rampsgill Head
Dollywaggon Pike	High Raise	Red Screes
Dove Crag	High Street	Rest Dodd
	The Knott	Saint Sunday Crag

The combined heights and distances of the 36 ascents of these 20 fells are:

Height of ascents	–	over 73,000 feet
Distance of ascents	–	over 145 miles
Time of 'round trips':		
Faster	–	over 133 hours
Slower	–	over 165 hours

However, a fellwalker may be able to make arrangements to get to other starting points within, say, 6 miles from Patterdale (by public transport, by bicycle or by arranging a lift with other fellwalkers), and this will offer an even greater choice of ascents and fells. The list is as follows:

Angletarn Pikes	Gray Crag	Middle Dodd
Arnison Crag	Great Dodd	Nethermost Pike
Birkhouse Moor	Hart Crag	Place Fell
Birks	Hart Side	Raise
Brock Crags	Hartsop Above How	Rampsgill Head
Catstycam	Hartsop Dodd	Red Screes
Caudale Moor	Helvellyn	Rest Dodd
Dollywaggon Pike	High Hartsop Dodd	Saint Sunday Crag
Dove Crag	High Raise	Sheffield Pike
Fairfield	High Street	Stybarrow Dodd
Glenridding Dodd	The Knott	Thornthwaite Crag
Gowbarrow Fell	Little Hart Crag	White Side

By close examination of the seven guide books, it will be noted that:

There are 178 listed Starting Points.

Some 80% of the 759 listed ascents start from less than 42% of the named Starting Points.

About 25% of the listed ascents start from locations with fewer than 4 ascents.

HALF-DAY EXCURSIONS

Many fellwalkers will not want an eight-hour 'walking day' on every occasion and, indeed, would like to know which fells can be climbed in a round trip of, say, 4 hours or less.

If we apply the four-hour limit to the slower speed, then some 493 ascents result. They can be easily identified in the main tables which follow. Table 9 shown below examines the distribution of these 'half-day excursions' by reference to round trip time and guide book.

TABLE 9: **Distribution of 'Half-Day' Ascents by Round Trip Time (Slower Rate)**

HOURS OF ROUND TRIP	GUIDE BOOK NUMBER							
	1	2	3	4	5	6	7	ALL
0–1	1	2	1	1	0	0	0	5
1–2	11	11	19	7	6	24	11	89
2–3	16	32	35	15	32	24	42	196
3–4	28	26	22	15	44	29	39	203
ALL TRIPS	56	71	77	38	82	77	92	493

Within the alphabetical order of Starting Point, the fells which may be visited are listed in descending order of Round Trip Time using the faster time. Remember, these times do not allow for any stops for lunch or rest which need to be added according to individual needs.

STARTING POINTS
listed in alphabetical order of starting point

FELL NAME & ROUTE	BOOK & FELL NUMBER	HEIGHT ABOVE SEA LEVEL (feet)	HEIGHT OF ASCENT (feet)	DISTANCE OF ASCENT (miles)	ROUND TRIP FASTER TIME (hours)	SLOWER TIME (hours)
Ambleside						
DOVE CRAG via HIGH PIKE	1·12	2603	2500	5·00	4·58	5·67
DOVE CRAG via Scandale	1·12	2603	2500	5·00	4·58	5·67
RED SCREES via Scandale Pass	1·14	2541	2400	5·00	4·53	5·60
DOVE CRAG via Scandale and High Bakestones	1·12	2603	2500	4·75	4·42	5·47
LITTLE HART CRAG	1·23	2091	2000	4·25	3·83	4·73
HIGH PIKE	1·21	2155	2000	4·00	3·67	4·53
LOUGHRIGG FELL via Fox Gill	3·27	1101	1050	3·00	2·52	3·10
WANSFELL via Stock Ghyll Force	2·32	1597	1500	2·50	2·42	3·00
WANSFELL via Blue Hill road	2·32	1597	1500	2·50	2·42	3·00
LOW PIKE via Low Sweden Bridge	1·30	1657	1500	2·25	2·25	2·80
LOW PIKE via High Sweden Bridge	1·30	1657	1500	2·25	2·25	2·80
LOUGHRIGG FELL via Browhead Farm	3·27	1101	1050	2·50	2·19	2·70
Applethwaite						
SKIDDAW direct	5·1	3053	2700	3·00	3·35	4·20
SKIDDAW via Howgill Tongue	5·1	3053	2700	3·00	3·35	4·20
SKIDDAW LITTLE MAN via Howgill Tongue	5·3	2837	2450	2·00	2·56	3·23
SKIDDAW LITTLE MAN direct	5·3	2837	2450	1·75	2·39	3·03
Armaside						
GRAYSTONES direct	6·25	1476	1200	2·75	2·43	3·00
GRAYSTONES via Kirk Fell	6·25	1476	1200	2·75	2·43	3·00
Armboth						
HIGH SEAT	3·9	1995	1450	2·00	2·06	2·57
HIGH TOVE	3·16	1665	1100	1·33	1·44	1·80
Ashness Bridge						
HIGH SEAT via the falls	3·9	1995	1500	2·00	2·08	2·60
HIGH SEAT via Dodd	3·9	1995	1500	2·00	2·08	2·60
Askham						
LOADPOT HILL	2·18	2201	1600	6·50	5·13	6·27
Bampton						
WETHER HILL	2·17	2210	1750	5·00	4·21	5·17
LOADPOT HILL	2·18	2201	1650	4·50	3·83	4·70

STARTING POINT FELL NAME & ROUTE	BOOK & FELL NUMBER	HEIGHT ABOVE SEA LEVEL (feet)	HEIGHT OF ASCENT (feet)	DISTANCE OF ASCENT (miles)	ROUND TRIP	
					FASTER TIME (hours)	SLOWER TIME (hours)
Bassenthwaite Lake Station						
SALE FELL direct	6·27	1170	930	2·00	1·80	2·22
SALE FELL via Dodd Crag	6·27	1170	930	2·00	1·80	2·22
Bassenthwaite village						
SKIDDAW via Barkbethdale	5·1	3053	2800	5·00	4·73	5·87
SKIDDAW via Southerndale	5·1	3053	2800	4·50	4·40	5·47
SKIDDAW via north-west ridge	5·1	3053	2800	4·00	4·07	5·07
BAKESTALL	5·12	2189	1750	4·67	3·99	4·90
ULLOCK PIKE	5·11	2230	2000	3·25	3·17	3·93
Beck House						
WHITESIDE	6·10	2317	1950	1·25	1·81	2·30
Bewaldeth						
BINSEY	5·23	1466	950	1·75	1·64	2·03
Binsey Lodge						
BINSEY	5·23	1466	620	1·00	0·98	1·21
Black Sail Youth Hostel						
PILLAR via High Level Route	7·2	2927	2100	3·00	3·05	3·80
PILLAR direct	7·2	2927	2000	2·75	2·83	3·53
GREAT GABLE via Windy Gap	7·1	2949	2000	2·25	2·50	3·13
GREAT GABLE via Beck Head	7·1	2949	2000	2·25	2·50	3·13
GREEN GABLE via The Tongue	7·9	2603	1650	2·25	2·33	2·90
GREEN GABLE via River Liza	7·9	2603	1650	2·25	2·33	2·90
HIGH CRAG	7·11	2443	1500	1·75	1·92	2·40
BRANDRETH via Loft Beck	7·12	2344	1400	1·75	1·87	2·33
BRANDRETH via The Tongue	7·12	2344	1400	1·75	1·87	2·33
KIRK FELL	7·7	2630	1700	1·50	1·85	2·33
HAYSTACKS	7·22	1900	970	1·25	1·32	1·65
Blengdale						
CAW FELL	7·13	2288	2100	5·50	4·72	5·80
Boardale						
BEDA FELL	2·31	1664	1100	1·75	1·72	2·13
Boot						
ESK PIKE via Cam Spout	4·5	2903	2800	9·50	7·73	9·47
ESK PIKE via Lingcove Bridge	4·5	2903	2800	8·50	7·07	8·67
BOWFELL via Ore Gap	4·4	2960	2900	8·00	6·78	8·33
CRINKLE CRAGS via Three Tarns	4·6	2816	2650	8·00	6·66	8·17
SCAFELL PIKE via Mickledore	4·1	3210	3100	7·50	6·55	8·07
SCAFELL PIKE via Broad	4·1	3210	3100	7·50	6·55	8·07

STARTING POINT FELL NAME & ROUTE	BOOK & FELL NUMBER	HEIGHT ABOVE SEA LEVEL (feet)	HEIGHT OF ASCENT (feet)	DISTANCE OF ASCENT (miles)	ROUND TRIP	
					FASTER TIME (hours)	SLOWER TIME (hours)
Boot *(continued)*						
BOWFELL via Three Tarns	4·4	2960	2900	7·50	6·45	7·93
SCAFELL via Cam Spout Crag	4·2	3162	3050	7·25	6·36	7·83
SCAFELL via Cam Spout						
and Foxes Tarn	4·2	3162	3050	7·25	6·36	7·83
CRINKLE CRAGS via Rest Gill	4·6	2816	2650	7·50	6·33	7·77
CRINKLE CRAGS via Swinsty Gill	4·6	2816	2650	7·50	6·33	7·77
SCAFELL direct	4·2	3162	3100	6·00	5·55	6·87
SLIGHT SIDE	4·17	2499	2350	4·75	4·34	5·37
ILLGILL HEAD via old corpse-road	4·22	1983	1700	4·75	4·02	4·93
HARTER FELL	4·20	2140	2000	3·50	3·33	4·13
Borrowdale road						
BLEABERRY FELL	3·10	1932	1650	1·75	1·99	2·50
WALLA CRAG	3·25	1234	950	1·00	1·14	1·43
Borwick Lodge						
BLACK FELL via Iron Keld	4·29	1056	600	1·33	1·19	1·46
Bowscale						
BOWSCALE FELL	5·8	2306	1550	2·50	2·44	3·03
Braithwaite						
CAUSEY PIKE via Sail Pass	6·14	2035	2150	4·50	4·08	5·03
CAUSEY PIKE direct	6·14	2035	2150	4·50	4·08	5·03
EEL CRAG via Shelf Route	6·2	2749	2500	4·00	3·92	4·87
EEL CRAG via Tower Ridge	6·2	2749	2500	3·75	3·75	4·67
SAIL	6·5	2530	2350	3·50	3·51	4·37
GRISEDALE PIKE	6·3	2593	2400	3·00	3·20	4·00
OUTERSIDE	6·16	1863	1650	2·50	2·49	3·10
BARROW via Barrow door	6·23	1494	1250	2·00	1·96	2·43
BARROW direct	6·23	1494	1250	1·50	1·63	2·03
Brothers Water						
CAUDALE MOOR	2·7	2502	2000	2·50	2·67	3·33
Burn Banks						
WETHER HILL via Measand Beck	2·17	2210	1550	5·00	4·11	5·03
WETHER HILL direct	2·17	2210	1550	4·50	3·77	4·63
Buttermere						
RED PIKE (Buttermere)						
via Scale Force	7·10	2479	2200	4·00	3·77	4·67
WANDOPE via the Addacomb Ridge	6·4	2533	2250	3·50	3·46	4·30
WANDOPE via Third Gill	6·4	2533	2250	2·75	2·96	3·70

STARTING POINT FELL NAME & ROUTE	BOOK & FELL NUMBER	HEIGHT ABOVE SEA LEVEL (feet)	HEIGHT OF ASCENT (feet)	DISTANCE OF ASCENT (miles)	ROUND TRIP	
					FASTER TIME (hours)	SLOWER TIME (hours)
Buttermere *(continued)*						
RED PIKE (Buttermere)						
via Lingcomb Edge	7·10	2479	2150	2·75	2·91	3·63
WANDOPE direct	6·4	2533	2300	2·50	2·82	3·53
ROBINSON	6·8	2417	2100	2·50	2·72	3·40
HIGH CRAG	7·11	2443	2100	2·50	2·72	3·40
HIGH STILE direct	7·6	2644	2350	2·25	2·67	3·37
HIGH STILE via north-east ridge	7·6	2644	2350	2·25	2·67	3·37
RED PIKE (Buttermere)						
via Far Ruddy Beck	7·10	2479	2150	2·25	2·58	3·23
MELLBREAK to the south top	7·27	1676	1300	2·50	2·32	2·87
RED PIKE (Buttermere)						
via Bleaberry Tarn	7·10	2479	2150	1·75	2·24	2·83
WHITELESS PIKE	6·12	2159	1800	1·75	2·07	2·60
RANNERDALE KNOTTS	6·28	1160	850	1·50	1·43	1·77
Calebrack						
CARROCK FELL	5·13	2174	1300	3·50	2·98	3·67
HIGH PIKE	5·14	2157	1300	2·75	2·48	3·07
Caudale Bridge						
HARTSOP DODD via Caudale Beck	2·23	2018	1400	1·50	1·70	2·13
HARTSOP DODD direct	2·23	2018	1400	0·75	1·20	1·53
Chapel Stile						
LINGMOOR FELL	4·28	1530	1350	2·50	2·34	2·90
SILVER HOW via Spedding Crag	3·24	1292	1050	1·75	1·69	2·10
SILVER HOW direct	3·24	1292	1050	1·25	1·36	1·70
Clappersgate						
LOUGHRIGG FELL	3·27	1101	1050	2·50	2·19	2·70
Cockley Beck Bridge						
CRINKLE CRAGS	4·6	2816	2350	3·00	3·17	3·97
Coldfell Gate						
LANK RIGG	7·24	1775	1100	4·00	3·22	3·93
Coldfell road						
LANK RIGG	7·24	1775	1400	2·50	2·37	2·93
Coledale Hause						
GRASMOOR	6·1	2791	850	1·25	1·26	1·57
GRISEDALE PIKE	6·3	2593	700	1·25	1·18	1·47
EEL CRAG direct	6·2	2749	850	1·00	1·09	1·37

STARTING POINT FELL NAME & ROUTE	BOOK & FELL NUMBER	HEIGHT ABOVE SEA LEVEL (feet)	HEIGHT OF ASCENT (feet)	DISTANCE OF ASCENT (miles)	ROUND TRIP	
					FASTER TIME (hours)	SLOWER TIME (hours)
Coledale Hause *(continued)*						
EEL CRAG via the pools	6·2	2749	850	1·00	1·09	1·37
HOPEGILL HEAD via Sand Hill	6·6	2525	600	0·75	0·80	1·00
HOPEGILL HEAD via Hobcarton Crag	6·6	2525	600	0·75	0·80	1·00
Coniston						
DOW CRAG via Walna Scar Pass	4·14	2555	2350	4·25	4·01	4·97
DOW CRAG via Goat's Hause	4·14	2555	2350	4·00	3·84	4·77
BRIM FELL via Gill Cove	4·10	2611	2450	3·50	3·56	4·43
SWIRL HOW via Levers Hause	4·9	2630	2450	3·50	3·56	4·43
SWIRL HOW via Swirl Hause	4·9	2630	2450	3·50	3·56	4·43
WETHERLAM via Red Dell Copper Works	4·16	2502	2350	3·50	3·51	4·37
WETHERLAM via Lad Stones	4·16	2502	2350	3·50	3·51	4·37
BRIM FELL direct	4·10	2611	2450	3·00	3·23	4·03
CONISTON OLD MAN direct	4·8	2633	2450	3·00	3·23	4·03
CONISTON OLD MAN via Boo Tarn	4·8	2633	2400	3·00	3·20	4·00
CONISTON OLD MAN via Church Beck	4·8	2633	2450	2·50	2·89	3·63
Croasdale						
GAVEL FELL direct	7·25	1720	1250	2·00	1·96	2·43
GAVEL FELL via Banna Fell	7·25	1720	1250	2·00	1·96	2·43
Crummock Water						
MELLBREAK to the south top	7·27	1676	1450	1·00	1·39	1·77
MELLBREAK to the north top	7·27	1676	1350	0·75	1·18	1·50
Dale Bottom						
HIGH SEAT via Mere Gill	3·9	1995	1600	4·00	3·47	4·27
HIGH SEAT via Litt's Memorial	3·9	1995	1600	4·00	3·47	4·27
BLEABERRY FELL	3·10	1932	1600	3·00	2·80	3·47
Dale End						
LINGMOOR FELL	4·28	1530	1100	1·50	1·55	1·93
Dancing Gate						
DODD	5·21	1612	1320	1·50	1·66	2·08
Dash Falls						
SKIDDAW via the Skiddaw House road	5·1	3053	1800	2·00	2·23	2·80
BAKESTALL via Birkett Edge	5·12	2189	900	0·67	0·90	1·14

STARTING POINT FELL NAME & ROUTE	BOOK & FELL NUMBER	HEIGHT ABOVE SEA LEVEL (feet)	HEIGHT OF ASCENT (feet)	DISTANCE OF ASCENT (miles)	ROUND TRIP	
					FASTER TIME (hours)	SLOWER TIME (hours)
Dockray						
STYBARROW DODD via Green Side	1·9	2770	1900	5·50	4·62	5·67
STYBARROW DODD via Deep Dale	1·9	2770	1900	5·50	4·62	5·67
GREAT DODD direct	1·8	2807	2000	4·75	4·17	5·13
GREAT DODD via Groove Beck	1·8	2807	2000	4·75	4·17	5·13
HART SIDE via Brown Hills	1·16	2481	1600	4·00	3·47	4·27
HART SIDE via Dowthwaitehead	1·16	2481	1600	4·00	3·47	4·27
GOWBARROW FELL direct	1·32	1579	650	1·00	0·99	1·23
Dungeon Ghyll New Hotel						
HIGH RAISE	3·1	2500	2250	2·50	2·79	3·50
SERGEANT MAN direct	3·2	2414	2200	2·25	2·60	3·27
SERGEANT MAN via Stickle Tarn	3·2	2414	2200	2·00	2·43	3·07
THUNACAR KNOTT	3·5	2351	2100	2·00	2·38	3·00
HARRISON STICKLE via Stickle Tarn	3·3	2403	2100	1·75	2·22	2·80
PAVEY ARK via south-west ridge	3·7	2288	2050	1·75	2·19	2·77
PAVEY ARK via Easy Gully	3·7	2288	2050	1·75	2·19	2·77
PAVEY ARK via North Rake	3·7	2288	2050	1·75	2·19	2·77
LOFT CRAG	3·8	2270	2000	1·75	2·17	2·73
BLEA RIGG via Tarn Crag	3·14	1776	1550	2·00	2·11	2·63
HARRISON STICKLE via Pike How	3·3	2403	2100	1·50	2·05	2·60
PAVEY ARK via Jack's Rake	3·7	2288	2050	1·50	2·02	2·57
BLEA RIGG via Whitegill Crag	3·14	1776	1500	1·50	1·75	2·20
Dungeon Ghyll Old Hotel						
SCAFELL PIKE via Esk Hause	4·1	3210	3400	5·50	5·37	6·67
GREAT END	4·3	2984	2900	5·00	4·78	5·93
ESK PIKE via Ore Gap	4·5	2903	2800	4·25	4·23	5·27
ESK PIKE via Esk Hause	4·5	2903	2800	4·25	4·23	5·27
CRINKLE CRAGS via Hell Gill and Three Tarns	4·6	2816	2650	4·00	3·99	4·97
CRINKLE CRAGS via The Band and Three Tarns	4·6	2816	2650	4·00	3·99	4·97
CRINKLE CRAGS via Red Tarn direct	4·6	2816	2600	4·00	3·97	4·93
CRINKLE CRAGS via Red Tarn and Isaac Gill	4·6	2816	2600	4·00	3·97	4·93
CRINKLE CRAGS via Oxendale	4·6	2816	2550	3·50	3·61	4·50
BOWFELL via Three Tarns	4·4	2960	2700	3·25	3·52	4·40
BOWFELL direct	4·4	2960	2700	3·00	3·35	4·20
PIKE O'BLISCO via Stool End	4·18	2304	2100	2·50	2·72	3·40
HARRISON STICKLE via Stickle Tarn	3·3	2403	2100	2·25	2·55	3·20
PIKE O'BLISCO via Wall End	4·18	2304	2100	2·25	2·55	3·20
LINGMOOR FELL via Side Pike	4·28	1530	1500	2·50	2·42	3·00

FELL NAME & ROUTE	BOOK & FELL NUMBER	HEIGHT ABOVE SEA LEVEL (feet)	HEIGHT OF ASCENT (feet)	DISTANCE OF ASCENT (miles)	ROUND TRIP	
					FASTER TIME (hours)	SLOWER TIME (hours)

ungeon Ghyll Old Hotel *(continued)*

FELL NAME & ROUTE	BOOK & FELL NUMBER	HEIGHT ABOVE SEA LEVEL	HEIGHT OF ASCENT	DISTANCE OF ASCENT	FASTER TIME	SLOWER TIME
HARRISON STICKLE						
via Thorn Crag	3·3	2403	2150	2·00	2·41	3·03
HARRISON STICKLE						
via The Ravines	3·3	2403	2150	1·75	2·24	2·83
PIKE O'STICKLE via Mickleden	3·6	2323	2000	1·75	2·17	2·73
LINGMOOR FELL direct	4·28	1530	1250	2·00	1·96	2·43
LINGMOOR FELL						
via Bleatarn House	4·28	1530	1250	2·00	1·96	2·43
LOFT CRAG	3·8	2270	2000	1·25	1·83	2·33
unmail Raise						
DOLLYWAGGON PIKE						
via Birkside Gill	1·7	2810	2100	2·00	2·38	3·00
DOLLYWAGGON PIKE						
via Reggle Knott	1·7	2810	2100	2·00	2·38	3·00
DOLLYWAGGON PIKE						
via Raise Beck	1·7	2810	2100	2·00	2·38	3·00
SEAT SANDAL	1·17	2415	1700	1·50	1·85	2·33
STEEL FELL	3·12	1811	1050	1·00	1·19	1·50
terwater						
LINGMOOR FELL	4·28	1530	1350	2·50	2·34	2·90
SILVER HOW	3·24	1292	1200	2·25	2·10	2·60
mbleton Church						
GRAYSTONES	6·25	1476	1200	2·50	2·27	2·80
nnerdale Bridge						
GREAT BORNE via Floutern Pass	7·20	2019	1600	4·00	3·47	4·27
GREAT BORNE direct	7·20	2019	1600	4·00	3·47	4·27
CRAG FELL via Anglers' Crag	7·26	1710	1350	2·50	2·34	2·90
CRAG FELL direct	7·26	1710	1350	2·50	2·34	2·90
GRIKE	7·29	1596	1250	2·50	2·29	2·83
skdale Green						
ILLGILL HEAD via WHIN RIGG	4·22	1983	2100	4·83	4·27	5·26
WHIN RIGG	4·26	1755	1650	3·50	3·16	3·90
angs						
BURNBANK FELL	7·30	1580	1100	2·75	2·38	2·93
ell Foot						
PIKE O'BLISCO via Little Langdale	4·18	2304	1800	2·50	2·57	3·20

STARTING POINT FELL NAME & ROUTE	BOOK & FELL NUMBER	HEIGHT ABOVE SEA LEVEL (feet)	HEIGHT OF ASCENT (feet)	DISTANCE OF ASCENT (miles)	ROUND TRIP	
					FASTER TIME (hours)	SLOW TIME (hour)
Fell Side						
KNOTT	5·7	2329	1500	3·50	3·08	3·8
GREAT SCA FELL via Roughton Gill	5·15	2131	1300	3·00	2·65	3·2
GREAT SCA FELL via Ward Steel	5·15	2131	1300	3·00	2·65	3·2
HIGH PIKE	5·14	2157	1350	2·50	2·34	2·9
BRAE FELL	5·17	1920	1150	2·50	2·24	2·7
Fornside						
GREAT DODD	1·8	2807	2300	2·50	2·82	3·5
Garburn Pass						
ILL BELL	2·9	2476	1050	2·50	2·19	2·7
YOKE	2·14	2309	850	1·75	1·59	1·9
SOUR HOWES	2·33	1568	100	1·00	0·72	0·8
Gatesgarth						
GREAT GABLE via GREEN GABLE	7·1	2949	2800	4·00	4·07	5·0
GREAT GABLE via Beck Head	7·1	2949	2800	4·00	4·07	5·0
HINDSCARTH via Littledale Edge	6·9	2385	2050	3·00	3·02	3·7
HINDSCARTH via Hindscarth Edge	6·9	2385	2050	3·00	3·02	3·7
ROBINSON	6·8	2417	2050	3·00	3·02	3·7
BRANDRETH via Dubbs Quarry	7·12	2344	2000	3·00	3·00	3·7
BRANDRETH via Warnscale Bottom	7·12	2344	2000	3·00	3·00	3·7
HAYSTACKS via Warnscale	7·22	1900	1600	2·75	2·63	3·2
HIGH STILE	7·6	2644	2300	2·00	2·48	3·1
HIGH CRAG via Scarth Gap	7·11	2443	2100	1·75	2·22	2·8
HIGH CRAG direct	7·11	2443	2100	1·75	2·22	2·8
HAYSTACKS via Scarth Gap	7·22	1900	1550	1·75	1·94	2·4
FLEETWITH PIKE	7·16	2126	1750	1·13	1·63	2·0
Glencoyne						
SHEFFIELD PIKE via HERON PIKE	1·20	2232	1800	2·50	2·57	3·2
SHEFFIELD PIKE via Nick Head	1·20	2232	1800	2·50	2·57	3·2
Glenridding						
HELVELLYN via the old pony-route and Keppel Cove	1·1	3118	2750	5·50	5·04	6·2
HELVELLYN via Red Tarn and Swirral Edge	1·1	3118	2750	4·50	4·38	5·4
CATSTYCAM via Redtarn Beck	1·3	2917	2500	4·00	3·92	4·8
CATSTYCAM via north-west ridge	1·3	2917	2500	4·00	3·92	4·8
RAISE direct	1·4	2889	2500	4·00	3·92	4·8
RAISE via Sticks Pass	1·4	2889	2500	4·00	3·92	4·8
WHITE SIDE	1·6	2832	2400	4·00	3·87	4·8

STARTING POINT FELL NAME & ROUTE	BOOK & FELL NUMBER	HEIGHT ABOVE SEA LEVEL (feet)	HEIGHT OF ASCENT (feet)	DISTANCE OF ASCENT (miles)	ROUND TRIP	
					FASTER TIME (hours)	SLOWER TIME (hours)
Glenridding *(continued)*						
SHEFFIELD PIKE via Lead Mine	1·20	2232	1800	3·25	3·07	3·80
BIRKHOUSE MOOR via Mires Beck	1·19	2350	1900	2·00	2·28	2·87
SHEFFIELD PIKE via south-east ridge	1·20	2232	1800	2·00	2·23	2·80
BIRKHOUSE MOOR						
via north-east ridge	1·19	2350	1900	1·50	1·95	2·47
GLENRIDDING DODD	1·34	1425	1000	1·00	1·17	1·47
Gosforth						
CAW FELL	7·13	2288	2100	7·50	6·05	7·40
Grange						
HIGH SPY via Narrow Moor	6·13	2143	1950	2·50	2·64	3·30
MAIDEN MOOR via Manesty	6·15	1887	1600	2·50	2·47	3·07
GRANGE FELL to Brund Fell						
via Troutdale and King's How	3·22	1363	1300	2·50	2·32	2·87
HIGH SPY via High White Rake	6·13	2143	1950	2·00	2·31	2·90
MAIDEN MOOR via Peace How	6·15	1887	1600	2·00	2·13	2·67
GRANGE FELL to Brund Fell via						
King's How	3·22	1363	1300	2·00	1·98	2·47
CATBELLS	6·24	1481	1250	2·00	1·96	2·43
GRANGE FELL to King's How						
viaTroutdale	3·22	1363	1050	2·00	1·86	2·30
GRANGE FELL to King's How only	3·22	1363	1050	1·25	1·36	1·70
CASTLE CRAG	6·29	985	700	1·50	1·35	1·67
Grasmere						
HELVELLYN	1·1	3118	3050	6·50	5·86	7·23
HARRISON STICKLE via SERGEANT						
MAN and THUNACAR KNOTT	3·3	2403	2450	5·50	4·89	6·03
HIGH RAISE	3·1	2500	2350	5·50	4·84	5·97
SERGEANT MAN via Far Easedale	3·2	2414	2200	5·50	4·77	5·87
DOLLYWAGGON PIKE						
via Little Tongue Gill	1·7	2810	2700	5·00	4·68	5·80
DOLLYWAGGON PIKE						
via Tongue Gill	1·7	2810	2700	5·00	4·68	5·80
HARRISON STICKLE via BLEA						
RIGG and Stickle Tarn	3·3	2403	2450	5·16	4·67	5·76
FAIRFIELD via Little Tongue Gill	1·5	2863	2650	4·25	4·16	5·17
FAIRFIELD via Tongue Gill	1·5	2863	2650	4·25	4·16	5·17
SERGEANT MAN by Codale Tarn	3·2	2414	2200	4·25	3·93	4·87
CALF CRAG via Far Easedale	3·15	1762	1650	4·50	3·83	4·70
CALF CRAG via Green Burn	3·15	1762	1650	4·50	3·83	4·70
SERGEANT MAN via Easedale Tarn	3·2	2414	2200	4·00	3·77	4·67

STARTING POINT FELL NAME & ROUTE	BOOK & FELL NUMBER	HEIGHT ABOVE SEA LEVEL (feet)	HEIGHT OF ASCENT (feet)	DISTANCE OF ASCENT (miles)	ROUND TRIP FASTER TIME (hours)	ROUND TRIP SLOWER TIME (hours)
Grasmere *(continued)*						
GIBSON KNOTT	3·21	1379	1300	4·50	3·65	4·47
SEAT SANDAL via Little Tongue Gill	1·17	2415	2200	3·50	3·43	4·27
SEAT SANDAL via Tongue Gill	1·17	2415	2200	3·50	3·43	4·27
TARN CRAG via Stythwaite Steps	3·13	1801	1650	3·50	3·16	3·90
TARN CRAG via Deer Bield Crag	3·13	1801	1650	3·50	3·16	3·90
GREAT RIGG via Greenhead Gill	1·15	2513	2300	3·00	3·15	3·93
GREAT RIGG via STONE ARTHUR	1·15	2513	2300	3·00	3·15	3·93
BLEA RIGG	3·14	1776	1600	3·50	3·13	3·87
STEEL FELL	3·12	1811	1650	3·25	2·99	3·70
SEAT SANDAL via south ridge	1·17	2415	2200	2·75	2·93	3·67
TARN CRAG via Sour Milk Gill	3·13	1801	1600	3·00	2·80	3·47
TARN CRAG via the east ridge	3·13	1801	1600	3·00	2·80	3·47
LOUGHRIGG FELL	3·27	1101	920	2·25	1·96	2·41
HELM CRAG	3·23	1299	1100	1·50	1·55	1·93
SILVER HOW direct	3·24	1292	1100	1·50	1·55	1·93
SILVER HOW via Wray Gill	3·24	1292	1100	1·50	1·55	1·93
Grasmere, Swan Hotel						
HERON PIKE via Alcock Tarn	1·25	2003	1750	1·25	1·71	2·17
NAB SCAR	1·33	1450	1200	1·50	1·60	2·00
STONE ARTHUR	1·31	1652	1400	1·00	1·37	1·73
Greendale						
HAYCOCK	7·8	2618	2500	4·25	4·08	5·07
SEATALLAN	7·15	2266	2050	2·00	2·36	2·97
MIDDLE FELL	7·21	1908	1650	1·50	1·82	2·30
Greenhead						
BRAE FELL	5·17	1920	1100	2·00	1·88	2·33
Grisedale Tarn						
SAINT SUNDAY CRAG	1·10	2756	1000	1·75	1·67	2·07
Hardknott Pass						
HARTER FELL	4·20	2140	900	1·50	1·45	1·80
HARD KNOTT	4·25	1803	550	0·75	0·78	0·97
Harrow Head						
BUCKBARROW	7·31	1410	1100	1·00	1·22	1·53
Hartsop						
HIGH STREET	2·1	2718	2300	3·75	3·65	4·53
GRAY CRAG via Threshthwaite Mouth	2·15	2286	1950	4·00	3·64	4·50

STARTING POINT FELL NAME & ROUTE	BOOK & FELL NUMBER	HEIGHT ABOVE SEA LEVEL (feet)	HEIGHT OF ASCENT (feet)	DISTANCE OF ASCENT (miles)	ROUND TRIP FASTER TIME (hours)	ROUND TRIP SLOWER TIME (hours)
Hartsop *(continued)*						
THORNTHWAITE CRAG						
via Hayeswater Gill	2·4	2569	2000	3·75	3·50	4·33
HIGH RAISE	2·2	2634	2250	3·50	3·46	4·30
THORNTHWAITE CRAG						
via GRAY CRAG	2·4	2569	2000	3·25	3·17	3·93
THORNTHWAITE CRAG						
via Threshthwaite Mouth	2·4	2569	2000	3·25	3·17	3·93
RAMPSGILL HEAD	2·3	2581	2050	2·75	2·86	3·57
THE KNOTT	2·10	2423	1850	2·00	2·26	2·83
GRAY CRAG direct	2·15	2286	1800	2·00	2·23	2·80
REST DODD	2·16	2278	1700	2·00	2·18	2·73
BROCK CRAGS via the filter house	2·27	1842	1300	2·00	1·98	2·47
HARTSOP DODD	2·23	2018	1450	1·25	1·56	1·97
BROCK CRAGS direct	2·27	1842	1300	1·00	1·32	1·67
Hartsop Hall						
MIDDLE DODD	1·22	2106	1650	2·00	2·16	2·70
HIGH HARTSOP DODD	1·28	1702	1200	0·75	1·10	1·40
Hassness						
ROBINSON	6·8	2417	1900	1·50	1·95	2·47
Haweswater Hotel						
BRANSTREE	2·13	2333	1500	3·00	2·75	3·40
Hawse End						
CATBELLS	6·24	1481	1250	1·50	1·63	2·03
Helton						
LOADPOT HILL	2·18	2201	1650	5·50	4·49	5·50
High Borrans						
SOUR HOWES	2·33	1568	850	2·00	1·76	2·17
High Gillerthwaite						
PILLAR via Wind Gap	7·2	2927	2500	3·25	3·42	4·27
PILLAR via the north-west ridge	7·2	2927	2500	2·75	3·08	3·87
HIGH STILE	7·6	2644	2200	2·50	2·77	3·47
RED PIKE (Buttermere)	7·10	2479	2000	1·75	2·17	2·73
High Ireby						
BINSEY	5·23	1466	700	1·50	1·35	1·67

STARTING POINT FELL NAME & ROUTE	BOOK & FELL NUMBER	HEIGHT ABOVE SEA LEVEL (feet)	HEIGHT OF ASCENT (feet)	DISTANCE OF ASCENT (miles)	ROUND TRIP	
					FASTER TIME (hours)	SLOWER TIME (hours)
High Lorton						
HOPEGILL HEAD	6·6	2525	2450	3·75	3·73	4·63
LORD'S SEAT	6·18	1811	1550	4·00	3·44	4·23
BROOM FELL	6·21	1670	1400	3·00	2·70	3·33
High Side						
SKIDDAW via Barkbethdale	5·1	3053	2700	4·25	4·18	5·20
BAKESTALL	5·12	2189	1750	4·67	3·99	4·90
SKIDDAW via Southerndale	5·1	3053	2700	3·75	3·85	4·80
SKIDDAW via north-west ridge	5·1	3053	2700	3·25	3·52	4·40
CARL SIDE	5·4	2420	2050	3·00	3·02	3·77
ULLOCK PIKE	5·11	2230	1900	2·50	2·62	3·27
Honister Pass						
GREAT GABLE via GREEN GABLE	7·1	2949	1950	3·00	2·98	3·70
GREAT GABLE via Beck Head	7·1	2949	1950	3·00	2·98	3·70
GREEN GABLE	7·9	2603	1550	2·50	2·44	3·03
HAYSTACKS	7·22	1900	1050	2·25	2·02	2·50
BRANDRETH	7·12	2344	1150	2·00	1·91	2·37
FLEETWITH PIKE via the old Drum House	7·16	2126	1000	1·75	1·67	2·07
FLEETWITH PIKE via the old tramway	7·16	2126	1000	1·75	1·67	2·07
DALE HEAD	6·7	2473	1300	1·25	1·48	1·87
GREY KNOTTS via the old Drum House	7·14	2287	1150	1·25	1·41	1·77
GREY KNOTTS direct	7·14	2287	1150	1·00	1·24	1·57
Hopebeck						
HOPEGILL HEAD	6·6	2525	2150	2·50	2·74	3·43
WHITESIDE via Dodd	6·10	2317	1950	2·25	2·48	3·10
WHITESIDE via Cold Gill	6·10	2317	1950	2·25	2·48	3·10
WHITESIDE via Penn	6·10	2317	1950	2·25	2·48	3·10
Howtown						
ARTHUR'S PIKE	2·28	1747	1200	3·50	2·93	3·60
WETHER HILL	2·17	2210	1750	3·00	2·88	3·57
LOADPOT HILL	2·18	2201	1750	2·25	2·38	2·97
BONSCALE PIKE via the breast	2·29	1718	1200	1·25	1·43	1·80
BONSCALE PIKE direct	2·29	1718	1200	1·25	1·43	1·80
STEEL KNOTTS	2·34	1414	900	1·00	1·12	1·40
Hucks Bridge						
TARN CRAG via GREY CRAG	2·19	2176	1950	5·75	4·81	5·90
GREY CRAG	2·22	2093	1700	5·00	4·18	5·13

STARTING POINT FELL NAME & ROUTE	BOOK & FELL NUMBER	HEIGHT ABOVE SEA LEVEL (feet)	HEIGHT OF ASCENT (feet)	DISTANCE OF ASCENT (miles)	ROUND TRIP	
					FASTER TIME (hours)	SLOWER TIME (hours)
Ings						
SOUR HOWES via Grassgarth	2·33	1568	1150	3·75	3·08	3·77
SOUR HOWES via Hugill Hall	2·33	1568	1150	3·75	3·08	3·77
Jungle Cafe						
TARN CRAG via GREY CRAG	2·19	2176	1900	6·75	5·45	6·67
GREY CRAG	2·22	2093	1650	6·00	4·83	5·90
Kendal-Shap road (summit)						
TARN CRAG via GREY CRAG	2·19	2176	1250	5·75	4·46	5·43
GREY CRAG	2·22	2093	1000	5·00	3·83	4·67
Kentmere						
HIGH STREET via Nan Bield Pass	2·1	2718	2300	6·00	5·15	6·33
HIGH STREET via Hall Cove	2·1	2718	2300	5·50	4·82	5·93
HIGH STREET via Lingmell End	2·1	2718	2300	5·50	4·82	5·93
HARTER FELL via Nan Bield Pass	2·6	2539	2200	5·25	4·60	5·67
FROSWICK via the reservoir	2·12	2359	1850	5·00	4·26	5·23
MARDALE ILL BELL via Lingmell End	2·8	2496	2100	4·75	4·22	5·20
MARDALE ILL BELL via Nan Bield Pass	2·8	2496	2100	4·75	4·22	5·20
HARTER FELL via KENTMERE PIKE	2·6	2539	2200	4·25	3·93	4·87
KENTMERE PIKE	2·11	2397	1900	3·00	2·95	3·67
YOKE via Garburn Pass	2·14	2309	1800	3·00	2·90	3·60
YOKE direct	2·14	2309	1800	2·50	2·57	3·20
SHIPMAN KNOTTS	2·24	1926	1400	2·25	2·20	2·73
SALLOWS	2·30	1691	1100	2·00	1·88	2·33
Kentmere Reservoir						
THORNTHWAITE CRAG via Hall Cove	2·4	2569	1650	2·25	2·33	2·90
THORNTHWAITE CRAG via Gavel Crag	2·4	2569	1650	2·00	2·16	2·70
ILL BELL	2·9	2476	1500	0·75	1·25	1·60
Keskadale						
KNOTT RIGG direct	6·19	1790	1000	1·25	1·33	1·67
KNOTT RIGG via the ridge	6·19	1790	1000	1·25	1·33	1·67
KNOTT RIGG via Ill Gill	6·19	1790	1000	1·25	1·33	1·67
Keswick						
HIGH SEAT via Dale Bottom	3·9	1995	1750	6·50	5·21	6·37
SKIDDAW	5·1	3053	2850	5·50	5·09	6·30

STARTING POINT FELL NAME & ROUTE	BOOK & FELL NUMBER	HEIGHT ABOVE SEA LEVEL (feet)	HEIGHT OF ASCENT (feet)	DISTANCE OF ASCENT (miles)	ROUND TRIP	
					FASTER TIME (hours)	SLOWER TIME (hours)
Keswick *(continued)*						
BLEABERRY FELL via Dale Bottom	3·10	1932	1650	5·50	4·49	5·50
SKIDDAW LITTLE MAN	5·3	2837	2630	4·50	4·31	5·35
LONSCALE FELL via shepherd's tracks	5·6	2344	2150	4·25	3·91	4·83
LONSCALE FELL via Lonscale Crags	5·6	2344	2150	4·25	3·91	4·83
HIGH SEAT via Ashness Bridge	3·9	1995	1750	4·50	3·88	4·77
LONSCALE FELL via Whit Beck	5·6	2344	2150	3·75	3·58	4·43
LONSCALE FELL via the central approach	5·6	2344	2150	3·75	3·58	4·43
BLEABERRY FELL direct	3·10	1932	1650	3·50	3·16	3·90
BLEABERRY FELL via Brown Knotts	3·10	1932	1650	3·50	3·16	3·90
WALLA CRAG	3·25	1234	1000	2·50	2·17	2·67
LATRIGG	5·24	1203	950	2·50	2·14	2·63
Kinniside Stone Circle						
CAW FELL	7·13	2288	1850	6·00	4·92	6·03
GRIKE	7·29	1596	850	2·00	1·76	2·17
Kirkstone Pass						
CAUDALE MOOR	2·7	2502	1150	2·50	2·24	2·77
RED SCREES	1·14	2541	1050	0·75	1·02	1·30
Lamplugh						
BLAKE FELL	7·23	1878	1400	3·25	2·87	3·53
BURNBANK FELL	7·30	1580	1000	1·75	1·67	2·07
Lanthwaite Green						
GRASMOOR via Dove Crags	6·1	2791	2300	2·00	2·48	3·13
GRASMOOR direct	6·1	2791	2300	1·50	2·15	2·73
WHITESIDE	6·10	2317	1850	1·50	1·93	2·43
Lanty Tarn						
STEEL KNOTTS	2·34	1414	750	1·00	1·04	1·30
Legburthwaite						
GREAT DODD	1·8	2807	2300	2·25	2·65	3·33
WATSON'S DODD	1·13	2584	2050	1·75	2·19	2·77
Little Crosthwaite						
LONG SIDE via Longside Edge	5·5	2405	2050	2·50	2·69	3·37
LONG SIDE via Gable Gill	5·5	2405	2050	2·50	2·69	3·37
CARL SIDE	5·4	2420	2070	2·25	2·54	3·18
DODD	5·21	1612	1300	2·50	2·32	2·87

STARTING POINT FELL NAME & ROUTE	BOOK & FELL NUMBER	HEIGHT ABOVE SEA LEVEL (feet)	HEIGHT OF ASCENT (feet)	DISTANCE OF ASCENT (miles)	ROUND TRIP	
					FASTER TIME (hours)	SLOWER TIME (hours)
Little Langdale						
SWIRL HOW via Greenburn Tarn	4·9	2630	2400	4·00	3·87	4·80
SWIRL HOW via Long Crag levels	4·9	2630	2400	4·00	3·87	4·80
WETHERLAM via High Fellside Quarry	4·16	2502	2250	3·00	3·13	3·90
WETHERLAM via Greenburn Copper Works	4·16	2502	2250	3·00	3·13	3·90
Little Langdale village						
GREAT CARRS via Broad Slack	4·11	2575	2350	4·00	3·84	4·77
GREAT CARRS via Wet Side Edge	4·11	2575	2350	4·00	3·84	4·77
Little Town						
DALE HEAD via Dalehead Tarn	6·7	2473	2000	4·00	3·67	4·53
HIGH SPY	6·13	2143	1650	4·00	3·49	4·30
DALE HEAD via Copper Mine	6·7	2473	2000	3·50	3·33	4·13
MAIDEN MOOR via Hause Gate	6·15	1887	1250	2·00	1·96	2·43
MAIDEN MOOR direct	6·15	1887	1250	1·50	1·63	2·03
CATBELLS	6·24	1481	950	1·33	1·36	1·70
Longlands						
KNOTT	5·7	2329	1700	3·50	3·18	3·93
GREAT SCA FELL via the bridle road	5·15	2131	1550	3·00	2·77	3·43
GREAT SCA FELL direct	5·15	2131	1550	2·50	2·44	3·03
MEAL FELL via Lowthwaite Fell	5·18	1770	1100	2·25	2·05	2·53
MEAL FELL via Trusmadoor	5·18	1770	1100	2·25	2·05	2·53
LONGLANDS FELL	5·22	1580	900	1·25	1·28	1·60
Low Gillerthwaite						
SCOAT FELL via Deep Gill	7·3	2760	2400	3·50	3·53	4·40
SCOAT FELL direct	7·3	2760	2400	3·00	3·20	4·00
STEEPLE	7·5	2687	2350	3·00	3·17	3·97
HAYCOCK	7·8	2618	2300	3·00	3·15	3·93
CAW FELL	7·13	2288	1950	2·75	2·81	3·50
Low Lorton						
FELLBARROW	7·32	1363	1200	3·00	2·60	3·20
Loweswater						
STARLING DODD	7·18	2085	1700	4·50	3·85	4·73
BLAKE FELL via High Nook Tarn	7·23	1878	1550	3·00	2·77	3·43
BLAKE FELL via Carling Knott	7·23	1878	1550	3·00	2·77	3·43
GAVEL FELL via the drove road	7·25	1720	1400	3·00	2·70	3·33
GAVEL FELL via Highnook Beck	7·25	1720	1400	3·00	2·70	3·33

FELL NAME & ROUTE	BOOK & FELL NUMBER	HEIGHT ABOVE SEA LEVEL (feet)	HEIGHT OF ASCENT (feet)	DISTANCE OF ASCENT (miles)	ROUND TRIP FASTER TIME (hours)	SLOWER TIME (hours)
Loweswater *(continued)*						
LOW FELL via Darling Fell	7·33	1360	1350	3·00	2·67	3·30
HEN COMB direct	7·28	1661	1300	2·50	2·32	2·87
HEN COMB via Little Dodd	7·28	1661	1300	2·50	2·32	2·87
MELLBREAK to the north top via the scree	7·27	1676	1300	2·25	2·15	2·67
MELLBREAK to the north top via the valley path	7·27	1676	1300	2·25	2·15	2·67
LOW FELL direct	7·33	1360	1050	2·00	1·86	2·30
MELLBREAK to the north top direct	7·27	1676	1300	1·25	1·48	1·87
Mardale Head						
HIGH STREET via Rough Crag	2·1	2718	2050	3·75	3·52	4·37
RAMPSGILL HEAD	2·3	2581	1950	3·50	3·31	4·10
HIGH STREET via Blea Water	2·1	2718	2050	3·00	3·02	3·77
KIDSTY PIKE	2·5	2560	1900	3·00	2·95	3·67
MARDALE ILL BELL via Blea Water	2·8	2496	1700	2·50	2·52	3·13
HARTER FELL	2·6	2539	1750	2·00	2·21	2·77
MARDALE ILL BELL via Small Water	2·8	2496	1700	2·00	2·18	2·73
BRANSTREE	2·13	2333	1500	1·50	1·75	2·20
Mardale road						
BRANSTREE	2·13	2333	1500	1·50	1·75	2·20
Martindale						
HIGH RAISE	2·2	2634	2100	5·00	4·38	5·40
THE NAB	2·25	1887	1300	4·00	3·32	4·07
ANGLETARN PIKES via Angle Tarn	2·26	1857	1300	3·50	2·98	3·67
ANGLETARN PIKES via Bedafell Knott	2·26	1857	1300	3·50	2·98	3·67
WETHER HILL	2·17	2210	1550	2·50	2·44	3·03
BEDA FELL	2·31	1664	1100	1·75	1·72	2·13
STEEL KNOTTS	2·34	1414	750	0·75	0·88	1·10
HALLIN FELL	2·35	1271	600	0·67	0·75	0·94
Measand						
HIGH RAISE via Long Grain	2·2	2634	1900	3·50	3·28	4·07
Melbecks						
SKIDDAW	5·1	3053	2500	3·00	3·25	4·07
Mellfell House						
LITTLE MELL FELL	1·29	1657	650	0·50	0·66	0·83

STARTING POINT FELL NAME & ROUTE	BOOK & FELL NUMBER	HEIGHT ABOVE SEA LEVEL (feet)	HEIGHT OF ASCENT (feet)	DISTANCE OF ASCENT (miles)	ROUND TRIP	
					FASTER TIME (hours)	SLOWER TIME (hours)
Memorial Footbridge						
PILLAR	7·2	2927	2250	1·25	1·96	2·50
Mickleden						
PIKE O'STICKLE via Troughton Beck	3·6	2323	2000	3·25	3·17	3·93
Mickleden sheepfold						
BOWFELL	4·4	2960	2500	1·75	2·42	3·07
ROSSETT PIKE via Rossett Gill	4·21	2106	1600	1·50	1·80	2·27
ROSSETT PIKE via Littlegill Head	4·21	2106	1600	1·50	1·80	2·27
Millbeck						
SKIDDAW	5·1	3053	2750	2·75	3·21	4·03
SKIDDAW LITTLE MAN via the two boulders	5·3	2837	2500	1·75	2·42	3·07
SKIDDAW LITTLE MAN via south-west arete	5·3	2837	2500	1·75	2·42	3·07
CARL SIDE via White Stones	5·4	2420	2100	1·75	2·22	2·80
CARL SIDE via cliffs of Doups	5·4	2420	2100	1·75	2·22	2·80
CARL SIDE via Carsleddam	5·4	2420	2100	1·75	2·22	2·80
CARL SIDE via Slades Beck	5·4	2420	2100	1·75	2·22	2·80
DODD	5·21	1612	1250	1·50	1·63	2·03
Moor Divock						
LOADPOT HILL	2·18	2201	1300	4·50	3·65	4·47
Mosedale						
KNOTT	5·7	2329	1650	4·50	3·83	4·70
CARROCK FELL direct	5·13	2174	1450	2·00	2·06	2·57
CARROCK FELL via east peak	5·13	2174	1450	2·00	2·06	2·57
Mungrisdale						
BLENCATHRA	5·2	2847	2250	4·00	3·79	4·70
MUNGRISDALE COMMON via Glendermackin col	5·16	2068	1300	4·25	3·48	4·27
BANNERDALE CRAGS via The Tongue	5·10	2230	1500	3·00	2·75	3·40
BOWSCALE FELL via east ridge	5·8	2306	1550	2·50	2·44	3·03
BOWSCALE FELL via The Tongue	5·8	2306	1470	2·25	2·23	2·78
BOWSCALE FELL via old bridle path	5·8	2306	1450	2·25	2·23	2·77
BOWSCALE FELL via Bullfell Beck	5·8	2306	1450	2·25	2·23	2·77
BANNERDALE CRAGS via east ridge	5·10	2230	1500	2·00	2·08	2·60
SOUTHER FELL	5·20	1680	950	1·25	1·31	1·63

STARTING POINT FELL NAME & ROUTE	BOOK & FELL NUMBER	HEIGHT ABOVE SEA LEVEL (feet)	HEIGHT OF ASCENT (feet)	DISTANCE OF ASCENT (miles)	ROUND TRIP FASTER TIME (hours)	ROUND TRIP SLOWER TIME (hours)
Nether Row						
HIGH PIKE via Sandbed Mine	5·14	2157	1300	2·50	2·32	2·87
HIGH PIKE via Potts Gill Mine	5·14	2157	1300	2·50	2·32	2·87
Netherbeck Bridge						
SCOAT FELL direct	7·3	2760	2550	4·25	4·11	5·10
SCOAT FELL via Scoat Tarn	7·3	2760	2550	4·25	4·11	5·10
HAYCOCK via Little Lad Crag	7·8	2618	2400	4·00	3·87	4·80
HAYCOCK via Ladcrag Beck	7·8	2618	2400	4·00	3·87	4·80
SEATALLAN	7·15	2266	2100	3·00	3·05	3·80
Newlands Church						
ROBINSON via Scope Beck	6·8	2417	2000	3·00	3·00	3·73
ROBINSON via High Snab Bank	6·8	2417	2000	3·00	3·00	3·73
HINDSCARTH	6·9	2385	2000	2·50	2·67	3·33
Newlands Hause						
ROBINSON	6·8	2417	1400	1·25	1·53	1·93
KNOTT RIGG	6·19	1790	720	1·00	1·03	1·28
Orthwaite						
GREAT CALVA direct	5·9	2265	1500	3·75	3·25	4·00
GREAT CALVA via Brockle Crag	5·9	2265	1500	3·75	3·25	4·00
KNOTT direct	5·7	2329	1500	3·75	3·25	4·00
KNOTT via Brockle Crag	5·7	2329	1500	3·75	3·25	4·00
GREAT SCA FELL direct	5·15	2131	1400	3·50	3·03	3·73
GREAT SCA FELL via Brockle Crag	5·15	2131	1400	3·50	3·03	3·73
MEAL FELL direct	5·18	1770	1050	3·00	2·52	3·10
MEAL FELL via Brockle Crag	5·18	1770	1050	3·00	2·52	3·10
GREAT COCKUP	5·19	1720	950	2·00	1·81	2·23
Overbeck Bridge						
RED PIKE (Wasdale) via Dore Head	7·4	2707	2500	3·00	3·25	4·07
RED PIKE (Wasdale) via Low Tarn	7·4	2707	2500	3·00	3·25	4·07
YEWBARROW	7·19	2058	1900	1·50	1·95	2·47
Park Brow Foot						
GOWBARROW FELL via Yew Crag	1·32	1579	1000	2·50	2·17	2·67
GOWBARROW FELL via Aira Force	1·32	1579	1000	1·50	1·50	1·87
Patterdale						
HELVELLYN via Grisedale Tarn	1·1	3118	2700	7·25	6·18	7·60
HELVELLYN via Ruthwaite cove and DOLLYWAGGON PIKE	1·1	3118	2700	6·25	5·52	6·80
RED SCREES	1·14	2541	2200	6·50	5·43	6·67

STARTING POINT FELL NAME & ROUTE	BOOK & FELL NUMBER	HEIGHT ABOVE SEA LEVEL (feet)	HEIGHT OF ASCENT (feet)	DISTANCE OF ASCENT (miles)	ROUND TRIP	
					FASTER TIME (hours)	SLOWER TIME (hours)
Patterdale (*continued*)						
HELLVELLYN via Red Tarn and Swirral Edge	1·1	3118	2700	5·50	5·02	6·20
HIGH STREET	2·1	2718	2450	5·50	4·89	6·03
FAIRFIELD via Greenhow End	1·5	2863	2400	5·50	4·87	6·00
FAIRFIELD via Deepdale Hause	1·5	2863	2400	5·50	4·87	6·00
HELVELLYN via Striding Edge	1·1	3118	2700	5·25	4·85	6·00
HIGH RAISE	2·2	2634	2400	5·25	4·70	5·80
HELVELLYN via Nethermost Cove and NETHERMOST PIKE	1·1	3118	2700	5·00	4·68	5·80
NETHERMOST PIKE via Grisedale	1·2	2920	2500	5·00	4·58	5·67
DOLLYWAGGON PIKE via Grisedale	1·7	2810	2400	5·00	4·53	5·60
DOVE CRAG via Black Brow	1·12	2603	2200	5·00	4·43	5·47
DOVE CRAG direct	1·12	2603	2200	5·00	4·43	5·47
LITTLE HART CRAG via Scandale Pass	1·23	2091	1700	5·00	4·18	5·13
LITTLE HART CRAG via HIGH HARTSOP DODD	1·23	2091	1700	5·00	4·18	5·13
LITTLE HART CRAG via Hogget Gill	1·23	2091	1700	5·00	4·18	5·13
HART CRAG via Wallend	1·11	2698	2300	4·50	4·15	5·13
HART CRAG via HARTSOP ABOVE HOW	1·11	2698	2300	4·50	4·15	5·13
RAMPSGILL HEAD	2·3	2581	2200	4·50	4·10	5·07
SAINT SUNDAY CRAG via east ridge	1·10	2756	2300	4·00	3·82	4·73
THE KNOTT	2·10	2423	1850	4·00	3·59	4·43
BIRKHOUSE MOOR via Grisedale	1·19	2350	1900	3·50	3·28	4·07
REST DODD	2·16	2278	1900	3·50	3·28	4·07
SAINT SUNDAY CRAG via Trough Head	1·10	2756	2300	3·00	3·15	3·93
SAINT SUNDAY CRAG via Thornhow End	1·10	2756	2300	3·00	3·15	3·93
HARTSOP ABOVE HOW	1·26	1870	1400	3·00	2·70	3·33
BIRKS via Trough Head	1·24	2040	1600	2·50	2·47	3·07
PLACE FELL via The Knight	2·20	2154	1700	2·00	2·18	2·73
PLACE FELL via Boardale Hause	2·20	2154	1700	2·00	2·18	2·73
PLACE FELL direct	2·20	2154	1700	1·75	2·02	2·53
BIRKS via Thornhow End	1·24	2040	1600	1·75	1·97	2·47
ANGLETARN PIKES via Freeze Beck	2·26	1857	1400	1·75	1·87	2·33
ANGLETARN PIKES direct	2·26	1857	1400	1·75	1·87	2·33
ARNISON CRAG via Trough Head	1·35	1424	900	1·75	1·62	2·00
ARNISON CRAG direct	1·35	1424	900	0·67	0·90	1·14
Pooley Bridge						
LOADPOT HILL	2·18	2201	1800	6·00	4·90	6·00

STARTING POINT FELL NAME & ROUTE	BOOK & FELL NUMBER	HEIGHT ABOVE SEA LEVEL (feet)	HEIGHT OF ASCENT (feet)	DISTANCE OF ASCENT (miles)	ROUND TRIP FASTER TIME (hours)	ROUND TRIP SLOWER TIME (hours)
Rannerdale						
EEL CRAG	6·2	2749	2400	2·50	2·87	3·60
GRASMOOR via Lad Hows	6·1	2791	2450	1·75	2·39	3·03
GRASMOOR via Red Gill	6·1	2791	2430	1·25	2·05	2·62
RANNERDALE KNOTTS	6·28	1160	800	0·75	0·90	1·13
Ravenstone						
LONG SIDE	5·5	2405	2150	2·25	2·58	3·23
ULLOCK PIKE	5·11	2230	1850	1·75	2·09	2·63
Rigg Beck						
ARD CRAGS	6·17	1860	1350	1·50	1·68	2·10
Riggindale						
HIGH RAISE via Mardale	2·2	2634	1900	2·50	2·62	3·27
Rosgill						
TARN CRAG via Swindale and Brunt Tongue	2·19	2176	1730	7·00	5·53	6·75
Rosthwaite						
GLARAMARA via Comb Gill	4·13	2560	2300	3·75	3·65	4·53
GLARAMARA via Thornythwaite Fell	4·13	2560	2300	3·75	3·65	4·53
DALE HEAD	6·7	2473	2250	3·75	3·63	4·50
HIGH SPY	6·13	2143	1900	2·50	2·62	3·27
GRANGE FELL to Brund Fell via the bridle path	3·22	1363	1100	2·00	1·88	2·33
GRANGE FELL to Brund Fell via Hazel Bank	3·22	1363	1100	1·50	1·55	1·93
GRANGE FELL to King's How, direct	3·22	1363	1000	1·50	1·50	1·87
CASTLE CRAG	6·29	985	700	1·50	1·35	1·67
Rydal						
HART CRAG via Rydal Head	1·11	2698	2600	4·50	4·30	5·33
HART CRAG direct	1·11	2698	2600	4·50	4·30	5·33
HERON PIKE via Blind Cove	1·25	2003	1750	2·50	2·54	3·17
HERON PIKE via NAB SCAR	1·25	2003	1750	1·67	1·99	2·50
LOUGHRIGG FELL	3·27	1101	1000	2·50	2·17	2·67
LOW PIKE	1·30	1657	1500	2·00	2·08	2·60
NAB SCAR	1·33	1450	1200	1·00	1·27	1·60
Sadgill						
HARTER FELL via Wren Gill	2·6	2539	1950	4·25	3·81	4·70
HARTER FELL via Gatescarth Pass	2·6	2539	1950	4·25	3·81	4·70
BRANSTREE	2·13	2333	1750	3·50	3·21	3·97

STARTING POINT FELL NAME & ROUTE	BOOK & FELL NUMBER	HEIGHT ABOVE SEA LEVEL (feet)	HEIGHT OF ASCENT (feet)	DISTANCE OF ASCENT (miles)	ROUND TRIP	
					FASTER TIME (hours)	SLOWER TIME (hours)
Sadgill *(continued)*						
KENTMERE PIKE	2·11	2397	1850	3·00	2·92	3·63
TARN CRAG	2·19	2176	1600	2·00	2·13	2·67
GREY CRAG	2·22	2093	1500	1·50	1·75	2·20
SHIPMAN KNOTTS	2·24	1926	1300	1·50	1·65	2·07
Sandwick						
PLACE FELL via Nettleslack	2·20	2154	1700	3·00	2·85	3·53
PLACE FELL via High Dodd	2·20	2154	1700	2·50	2·52	3·13
PLACE FELL via Sleet Fell	2·20	2154	1700	2·50	2·52	3·13
PLACE FELL via Scalehow Beck	2·20	2154	1700	2·50	2·52	3·13
Scales						
BLENCATHRA via Sharp Edge	5·2	2847	2250	2·75	2·96	3·70
BLENCATHRA via Scales Fell	5·2	2847	2150	2·25	2·58	3·23
BANNERDALE CRAGS direct	5·10	2230	1550	2·50	2·44	3·03
BANNERDALE CRAGS via Glendermackin col	5·10	2230	1550	2·50	2·44	3·03
BLENCATHRA via Scaley Beck	5·2	2847	2150	2·00	2·41	3·03
BLENCATHRA via Doddick Fell	5·2	2847	2150	1·75	2·24	2·83
SOUTHER FELL	5·20	1680	1000	2·00	1·83	2·27
Scawgill Bridge						
GRAYSTONES	6·25	1476	900	0·75	0·95	1·20
Seathwaite						
GREAT END via Sty Head	4·3	2984	2650	3·25	3·49	4·37
GREAT GABLE via Sty Head and the Breast Route	7·1	2949	2600	3·25	3·47	4·33
GREAT GABLE via Aaron Slack and Windy Gap	7·1	2949	2600	3·25	3·47	4·33
GREAT GABLE direct	7·1	2949	2700	2·75	3·18	4·00
GREEN GABLE	7·9	2603	2250	2·25	2·63	3·30
BRANDRETH	7·12	2344	2000	2·00	2·33	2·93
GREY KNOTTS	7·14	2287	1900	1·50	1·95	2·47
SEATHWAITE FELL via Black Waugh	4·23	1970	1550	1·75	1·94	2·43
SEATHWAITE FELL via Styhead Gill	4·23	1970	1550	1·75	1·94	2·43
BASE BROWN	7·17	2120	1750	1·50	1·88	2·37
Seathwaite (Duddon Valley)						
DOW CRAG via Seathwaite Tarn	4·14	2555	2300	4·50	4·15	5·13
GREY FRIAR	4·15	2536	2200	4·00	3·77	4·67
DOW CRAG via Walna Scar Pass	4·14	2555	2300	3·75	3·65	4·53

STARTING POINT FELL NAME & ROUTE	BOOK & FELL NUMBER	HEIGHT ABOVE SEA LEVEL (feet)	HEIGHT OF ASCENT (feet)	DISTANCE OF ASCENT (miles)	ROUND TRIP FASTER TIME (hours)	ROUND TRIP SLOWER TIME (hours)
Seatoller						
SCAFELL PIKE via Sty Head	4·1	3210	3000	6·00	5·50	6·80
SCAFELL PIKE via Esk Hause	4·1	3210	3200	5·50	5·27	6·53
GREAT END	4·3	2984	2650	5·00	4·66	5·77
ESK PIKE	4·5	2903	2550	4·75	4·44	5·50
ALLEN CRAGS direct	4·12	2572	2250	4·50	4·13	5·10
ALLEN CRAGS via Allen Gill	4·12	2572	2250	4·00	3·79	4·70
DALE HEAD	6·7	2473	2150	3·25	3·24	4·03
GREY KNOTTS	7·14	2287	1950	2·50	2·64	3·30
HIGH SPY	6·13	2143	1800	2·50	2·57	3·20
Selside						
TARN CRAG via GREY CRAG	2·19	2176	1950	7·75	6·14	7·50
GREY CRAG	2·22	2093	1700	7·00	5·52	6·73
Shap						
TARN CRAG via Peat Hill and Brunt Tongue	2·19	2176	1680	7·00	5·51	6·72
Skelwith Bridge						
LOUGHRIGG FELL	3·27	1101	1000	1·75	1·67	2·07
Skiddaw House						
SKIDDAW via Hare Crag	5·1	3053	1700	3·00	2·85	3·53
SKIDDAW via Sale How	5·1	3053	1600	2·50	2·47	3·07
SKIDDAW LITTLE MAN	5·3	2837	1350	2·25	2·17	2·70
GREAT CALVA direct	5·9	2265	900	2·00	1·78	2·20
GREAT CALVA via Dead Beck	5·9	2265	900	2·00	1·78	2·20
LONSCALE FELL to East Peak	5·6	2344	1000	1·75	1·67	2·07
LONSCALE FELL via Burnt Horse Ridge	5·6	2344	1000	1·75	1·67	2·07
St John's-in-the-Vale Church						
HIGH RIGG	3·26	1163	450	0·50	0·56	0·70
Stair						
EEL CRAG via Causey Pike	6·2	2749	2850	3·40	3·69	4·62
EEL CRAG via the mine road	6·2	2749	2700	3·50	3·68	4·60
SAIL	6·5	2530	2200	3·00	3·10	3·87
SCAR CRAGS	6·11	2205	1950	3·00	2·98	3·70
OUTERSIDE	6·16	1863	1550	2·25	2·27	2·83
BARROW	6·23	1494	1200	2·25	2·10	2·60
CAUSEY PIKE direct	6·14	2035	1750	1·50	1·88	2·37
CAUSEY PIKE via Rowling End	6·14	2035	1750	1·50	1·88	2·37
CATBELLS via Skelgill	6·24	1481	1200	1·33	1·49	1·86

STARTING POINT FELL NAME & ROUTE	BOOK & FELL NUMBER	HEIGHT ABOVE SEA LEVEL (feet)	HEIGHT OF ASCENT (feet)	DISTANCE OF ASCENT (miles)	ROUND TRIP	
					FASTER TIME (hours)	SLOWER TIME (hours)
take Pass						
PIKE O'STICKLE	3·6	2323	800	1·33	1·29	1·60
tanah						
RAISE	1·4	2889	2400	2·50	2·87	3·60
STYBARROW DODD via Stanah Gill	1·9	2770	2300	2·50	2·82	3·53
STYBARROW DODD via Sticks Pass	1·9	2770	2300	2·50	2·82	3·53
taveley						
SOUR HOWES via Browfoot	2·33	1568	1250	5·25	4·13	5·03
tone Ends						
CARROCK FELL	5·13	2174	1400	1·25	1·53	1·93
tonethwaite						
BOWFELL via Stake Beck	4·4	2960	2650	6·50	5·66	6·97
BOWFELL via Angletarn Gill	4·4	2960	2650	6·50	5·66	6·97
HARRISON STICKLE via Langstrath, Stake Pass and PIKE	3·3	2403	2360	5·83	5·07	6·24
HARRISON STICKLE via HIGH RAISE and THUNACAR KNOTT	3·3	2403	2410	4·75	4·37	5·41
GLARAMARA via Langstrath and Tray Dub	4·13	2560	2300	4·50	4·15	5·13
GLARAMARA via Langstrath and shepherd's track	4·13	2560	2300	4·50	4·15	5·13
SERGEANT'S CRAG	3·11	1873	1600	4·50	3·80	4·67
HIGH RAISE	3·1	2500	2200	3·75	3·60	4·47
ULLSCARF via Coldbarrow Fell	3·4	2370	2100	3·25	3·22	4·00
ULLSCARF via Lining Crag	3·4	2370	2100	3·25	3·22	4·00
EAGLE CRAG via Greenup path	3·17	1650	1300	3·00	2·65	3·27
EAGLE CRAG direct	3·17	1650	1300	2·00	1·98	2·47
ROSTHWAITE FELL	4·24	1807	1500	1·50	1·75	2·20
GREAT CRAG via Knotts	3·20	1500	1200	1·50	1·60	2·00
GREAT CRAG via Dock Tarn	3·20	1500	1200	1·50	1·60	2·00
trands						
SEATALLAN via BUCKBARROW	7·15	2266	2150	4·50	4·08	5·03
SEATALLAN	7·15	2266	2150	4·00	3·74	4·63
ty Head						
GREAT END	4·3	2984	1450	1·00	1·39	1·77
GREAT GABLE	7·1	2949	1350	1·00	1·34	1·70

STARTING POINT FELL NAME & ROUTE	BOOK & FELL NUMBER	HEIGHT ABOVE SEA LEVEL (feet)	HEIGHT OF ASCENT (feet)	DISTANCE OF ASCENT (miles)	ROUND TRIP	
					FASTER TIME (hours)	SLOWER TIME (hours)
Styhead Gill						
GREEN GABLE via Aaron Slack	7·9	2603	1200	0·75	1·10	1·40
GREEN GABLE via Mitchell Cove	7·9	2603	1200	0·75	1·10	1·40
Swindale Head						
SELSIDE PIKE via Mosedale path	2·21	2142	1350	2·25	2·17	2·70
SELSIDE PIKE via north-east ridge	2·21	2142	1200	1·50	1·60	2·00
Thackthwaite						
LITTLE MELL FELL	1·29	1657	750	1·00	1·04	1·30
Thackthwaite (Lorton Vale)						
LOW FELL via the drove road	7·33	1360	1250	2·00	1·96	2·43
FELLBARROW via Watching Crag	7·32	1363	1150	2·00	1·91	2·37
LOW FELL via Watching Gill	7·33	1360	1250	1·50	1·63	2·03
FELLBARROW direct	7·32	1363	1000	1·25	1·33	1·67
Thirlmere						
ARMBOTH FELL via Dob Gill	3·18	1570	850	2·50	2·09	2·57
ARMBOTH FELL via Brown Rigg	3·18	1570	850	1·75	1·59	1·97
ARMBOTH FELL via Launchy Gill	3·18	1570	850	1·25	1·26	1·57
ARMBOTH FELL via Fisher Gill	3·18	1570	850	1·25	1·26	1·57
Thirlmere Dam						
RAVEN CRAG	3·19	1520	950	1·00	1·14	1·43
Thirlspot						
HELVELLYN via the old pony-route	1·1	3118	2600	4·00	3·97	4·93
HELVELLYN via the 'White Stones' Route	1·1	3118	2600	3·50	3·63	4·53
HELVELLYN via Helvellyn Gill	1·1	3118	2600	3·50	3·63	4·53
RAISE direct	1·4	2889	2400	2·50	2·87	3·60
RAISE via Brund Gill	1·4	2889	2400	2·50	2·87	3·60
WHITE SIDE	1·6	2832	2300	2·50	2·82	3·53
Thornthwaite						
GRISEDALE PIKE via north ridge	6·3	2593	2400	3·75	3·70	4·60
GRISEDALE PIKE via north-east ridge	6·3	2593	2350	3·25	3·34	4·17
LORD'S SEAT	6·18	1811	1550	2·50	2·44	3·03
Thornthwaite, Swan Hotel						
BARF via Beckstones Plantation	6·22	1536	1220	1·00	1·28	1·61
BARF via The Bishop	6·22	1536	1200	0·75	1·10	1·40

STARTING POINT FELL NAME & ROUTE	BOOK & FELL NUMBER	HEIGHT ABOVE SEA LEVEL (feet)	HEIGHT OF ASCENT (feet)	DISTANCE OF ASCENT (miles)	ROUND TRIP FASTER TIME (hours)	ROUND TRIP SLOWER TIME (hours)
Threlkeld						
BLENCATHRA via Roughten Gill	5·2	2847	2400	5·00	4·53	5·60
MUNGRISDALE COMMON via The Stake and Cloven Stone	5·16	2068	1500	4·50	3·75	4·60
MUNGRISDALE COMMON via Sinen Gill	5·16	2068	1500	4·25	3·58	4·40
BLENCATHRA via Doddick Gill	5·2	2847	2150	2·75	2·91	3·63
BLENCATHRA via Blease Fell	5·2	2847	2450	2·50	2·89	3·63
BLENCATHRA via Gategill Fell	5·2	2847	2450	2·00	2·56	3·23
BLENCATHRA via Blease Gill	5·2	2847	2400	2·00	2·53	3·20
BLENCATHRA via Middle Tongue	5·2	2847	2400	2·00	2·53	3·20
BLENCATHRA via Hall's Fell	5·2	2847	2400	2·00	2·53	3·20
LATRIGG	5·24	1203	900	3·00	2·45	3·00
Tilberthwaite						
WETHERLAM	4·16	2502	2100	2·00	2·38	3·00
Torver						
CONISTON OLD MAN via Goat's Hause	4·8	2633	2350	3·75	3·67	4·57
DOW CRAG via Goat's Hause	4·14	2555	2250	3·75	3·63	4·50
DOW CRAG via Walna Scar Pass	4·14	2555	2250	3·50	3·46	4·30
CONISTON OLD MAN direct	4·8	2633	2350	3·25	3·34	4·17
Troutal						
GREY FRIAR	4·15	2536	2000	2·25	2·50	3·13
Troutbeck						
CAUDALE MOOR via St Ravens Edge	2·7	2502	2350	6·00	5·17	6·37
CAUDALE MOOR via Threshthwaite Mouth	2·7	2502	2350	6·00	5·17	6·37
HIGH STREET	2·1	2718	2350	6·00	5·17	6·37
CAUDALE MOOR via Woundale	2·7	2502	2200	5·50	4·77	5·87
THORNTHWAITE CRAG via Threshthwaite Mouth	2·4	2569	2200	5·50	4·77	5·87
CAUDALE MOOR via Sad Gill	2·7	2502	2200	5·00	4·43	5·47
THORNTHWAITE CRAG via Scot Rake	2·4	2569	2200	5·00	4·43	5·47
FROSWICK via Blue Gill	2·12	2359	1850	3·75	3·42	4·23
ILL BELL via Hagg Gill	2·9	2476	1700	3·75	3·35	4·13
WANSFELL	2·32	1597	1100	1·75	1·72	2·13

STARTING POINT FELL NAME & ROUTE	BOOK & FELL NUMBER	HEIGHT ABOVE SEA LEVEL (feet)	HEIGHT OF ASCENT (feet)	DISTANCE OF ASCENT (miles)	ROUND TRIP	
					FASTER TIME (hours)	SLOWER TIME (hours)
Troutbeck Old Railway Station						
GREAT MELL FELL	1·27	1760	850	1·00	1·09	1·37
Troutbeck Park Farm						
TROUTBECK TONGUE						
via the Tongue	2·36	1191	650	3·00	2·33	2·83
TROUTBECK TONGUE	2·36	1191	650	0·75	0·82	1·03
Wanthwaite						
CLOUGH HEAD via Hause Well	1·18	2381	1900	3·00	2·95	3·67
CLOUGH HEAD direct	1·18	2381	1900	2·00	2·28	2·87
Wasdale Head						
BOWFELL via ESK PIKE	4·4	2960	3100	5·25	5·05	6·27
PILLAR via Black Sail Pass	7·2	2927	2700	4·50	4·35	5·40
ESK PIKE	4·5	2903	2700	4·25	4·18	5·20
GREAT END						
via Corridor Route	4·3	2984	2750	4·00	4·04	5·03
SCAFELL PIKE via Piers Gill and Lingmell col	4·1	3210	3000	3·75	4·00	5·00
SCAFELL PIKE via Piers Gill and Broad Crag col	4·1	3210	3000	3·75	4·00	5·00
SCAFELL via Green How	4·2	3162	2950	3·75	3·98	4·97
SCAFELL PIKE via Brown Tongue and Lingmell col	4·1	3210	3000	3·50	3·83	4·80
SCAFELL PIKE via Brown Tongue and Mickledore	4·1	3210	3000	3·50	3·83	4·80
GREAT END via Sty Head	4·3	2984	2800	3·25	3·57	4·47
LINGMELL via Piers Gill	4·7	2649	2450	3·50	3·56	4·43
ILLGILL HEAD	4·22	1983	1750	4·00	3·54	4·37
GREAT GABLE via Sty Head	7·1	2949	2750	3·25	3·54	4·43
PILLAR via Wind Gap	7·2	2927	2700	3·25	3·52	4·40
SCAFELL via Brown Tongue	4·2	3162	3000	3·00	3·50	4·40
SCOAT FELL	7·3	2760	2500	3·00	3·25	4·07
LINGMELL via Brown Tongue	4·7	2649	2450	3·00	3·23	4·03
GREAT GABLE via Gavel Neese and Beck Head	7·1	2949	2700	2·50	3·02	3·80
GREAT GABLE via Gavel Neese and Moses' Finger	7·1	2949	2700	2·50	3·02	3·80
LINGMELL via The Shoulder	4·7	2649	2450	2·50	2·89	3·63
RED PIKE (Wasdale)	7·4	2707	2450	2·50	2·89	3·63
YEWBARROW	7·19	2058	1900	2·50	2·62	3·27
KIRK FELL	7·7	2630	2330	1·25	2·00	2·55

STARTING POINT FELL NAME & ROUTE	BOOK & FELL NUMBER	HEIGHT ABOVE SEA LEVEL (feet)	HEIGHT OF ASCENT (feet)	DISTANCE OF ASCENT (miles)	ROUND TRIP	
					FASTER TIME (hours)	SLOWER TIME (hours)
Watendlath						
ULLSCARF	3·4	2370	1600	3·50	3·13	3·87
HIGH SEAT via HIGH TOVE	3·9	1995	1200	2·00	1·93	2·40
HIGH SEAT via Raise Gill	3·9	1995	1200	2·00	1·93	2·40
HIGH TOVE	3·16	1665	800	1·00	1·07	1·33
GRANGE FELL to Brund Fell	3·22	1363	550	1·00	0·94	1·17
Waterend						
BURNBANK FELL	7·30	1580	1250	2·75	2·46	3·03
Whinlatter Pass						
HOPEGILL HEAD	6·6	2525	1850	2·50	2·59	3·23
GRISEDALE PIKE	6·3	2593	1600	2·25	2·30	2·87
LORD'S SEAT	6·18	1811	800	2·00	1·73	2·13
WHINLATTER	6·20	1696	750	1·75	1·54	1·90
White Moss						
LOUGHRIGG FELL	3·27	1101	925	1·50	1·46	1·82
Windermere						
SOUR HOWES	2·33	1568	1200	4·25	3·43	4·20
Woodhow Farm						
WHIN RIGG	4·26	1755	1600	2·00	2·13	2·67
Woolpack Inn						
GREEN CRAG via Crook Crag	4·27	1602	1450	2·50	2·39	2·97
GREEN CRAG via Low Birker Tarn	4·27	1602	1450	2·50	2·39	2·97
Wrynose Bottom						
GREY FRIAR	4·15	2536	1750	1·25	1·71	2·17
COLD PIKE	4·19	2259	1500	1·25	1·58	2·00
Wrynose Pass						
CRINKLE CRAGS	4·6	2816	1650	2·75	2·66	3·30
GREY FRIAR	4·15	2536	1350	2·25	2·17	2·70
PIKE O'BLISCO	4·18	2304	1100	1·25	1·38	1·73
COLD PIKE	4·19	2259	1000	1·25	1·33	1·67
Wythburn						
HIGH RAISE	3·1	2500	1950	5·00	4·31	5·30
SERGEANT MAN via Far Easedale	3·2	2414	1850	5·00	4·26	5·23
CALF CRAG	3·15	1762	1250	4·00	3·29	4·03

STARTING POINT FELL NAME & ROUTE	BOOK & FELL NUMBER	HEIGHT ABOVE SEA LEVEL (feet)	HEIGHT OF ASCENT (feet)	DISTANCE OF ASCENT (miles)	ROUND TRIP	
					FASTER TIME (hours)	SLOWER TIME (hours)
Wythburn *(continued)*						
ULLSCARF via West Head	3·4	2370	1800	3·50	3·23	4·00
HELVELLYN via Birk Side	1·1	3118	2550	2·75	3·11	3·90
HELVELLYN via old lead mine	1·1	3118	2550	2·50	2·94	3·70
HELVELLYN via Whelpside Gill	1·1	3118	2550	2·25	2·77	3·50
HELVELLYN via Comb Gill	1·1	3118	2550	2·25	2·77	3·50
NETHERMOST PIKE	1·2	2920	2400	2·00	2·53	3·20
STEEL FELL	3·12	1811	1250	2·00	1·96	2·43
Wythop Mill						
BROOM FELL	6·21	1670	1450	4·00	3·39	4·17
LING FELL	6·26	1224	850	1·50	1·43	1·77
SALE FELL	6·27	1170	750	1·50	1·38	1·70
Yew Tree House						
HOLME FELL	4·30	1040	750	1·00	1·04	1·30

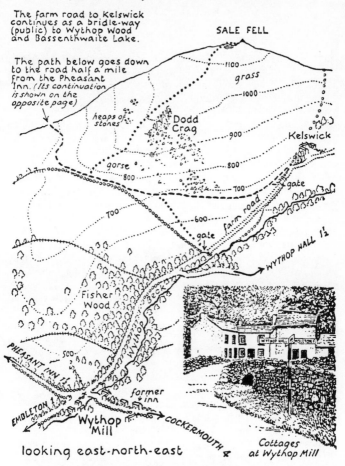

The farm road to Kelswick continues as a bridle-way (public) to Wythop Wood and Bassenthwaite Lake.

The path below goes down to the road half a mile from the Pheasant Inn. (Its continuation is shown on the opposite page)

SALE FELL

1100

grass

1000

heaps of stones

Dodd Crag

900

Kelswick

800

gorse

800

700

gate

700

600

farm road

gate

WYTHOP HALL 1½

Fisher Wood

WYTHOP BECK

PHEASANT INN 1½

500

former inn

Wythop Mill

EMBLETON 1

COCKERMOUTH 8

looking east-north-east

Cottages at Wythop Mill

A sylvan approach gives added pleasure to this simple climb. As an introduction to the Wythop Valley (an introduction warmly to be commended) this route is excellent and instructive.

CHAPTER 4

RIDGE ROUTES

Routes along the ridges which connect two or more fells are one of the most exciting aspects of fellwalking. Most of the 214 fells, at least those of any significance, form part of a group of fells which are connected to one another by high-level ridges. These ridges enable the walker to keep the advantage of high ground to visit neighbouring fells without a complete descent and re-ascent. Often the ridge routes are used to make a diversion to a neighbouring fell before the return journey to the valley below is started.

A more challenging use of these ridge connections, however, is when they form a continuous route along a number of fells, and some careful pre-planning can make an exciting all-day excursion – so long, of course, one has the means of transport at the other end.

Table 10 facing shows an example of one such through route: the first summit to be reached is Low Pike (climbed from Ambleside) and the final fell is Clough Head (with the walk finishing at Wanthwaite, near Threlkeld). The table shows the 'route card' for this marathon walk, and below that is a diagram of the elevation of the journey.

This particular route includes 15 fells of which 11 are over 2500 feet in height but no more than 6700 feet of ascent is climbed – a decent amount of climbing but averaging less than 500 feet per fell. The walk covers a distance of 19 miles but the important point is that there are more than 12 miles at heights above 2500 feet because of the use of connecting ridges.

There must have been many walking tours planned which use the principal of ridge walking to cover distance at height, but I cannot imagine any better than that encapsulated in Wainwright's tour of the Lake District in 1931. This ambitious tour covers 102.5 miles in 6 days, climbs 35,000 feet of ascent and visits 65 fells. AW, in his notes for the walk, promises that 'every lake, every valley, every mountain will be seen, if not actually visited'. It is hard to believe that AW planned this route, tucked up in his home in Blackburn, with the aid only of the 1″ to 1 mile Ordnance Survey map then available, and having visited the Lake District just once previously. The Tour follows the itinerary shown on p 142.

TABLE 10: Through Route – Ambleside to Wanthwaite

FROM	ASCENT, RIDGE ROUTE OR DESCENT BOOK & FELL NUMBER	TO	BOOK & FELL NUMBER	ASCENT HEIGHT (feet)	DISTANCE (miles)	TIME AT FASTER RATE (hours)	SLOWER RATE (hours)
Ambleside		LOW PIKE	1.30	1500	2.25	1.50	1.90
LOW PIKE	1.30	HIGH PIKE	1.21	600	0.67	0.52	0.67
HIGH PIKE	1.21	DOVE CRAG	1.12	470	1.00	0.57	0.71
DOVE CRAG	1.12	HART CRAG	1.11	350	0.75	0.43	0.53
HART CRAG	1.11	FAIRFIELD	1.5	330	1.00	0.50	0.62
FAIRFIELD	1.5	SEAT SANDAL	1.17	490	1.33	0.69	0.86
SEAT SANDAL	1.17	DOLLYWAGGON PIKE	1.7	1000	1.25	0.92	1.17
DOLLYWAGGON PIKE	1.7	NETHERMOST PIKE	1.2	220	1.00	0.44	0.55
NETHERMOST PIKE	1.2	HELVELLYN	1.1	280	0.75	0.39	0.49
HELVELLYN	1.1	WHITE SIDE	1.6	300	1.50	0.65	0.80
WHITE SIDE	1.6	RAISE	1.4	250	0.75	0.38	0.47
RAISE	1.4	STYBARROW DODD	1.9	350	1.00	0.51	0.63
STYBARROW DODD	1.9	WATSON'S DODD	1.13	0	0.67	0.22	0.27
WATSON'S DODD	1.13	GREAT DODD	1.8	250	0.75	0.38	0.47
GREAT DODD	1.8	CLOUGH HEAD	1.18	300	2.00	0.82	1.00
CLOUGH HEAD	1.18	**Wanthwaite**		0	2.00	0.67	0.80
TOTALS OF HEIGHTS, DISTANCES AND TIMES				**6690**	**18.67**	**9.59**	**11.94**

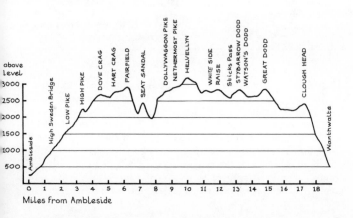

DAY AND ROUTE	MILES	CLIMBING	PRINCIPLE FELLS VISITED
1 Windermere to Patterdale	16	3850	ORREST HEAD, YOKE, ILL BELL, FROSWICK, THORNTHWAITE CRAG, HIGH STREET, THE KNOTT, ANGLETARN PIKES.
2. Patterdale to Threlkeld (for Keswick)	20	6900	STRIDING EDGE, HELVELLYN, RAISE, STYBARROW DODD, WATSON'S DODD, GREAT DODD, CALFHOW PIKE, WHITE PIKE, SHARP EDGE, BLENCATHRA.
3. Keswick to Buttermere	19	6650	CATBELLS, MAIDEN MOOR, EEL CRAGS, DALE HEAD, HINDSCARTH, ROBINSON, KNOTT RIGG, ARD CRAGS, SAIL, EEL CRAG, GRASMOOR, WANDOPE, WHITELESS PIKE.
4. Buttermere to Wasdale	18	7750	RED PIKE (B), HIGH STILE, HIGH CRAG, HAYSTACKS, BRANDRETH, GREEN GABLE, GREAT GABLE, KIRK FELL, LOOKING STEAD, PILLAR, SCOAT FELL, RED PIKE (W), DORE HEAD.
5. Wasdale to Langdale	14.5	6300	BROWN TONGUE, SCAFELL PIKE, BROAD CRAG, GREAT END, ESK PIKE, BOWFELL, SHELTER CRAGS, CRINKLE CRAGS, COLD PIKE, PIKE O'BLISCO, BLAKE RIGG.
6. Langdale to Ambleside (for Windermere)	15	3400	PIKE O'STICKLE, HARRISON STICKLE, PAVEY ARK, SERGEANT MAN, HIGH RAISE, CALF CRAG, GIBSON KNOTT, HELM CRAG.
TOTALS	102.5	34,850	

This impressive walking tour has been documented excellently in *Wainwright's Tour in the Lake District* (Michael Joseph, 1993) and I have been fortunate enough to contribute some tables and maps of a similar nature to those appearing in this Gazetteer. Readers of that book will note that it is an extremely strenuous expedition but one offering unrivalled coverage of the high fells and scenery.

Another benefit of the ridge routes is when they form a circular route, sometimes more in the form of a horseshoe with a final connecting link. The great advantage is not having to retrace one's steps to the starting point and there are many favourite routes known to experienced fellwalkers.

An example of this type of ridge walk is the Fairfield Horseshoe, one of the eighteen favourite walks included by AW in his first book to be illustrated with photographs by Derry Brabbs, *Fellwalking with Wainwright*. Starting from Ambleside, the walk visits the summits of Low Pike, High Pike, Dove Crag, Hart Crag, Fairfield, Great Rigg, Heron Pike, the steep descent down Nab Scar to Rydal, and then the final pretty walk through Rydal Park back to Ambleside.

This horseshoe, with its final stage making it the perfect circular walk, covers about 12 miles of which 7 miles are at a height of over 2000 feet, and includes some 3600 feet of ascent; the time required to complete this classic horseshoe would be about 6½ hours at the faster rate, and just under 10 hours at the slower rate.

The following tables appear in Book order and the fells within each Book appear in the alphabetical order AW used, and within each fell, the ridge routes are also given in the order they appear in the Pictorial Guides.

RIDGE ROUTES
listed in order of Book and Fell

BOOK 1 THE EASTERN FELLS

START FELL NUMBER & NAME		END FELL NUMBER & NAME		HEIGHT OF ASCENT (feet)	LENGTH OF RIDGE (miles)	ROUTE FASTER TIME (hours)	ROUTE SLOWER TIME (hours)
19	BIRKHOUSE MOOR	1	HELVELLYN	800	2·00	1·07	1·33
24	BIRKS	10	SAINT SUNDAY CRAG	800	1·25	0·82	1·03
3	CATSTYCAM	1	HELVELLYN *	520	1·00	0·59	0·75
18	CLOUGH HEAD	8	GREAT DODD	720	2·00	1·03	1·28
7	DOLLYWAGGON PIKE	2	NETHERMOST PIKE	220	1·00	0·44	0·55
7	DOLLYWAGGON PIKE	17	SEAT SANDAL	600	1·25	0·72	0·90
12	DOVE CRAG	11	HART CRAG	350	0·75	0·42	0·53
12	DOVE CRAG	21	HIGH PIKE	0	1·00	0·33	0·40
12	DOVE CRAG	23	LITTLE HART CRAG	200	1·25	0·52	0·63
5	FAIRFIELD	10	SAINT SUNDAY CRAG	610	1·50	0·80	1·01
5	FAIRFIELD	15	GREAT RIGG	140	1·00	0·40	0·49
5	FAIRFIELD	11	HART CRAG	150	1·00	0·41	0·50
5	FAIRFIELD	17	SEAT SANDAL *	490	1·33	0·69	0·86
34	GLENRIDDING DODD	20	SHEFFIELD PIKE *	880	1·00	0·77	0·99
8	GREAT DODD	18	CLOUGH HEAD	300	2·00	0·82	1·00
8	GREAT DODD	13	WATSON'S DODD	0	0·75	0·25	0·30
15	GREAT RIGG	5	FAIRFIELD	500	1·00	0·58	0·73
15	GREAT RIGG	25	HERON PIKE	150	1·50	0·57	0·70
15	GREAT RIGG	31	STONE ARTHUR	0	1·25	0·42	0·50
11	HART CRAG	5	FAIRFIELD	330	1·00	0·50	0·62
11	HART CRAG	12	DOVE CRAG	260	0·75	0·38	0·47
11	HART CRAG	26	HARTSOP ABOVE HOW	150	1·50	0·57	0·70
16	HART SIDE	9	STYBARROW DODD	550	1·50	0·78	0·97
26	HARTSOP ABOVE HOW	11	HART CRAG	1000	1·50	1·00	1·27
1	HELVELLYN	3	CATSTYCAM	320	1·00	0·49	0·61
1	HELVELLYN	19	BIRKHOUSE MOOR	100	2·00	0·72	0·87
1	HELVELLYN	2	NETHERMOST PIKE	80	0·75	0·29	0·35
1	HELVELLYN	6	WHITE SIDE *	300	1·50	0·65	0·80
25	HERON PIKE	15	GREAT RIGG	550	1·50	0·78	0·97
25	HERON PIKE	33	NAB SCAR	0	0·67	0·22	0·27
21	HIGH PIKE	12	DOVE CRAG	470	1·00	0·57	0·71
21	HIGH PIKE	30	LOW PIKE	100	0·67	0·27	0·33
23	LITTLE HART CRAG	12	DOVE CRAG	700	1·25	0·77	0·97
23	LITTLE HART CRAG	14	RED SCREES	900	1·25	0·87	1·10
30	LOW PIKE	21	HIGH PIKE	600	0·67	0·52	0·67
33	NAB SCAR	25	HERON PIKE	570	0·67	0·51	0·65
2	NETHERMOST PIKE	1	HELVELLYN	280	0·75	0·39	0·49
2	NETHERMOST PIKE	7	DOLLYWAGGON PIKE	120	1·00	0·39	0·48
4	RAISE	9	STYBARROW DODD	350	1·00	0·51	0·63
4	RAISE	6	WHITE SIDE	200	0·75	0·35	0·43
14	RED SCREES	23	LITTLE HART CRAG	430	1·25	0·63	0·79
10	SAINT SUNDAY CRAG	5	FAIRFIELD	750	1·50	0·88	1·10
10	SAINT SUNDAY CRAG	24	BIRKS	50	1·25	0·44	0·53
17	SEAT SANDAL	5	FAIRFIELD	950	1·33	0·92	1·17
17	SEAT SANDAL	7	DOLLYWAGGON PIKE	1000	1·25	0·92	1·17

The ridge routes shown with an * following the End Fell Name were not evaluated explicitly by Wainwright in his guidebooks but have been computed for the Gazetteer from data given there

[144]

START FELL NUMBER & NAME		END FELL NUMBER & NAME	HEIGHT OF ASCENT (feet)	LENGTH OF RIDGE (miles)	ROUTE	
					FASTER TIME (hours)	SLOWER TIME (hours)
20	SHEFFIELD PIKE	9 STYBARROW DODD	1000	2·00	1·17	1·47
20	SHEFFIELD PIKE	34 GLENRIDDING DODD	150	1·00	0·41	0·50
31	STONE ARTHUR	15 GREAT RIGG *	860	1·25	0·85	1·07
9	STYBARROW DODD	4 RAISE	470	1·00	0·57	0·71
9	STYBARROW DODD	13 WATSON'S DODD	0	0·67	0·22	0·27
9	STYBARROW DODD	16 HART SIDE	300	1·50	0·65	0·80
9	STYBARROW DODD	20 SHEFFIELD PIKE	400	2·00	0·87	1·07
13	WATSON'S DODD	8 GREAT DODD	250	0·75	0·38	0·47
13	WATSON'S DODD	9 STYBARROW DODD	200	0·67	0·32	0·40
6	WHITE SIDE	4 RAISE	250	0·75	0·38	0·47
6	WHITE SIDE	1 HELVELLYN	600	1·50	0·80	1·00

						ROUTE	
START			END		HEIGHT OF ASCENT (feet)	LENGTH OF RIDGE (miles)	FASTER TIME (hours)	SLOWE TIME (hour
FELL NUMBER & NAME			FELL NUMBER & NAME				

	START			END	HEIGHT OF ASCENT (feet)	LENGTH OF RIDGE (miles)	FASTER TIME (hours)	SLOWE TIME (hour
26	ANGLETARN PIKES	31	BEDA FELL		300	2·00	0·82	1·00
26	ANGLETARN PIKES	16	REST DODD		700	1·75	0·93	1·17
28	ARTHUR'S PIKE	18	LOADPOT HILL		500	2·25	1·00	1·23
28	ARTHUR'S PIKE	29	BONSCALE PIKE		150	1·00	0·41	0·50
31	BEDA FELL	26	ANGLETARN PIKES *		400	2·00	0·87	1·07
29	BONSCALE PIKE	28	ARTHUR'S PIKE		200	1·00	0·43	0·53
29	BONSCALE PIKE	18	LOADPOT HILL		550	1·50	0·78	0·97
13	BRANSTREE	19	TARN CRAG		550	1·75	0·86	1·07
13	BRANSTREE	6	HARTER FELL		700	2·00	1·02	1·27
13	BRANSTREE	21	SELSIDE PIKE		200	1·50	0·60	0·73
7	CAUDALE MOOR	32	WANSFELL		500	4·50	1·75	2·13
7	CAUDALE MOOR	4	THORNTHWAITE CRAG		620	1·00	0·64	0·81
7	CAUDALE MOOR	23	HARTSOP DODD		120	1·33	0·50	0·61
12	FROSWICK	4	THORNTHWAITE CRAG		480	1·00	0·57	0·72
12	FROSWICK	9	ILL BELL		400	0·67	0·42	0·53
15	GRAY CRAG	4	THORNTHWAITE CRAG		350	1·25	0·59	0·73
22	GREY CRAG	19	TARN CRAG		250	0·75	0·38	0·47
6	HARTER FELL	13	BRANSTREE		465	2·00	0·90	1·11
6	HARTER FELL	11	KENTMERE PIKE		150	1·25	0·49	0·60
6	HARTER FELL	8	MARDALE ILL BELL		450	1·00	0·56	0·70
23	HARTSOP DODD	7	CAUDALE MOOR		620	1·33	0·75	0·95
2	HIGH RAISE	17	WETHER HILL		100	2·25	0·80	0·97
2	HIGH RAISE	3	RAMPSGILL HEAD		140	0·75	0·32	0·39
1	HIGH STREET	3	RAMPSGILL HEAD		250	1·25	0·54	0·67
1	HIGH STREET	8	MARDALE ILL BELL		150	0·80	0·34	0·42
1	HIGH STREET	4	THORNTHWAITE CRAG		100	1·25	0·47	0·57
9	ILL BELL	12	FROSWICK		285	0·67	0·37	0·46
9	ILL BELL	14	YOKE		130	0·67	0·29	0·35
11	KENTMERE PIKE	6	HARTER FELL		275	1·25	0·55	0·68
11	KENTMERE PIKE	24	SHIPMAN KNOTTS		80	1·25	0·46	0·55
5	KIDSTY PIKE	3	RAMPSGILL HEAD		60	0·33	0·14	0·17
10	THE KNOTT	3	RAMPSGILL HEAD		225	0·33	0·22	0·28
10	THE KNOTT	16	REST DODD		360	0·75	0·43	0·54
18	LOADPOT HILL	28	ARTHUR'S PIKE		50	2·25	0·78	0·93
18	LOADPOT HILL	29	BONSCALE PIKE		50	1·50	0·53	0·63
18	LOADPOT HILL	17	WETHER HILL		200	1·00	0·43	0·53
8	MARDALE ILL BELL	1	HIGH STREET		400	0·80	0·47	0·59
8	MARDALE ILL BELL	4	THORNTHWAITE CRAG		250	1·33	0·57	0·70
8	MARDALE ILL BELL	6	HARTER FELL		500	1·00	0·58	0·73
25	THE NAB	16	REST DODD		650	1·25	0·74	0·93
3	RAMPSGILL HEAD	2	HIGH RAISE		190	0·75	0·34	0·43
3	RAMPSGILL HEAD	10	THE KNOTT		65	0·33	0·14	0·18
3	RAMPSGILL HEAD	5	KIDSTY PIKE		35	0·33	0·13	0·16
3	RAMPSGILL HEAD	1	HIGH STREET		400	1·25	0·62	0·77
16	REST DODD	26	ANGLETARN PIKES		300	1·75	0·73	0·90
16	REST DODD	10	THE KNOTT		500	0·75	0·50	0·63
16	REST DODD	25	THE NAB		250	1·25	0·54	0·67
21	SELSIDE PIKE	13	BRANSTREE		450	1·50	0·72	0·90

START FELL NUMBER & NAME		END FELL NUMBER & NAME	HEIGHT OF ASCENT (feet)	LENGTH OF RIDGE (miles)	ROUTE	
					FASTER TIME (hours)	SLOWER TIME (hours)
SHIPMAN KNOTTS	11	KENTMERE PIKE	525	1·25	0·68	0·85
STEEL KNOTTS	17	WETHER HILL	1100	1·50	1·05	1·33
TARN CRAG	13	BRANSTREE	700	1·75	0·93	1·17
TARN CRAG	22	GREY CRAG	170	0·75	0·34	0·41
THORNTHWAITE CRAG	7	CAUDALE MOOR	560	1·00	0·61	0·77
THORNTHWAITE CRAG	15	GRAY CRAG	150	1·25	0·49	0·60
THORNTHWAITE CRAG	12	FROSWICK	300	1·00	0·48	0·60
THORNTHWAITE CRAG	1	HIGH STREET	250	1·25	0·54	0·67
THORNTHWAITE CRAG	8	MARDALE ILL BELL	200	1·33	0·54	0·67
WANSFELL	7	CAUDALE MOOR	1550	4·50	2·27	2·83
WETHER HILL	18	LOADPOT HILL	180	1·00	0·42	0·52
WETHER HILL	2	HIGH RAISE	500	2·25	1·00	1·23
WETHER HILL	34	STEEL KNOTTS *	210	1·50	0·60	0·74
YOKE	9	ILL BELL	300	0·67	0·37	0·47

THE CENTRAL FELLS

START FELL NUMBER & NAME	END FELL NUMBER & NAME	HEIGHT OF ASCENT (feet)	LENGTH OF RIDGE (miles)	ROUTE FASTER TIME (hours)	SLOWE TIME (hours
18 ARMBOTH FELL	16 HIGH TOVE	200	1·00	0·43	0·53
18 ARMBOTH FELL	4 ULLSCARF	950	3·00	1·48	1·83
10 BLEABERRY FELL	9 HIGH SEAT	200	1·25	0·52	0·63
10 BLEABERRY FELL	25 WALLA CRAG	170	1·25	0·50	0·61
14 BLEA RIGG	2 SERGEANT MAN	700	1·50	0·85	1·07
14 BLEA RIGG	24 SILVER HOW	150	2·00	0·74	0·90
15 CALF CRAG	12 STEEL FELL	350	1·50	0·68	0·83
15 CALF CRAG	21 GIBSON KNOTT	100	1·25	0·47	0·57
17 EAGLE CRAG	11 SERGEANT'S CRAG	250	0·50	0·29	0·37
21 GIBSON KNOTT	15 CALF CRAG	450	1·25	0·64	0·80
21 GIBSON KNOTT	23 HELM CRAG	320	1·00	0·49	0·61
20 GREAT CRAG	4 ULLSCARF	1300	2·75	1·57	1·97
3 HARRISON STICKLE	6 PIKE O'STICKLE	250	0·50	0·29	0·37
3 HARRISON STICKLE	8 LOFT CRAG	200	0·33	0·21	0·27
3 HARRISON STICKLE	5 THUNACAR KNOTT	140	0·50	0·24	0·29
3 HARRISON STICKLE	7 PAVEY ARK	100	0·50	0·22	0·27
23 HELM CRAG	21 GIBSON KNOTT	400	1·00	0·53	0·67
1 HIGH RAISE	5 THUNACAR KNOTT	130	1·00	0·40	0·49
1 HIGH RAISE	2 SERGEANT MAN	60	0·50	0·20	0·24
1 HIGH RAISE	11 SERGEANT'S CRAG	225	1·50	0·61	0·75
1 HIGH RAISE	4 ULLSCARF	400	2·25	0·95	1·17
9 HIGH SEAT	10 BLEABERRY FELL	150	1·25	0·49	0·60
9 HIGH SEAT	16 HIGH TOVE	25	1·00	0·35	0·42
16 HIGH TOVE	9 HIGH SEAT	300	1·00	0·48	0·60
16 HIGH TOVE	18 ARMBOTH FELL	100	1·00	0·38	0·47
8 LOFT CRAG	3 HARRISON STICKLE	340	0·50	0·34	0·43
8 LOFT CRAG	6 PIKE O'STICKLE	170	0·33	0·20	0·25
27 LOUGHRIGG FELL	24 SILVER HOW	950	2·50	1·31	1·63
7 PAVEY ARK	3 HARRISON STICKLE *	175	0·50	0·25	0·32
6 PIKE O'STICKLE	8 LOFT CRAG	100	0·33	0·16	0·20
6 PIKE O'STICKLE	3 HARRISON STICKLE *	350	0·50	0·34	0·43
2 SERGEANT MAN	1 HIGH RAISE	140	0·50	0·24	0·29
2 SERGEANT MAN	14 BLEA RIGG	100	1·50	0·55	0·67
2 SERGEANT MAN	13 TARN CRAG	100	1·25	0·47	0·57
2 SERGEANT MAN	5 THUNACAR KNOTT *	125	1·00	0·40	0·48
11 SERGEANT'S CRAG	17 EAGLE CRAG	50	0·50	0·19	0·23
11 SERGEANT'S CRAG	1 HIGH RAISE	850	1·50	0·93	1·17
24 SILVER HOW	27 LOUGHRIGG FELL	850	2·50	1·26	1·57
24 SILVER HOW	14 BLEA RIGG	650	2·00	0·99	1·23
12 STEEL FELL	15 CALF CRAG	300	1·50	0·65	0·80
13 TARN CRAG	2 SERGEANT MAN	700	1·25	0·77	0·97
5 THUNACAR KNOTT	1 HIGH RAISE	275	1·00	0·47	0·58
5 THUNACAR KNOTT	2 SERGEANT MAN	200	1·00	0·43	0·53
5 THUNACAR KNOTT	3 HARRISON STICKLE	150	0·50	0·24	0·30
4 ULLSCARF	18 ARMBOTH FELL	250	3·00	1·13	1·37
4 ULLSCARF	20 GREAT CRAG	200	2·75	1·02	1·23
4 ULLSCARF	1 HIGH RAISE	520	2·25	1·01	1·25
25 WALLA CRAG	10 BLEABERRY FELL	900	1·25	0·87	1·10

THE SOUTHERN FELLS

START		END		HEIGHT OF ASCENT (feet)	LENGTH OF RIDGE (miles)	ROUTE	
FELL NUMBER & NAME		FELL NUMBER & NAME				FASTER TIME (hours)	SLOWER TIME (hours)
12	ALLEN CRAGS	13	GLARAMARA	500	1·75	0·83	1·03
4	BOWFELL	6	CRINKLE CRAGS	600	1·50	0·80	1·00
4	BOWFELL	5	ESK PIKE	340	1·00	0·50	0·63
10	BRIM FELL	8	CONISTON OLD MAN	100	0·50	0·22	0·27
10	BRIM FELL	9	SWIRL HOW	400	1·50	0·70	0·87
19	COLD PIKE	6	CRINKLE CRAGS	850	1·50	0·93	1·17
19	COLD PIKE	18	PIKE O'BLISCO	700	1·25	0·77	0·97
8	CONISTON OLD MAN	10	BRIM FELL	80	0·50	0·21	0·25
8	CONISTON OLD MAN	14	DOW CRAG	425	1·00	0·55	0·68
6	CRINKLE CRAGS	4	BOWFELL	850	1·50	0·93	1·17
6	CRINKLE CRAGS	19	COLD PIKE	300	1·50	0·65	0·80
14	DOW CRAG	8	CONISTON OLD MAN	510	1·00	0·59	0·74
5	ESK PIKE	4	BOWFELL	400	1·00	0·53	0·67
5	ESK PIKE	3	GREAT END	525	1·25	0·68	0·85
13	GLARAMARA	12	ALLEN CRAGS	500	1·75	0·83	1·03
13	GLARAMARA	24	ROSTHWAITE FELL	200	1·75	0·68	0·83
1	GREAT CARRS	9	SWIRL HOW	130	0·33	0·17	0·22
1	GREAT CARRS	15	GREY FRIAR	265	0·88	0·42	0·53
3	GREAT END	5	ESK PIKE	425	1·25	0·63	0·78
3	GREAT END	1	SCAFELL PIKE	600	1·33	0·74	0·93
15	GREY FRIAR	9	SWIRL HOW	355	1·00	0·51	0·64
15	GREY FRIAR	11	GREAT CARRS	300	0·88	0·44	0·55
2	ILLGILL HEAD	26	WHIN RIGG	240	1·33	0·56	0·69
7	LINGMELL	1	SCAFELL PIKE	850	0·88	0·72	0·92
18	PIKE O'BLISCO	19	COLD PIKE	650	1·25	0·74	0·93
24	ROSTHWAITE FELL	13	GLARAMARA	1000	1·75	1·08	1·37
2	SCAFELL	17	SLIGHT SIDE	100	1·25	0·47	0·57
2	SCAFELL	1	SCAFELL PIKE via Lord's Rake	750	1·25	0·79	1·00
2	SCAFELL	1	SCAFELL PIKE via Foxes Tarn	900	1·25	0·87	1·10
1	SCAFELL PIKE	3	GREAT END	350	1·33	0·62	0·77
1	SCAFELL PIKE	7	LINGMELL	280	0·88	0·43	0·54
1	SCAFELL PIKE	2	SCAFELL Via Lord's Rake	700	1·25	0·77	0·97
1	SCAFELL PIKE	2	SCAFELL Via Foxes Tarn	850	1·25	0·84	1·07
17	SLIGHT SIDE	2	SCAFELL	750	1·25	0·79	1·00
9	SWIRL HOW	10	BRIM FELL	380	1·50	0·69	0·85
9	SWIRL HOW	16	WETHERLAM	500	1·25	0·67	0·83
9	SWIRL HOW	11	GREAT CARRS	75	0·33	0·15	0·18
9	SWIRL HOW	15	GREY FRIAR	270	1·00	0·47	0·58
16	WETHERLAM	9	SWIRL HOW	620	1·25	0·73	0·91
26	WHIN RIGG	22	ILLGILL HEAD	450	1·33	0·67	0·83

START		END		HEIGHT OF ASCENT (feet)	LENGTH OF RIDGE (miles)	ROUTE	
FELL NUMBER & NAME		FELL NUMBER & NAME				FASTER TIME (hours)	SLOWER TIME (hours)
12	BAKESTALL	1	SKIDDAW	900	1·25	0·87	1·10
10	BANNERDALE CRAGS	8	BOWSCALE FELL	250	1·25	0·54	0·67
10	BANNERDALE CRAGS	2	BLENCATHRA	850	1·50	0·93	1·17
2	BLENCATHRA	20	SOUTHER FELL	350	2·50	1·01	1·23
2	BLENCATHRA	10	BANNERDALE CRAGS	200	1·50	0·60	0·73
8	BOWSCALE FELL	10	BANNERDALE CRAGS	180	1·25	0·51	0·62
17	BRAE FELL	15	GREAT SCA FELL *	270	1·00	0·47	0·58
4	CARL SIDE	1	SKIDDAW	780	1·00	0·72	0·92
4	CARL SIDE	5	LONG SIDE	165	0·50	0·25	0·31
4	CARL SIDE	21	DODD *	260	1·50	0·63	0·77
13	CARROCK FELL	14	HIGH PIKE	330	2·00	0·83	1·02
21	DODD	4	CARL SIDE	1075	1·50	1·04	1·32
9	GREAT CALVA	7	KNOTT	550	1·50	0·78	0·97
19	GREAT COCKUP	18	MEAL FELL	300	1·00	0·48	0·60
15	GREAT SCA FELL	7	KNOTT	250	0·75	0·38	0·47
15	GREAT SCA FELL	17	BRAE FELL	75	1·00	0·37	0·45
15	GREAT SCA FELL	22	LONGLANDS FELL	250	1·75	0·71	0·87
15	GREAT SCA FELL	18	MEAL FELL	100	0·75	0·30	0·37
14	HIGH PIKE	7	KNOTT	550	2·50	1·11	1·37
14	HIGH PIKE	13	CARROCK FELL	350	2·00	0·84	1·03
7	KNOTT	14	HIGH PIKE	380	2·50	1·02	1·25
7	KNOTT	15	GREAT SCA FELL *	50	0·75	0·28	0·33
7	KNOTT	9	GREAT CALVA *	480	1·50	0·74	0·92
22	LONGLANDS FELL	15	GREAT SCA FELL	730	1·75	0·95	1·19
5	LONG SIDE	11	ULLOCK PIKE	50	0·33	0·14	0·17
5	LONG SIDE	4	CARL SIDE	180	0·50	0·26	0·32
6	LONSCALE FELL	3	SKIDDAW LITTLE MAN	675	1·50	0·84	1·05
18	MEAL FELL	15	GREAT SCA FELL	460	0·75	0·48	0·61
18	MEAL FELL	19	GREAT COCKUP	250	1·00	0·46	0·57
1	SKIDDAW	3	SKIDDAW LITTLE MAN	190	1·00	0·43	0·53
1	SKIDDAW	4	CARL SIDE	160	1·00	0·41	0·51
1	SKIDDAW	12	BAKESTALL	40	1·25	0·44	0·53
3	SKIDDAW LITTLE MAN	1	SKIDDAW	400	1·00	0·53	0·67
3	SKIDDAW LITTLE MAN	6	LONSCALE FELL	175	1·50	0·59	0·72
20	SOUTHER FELL	2	BLENCATHRA *	500	2·50	1·08	1·33
11	ULLOCK PIKE	5	LONG SIDE	230	0·33	0·23	0·29

THE NORTH WESTERN FELLS

START FELL NUMBER & NAME	END FELL NUMBER & NAME	HEIGHT OF ASCENT (feet)	LENGTH OF RIDGE (miles)	ROUTE FASTER TIME (hours)	SLOWER TIME (hours)
17 ARD CRAGS	19 KNOTT RIGG	130	1·00	0·40	0·49
22 BARF	18 LORD'S SEAT	420	0·75	0·46	0·58
23 BARROW	16 OUTERSIDE	800	1·25	0·82	1·03
21 BROOM FELL	18 LORD'S SEAT	260	0·88	0·42	0·53
21 BROOM FELL	25 GRAYSTONES	260	1·25	0·55	0·67
24 CAT BELLS	15 MAIDEN MOOR	720	1·50	0·86	1·08
14 CAUSEY PIKE	11 SCAR CRAGS	320	0·75	0·41	0·51
7 DALE HEAD	9 HINDSCARTH	250	1·25	0·54	0·67
7 DALE HEAD	13 HIGH SPY	550	1·50	0·78	0·97
2 EEL CRAG	5 SAIL	100	0·40	0·18	0·23
2 EEL CRAG	1 GRASMOOR	450	1·25	0·64	0·80
2 EEL CRAG	4 WANDOPE	120	0·75	0·31	0·38
1 GRASMOOR	2 EEL CRAG	400	1·25	0·62	0·77
1 GRASMOOR	4 WANDOPE *	160	1·25	0·50	0·61
25 GRAYSTONES	21 BROOM FELL	450	1·50	0·72	0·90
3 GRISEDALE PIKE	6 HOPEGILL HEAD	350	1·13	0·55	0·68
13 HIGH SPY	15 MAIDEN MOOR	100	1·50	0·55	0·68
13 HIGH SPY	7 DALE HEAD	900	1·50	0·95	1·20
9 HINDSCARTH	8 ROBINSON	550	1·50	0·78	0·97
9 HINDSCARTH	7 DALE HEAD	330	1·25	0·58	0·72
6 HOPEGILL HEAD	3 GRISEDALE PIKE	400	1·25	0·62	0·77
6 HOPEGILL HEAD	10 WHITESIDE	150	1·13	0·45	0·55
19 KNOTT RIGG	17 ARD CRAGS	200	1·00	0·43	0·53
18 LORD'S SEAT	21 BROOM FELL	120	0·88	0·35	0·43
18 LORD'S SEAT	22 BARF	150	0·75	0·33	0·40
15 MAIDEN MOOR	24 CAT BELLS	310	1·50	0·66	0·81
15 MAIDEN MOOR	13 HIGH SPY	300	1·50	0·65	0·80
16 OUTERSIDE	23 BARROW	400	1·25	0·62	0·77
8 ROBINSON	9 HINDSCARTH	520	1·50	0·76	0·95
5 SAIL	2 EEL CRAG	320	0·40	0·29	0·37
5 SAIL	11 SCAR CRAGS	160	0·75	0·33	0·41
1 SCAR CRAGS	5 SAIL	500	0·75	0·50	0·63
1 SCAR CRAGS	14 CAUSEY PIKE	150	0·75	0·33	0·40
4 WANDOPE	1 GRASMOOR	430	1·25	0·63	0·79
4 WANDOPE	2 EEL CRAG	340	0·75	0·42	0·53
4 WANDOPE	12 WHITELESS PIKE	110	0·88	0·35	0·42
2 WHITELESS PIKE	4 WANDOPE	500	0·88	0·54	0·68
10 WHITESIDE	6 HOPEGILL HEAD	360	1·13	0·56	0·69

THE WESTERN FELLS

START FELL NUMBER & NAME		END FELL NUMBER & NAME		HEIGHT OF ASCENT (feet)	LENGTH OF RIDGE (miles)	ROUTE FASTER TIME (hours)	ROUTE SLOWER TIME (hours)
17	BASE BROWN	9	GREEN GABLE	620	1·00	0·64	0·81
23	BLAKE FELL	25	GAVEL FELL	270	1·00	0·47	0·58
23	BLAKE FELL	30	BURNBANK FELL	150	1·00	0·41	0·50
12	BRANDRETH	14	GREY KNOTTS	50	0·50	0·19	0·23
12	BRANDRETH	9	GREEN GABLE	450	1·00	0·56	0·70
12	BRANDRETH	22	HAYSTACKS *	360	2·00	0·85	1·04
30	BURNBANK FELL	23	BLAKE FELL	420	1·00	0·54	0·68
13	CAW FELL	8	HAYCOCK	450	1·00	0·56	0·70
13	CAW FELL	26	CRAG FELL	550	3·50	1·44	1·77
26	CRAG FELL	29	GRIKE	150	1·00	0·41	0·50
26	CRAG FELL	24	LANK RIGG	750	2·00	1·04	1·30
26	CRAG FELL	13	CAW FELL	1200	3·50	1·77	2·20
32	FELLBARROW	33	LOW FELL	400	1·50	0·70	0·87
25	GAVEL FELL	23	BLAKE FELL	420	1·00	0·54	0·68
20	GREAT BORNE	18	STARLING DODD	480	1·50	0·74	0·92
1	GREAT GABLE	9	GREEN GABLE	150	0·50	0·24	0·30
1	GREAT GABLE	7	KIRK FELL	700	1·33	0·79	1·00
9	GREEN GABLE	12	BRANDRETH	200	1·00	0·43	0·53
9	GREEN GABLE	1	GREAT GABLE	500	0·50	0·42	0·53
9	GREEN GABLE	17	BASE BROWN *	130	1·00	0·40	0·49
14	GREY KNOTTS	12	BRANDRETH	100	0·50	0·22	0·27
29	GRIKE	26	CRAG FELL	260	1·00	0·46	0·57
8	HAYCOCK	3	SCOAT FELL	450	1·00	0·56	0·70
8	HAYCOCK	15	SEATALLAN	670	2·00	1·00	1·25
8	HAYCOCK	13	CAW FELL	120	1·00	0·39	0·48
22	HAYSTACKS	12	BRANDRETH	850	2·00	1·09	1·37
22	HAYSTACKS	11	HIGH CRAG	1100	1·25	0·97	1·23
11	HIGH CRAG	6	HIGH STILE	300	1·00	0·48	0·60
11	HIGH CRAG	22	HAYSTACKS	550	1·25	0·69	0·87
6	HIGH STILE	10	RED PIKE (Buttermere)	200	0·75	0·35	0·43
6	HIGH STILE	11	HIGH CRAG	80	1·00	0·37	0·45
7	KIRK FELL	2	PILLAR	1150	2·50	1·41	1·77
7	KIRK FELL	1	GREAT GABLE	990	1·33	0·94	1·19
24	LANK RIGG	26	CRAG FELL *	670	2·00	1·00	1·25
33	LOW FELL	32	FELLBARROW *	400	1·50	0·70	0·87
21	MIDDLE FELL	15	SEATALLAN	750	1·50	0·88	1·10
2	PILLAR	3	SCOAT FELL	300	1·25	0·57	0·70
2	PILLAR	7	KIRK FELL	850	2·50	1·26	1·57
10	RED PIKE (Buttermere)	6	HIGH STILE	350	0·75	0·42	0·53
10	RED PIKE (Buttermere)	18	STARLING DODD	240	1·25	0·54	0·66
4	RED PIKE (Wasdale)	3	SCOAT FELL	270	0·75	0·39	0·48
4	RED PIKE (Wasdale)	19	YEWBARROW	680	1·75	0·92	1·15
3	SCOAT FELL	5	STEEPLE	70	0·25	0·12	0·15
3	SCOAT FELL	8	HAYCOCK	330	1·00	0·50	0·62
3	SCOAT FELL	4	RED PIKE (Wasdale)	210	0·75	0·35	0·44
3	SCOAT FELL	2	PILLAR	500	1·25	0·67	0·83
15	SEATALLAN	8	HAYCOCK	1050	2·00	1·19	1·50
15	SEATALLAN	21	MIDDLE FELL *	360	1·50	0·68	0·84
18	STARLING DODD	10	RED PIKE (Buttermere)	650	1·25	0·74	0·93
18	STARLING DODD	20	GREAT BORNE	420	1·50	0·71	0·88
5	STEEPLE	3	SCOAT FELL	140	0·25	0·15	0·19
19	YEWBARROW	4	RED PIKE (Wasdale)	1350	1·75	1·26	1·60

CHAPTER 5

QUALITATIVE ANALYSIS

In addition to the wealth of physical data contained in the seven Pictorial Guides, AW has an opinion to offer on the following points:

the quality or severity the ascent
the qualitative attributes of the summit and the surrounding
    environment
the quality and extent of the view from the summit

While some fells merit only 4 pages of description, there are several with over 20 pages; Blencathra has the highest tally with 36 pages. This shows the degree of interest AW had in the fell and whilst the 'opinions' ventured regarding ascent, summit and view are not strictly related mathematically, AW is, as with the presentation of the physical data, consistent in style of description of the three features. There is one slight confusion, however, which relates to 'ascents'.

Most ascents have reference to 'difficulty', i.e. 'easy' and occasionally 'hard'. AW also offers his views on some ascents as to quality, e.g. 'exhilarating' or 'tedious' and one can often relate the degree of difficulty with the quality of the experience. 'Hard' is often equated to 'good', and 'easy' as 'tedious', although some of the relatively easy climbs are judged to be of high quality. The combination of the variables of 'ascent', 'summit' and 'view', together with the relative length of description as indicated by the number of pages, have been combined to give a Quality Factor, and when expressed as a percentage of the best possible Quality Factor produce a Quality Index for each ascent, thus enabling the relative merits of each ascent to be determined. The assessments of the three variables are mine but I hope closely reflect AW's expressed views.

These views on 'quality' occurred during the examination of the database and in reading all the descriptions in the seven Pictorial Guides. They were developed with the help of my good friend Geoffrey Myers who was the architect of the principle of 'Value For Effort' – which is simply the Quality Factor divided by the effort of making the ascent.

In the pages which follow I shall attempt to turn these subjective views into objective measurements, but I am acutely aware that the results are simply my interpretation of AW's opinions. For those who do not hold with such assessments, I suggest that you ignore these calculations and simply enjoy the walking, but for those who wish to have a full explanation of the mathematical processes which have been used to make the precise but not necessarily accurate evaluations, read on.

QUALITY INDEX

In order to make an analysis of the 'qualitative' data, it is necessary to assign numerical values to these quality descriptions. Because of the relative uncertainty of the description of the ascents, I have assigned only three grades:

> 3   hard or good
> 2   moderate or satisfactory
> 1   easy or tedious

In looking at the other two areas of interest, the summit and the view, I have felt able to assign 5 values:

> 5   excellent
> 4   good
> 3   indifferent
> 2   tedious
> 1   without interest

Finally the number of pages, in the fell description within the guide books, are also taken into the analysis.

If the four variables are combined, and it is reasonable to suggest that they should be combined arithmetically, it is necessary consider their relative 'weighting', and it is probably safest to give equal weighting to each feature. As two of the variables (summit and view) have identical ranges (1–5) then we can relate the other variables to this 'standard' range. As each of the variables vary in the form of a 'straight line' relationship, we can relate the 'ascents' and 'pages' ranges to the 'standard' range, using the following formula: $y = Mx + C$

where: y is the calculated value on the 'standard' range;
           M is the slope of the graph;
           x is the actual value of the variable, and
           C is the point where the graph crosses the 'y' axis.

Using 'simultaneous equations' the values of M and C for the two variables requiring conversion are found to be:

Variable	M	C
ascents	2.0	-1·0
pages	0·125	0·5

giving the following formulae:

for ascents: $y = 2x - 1$
for pages: $y = 0·125x + 0·5$.

The following table sets out the relative values of the variables using the base range of 1 to 5.

TABLE 11: **Relativity of Variables**

SUMMIT	VIEW	ASCENT	PAGES
1	1	1	4
2	2	1.5	12
3	3	2	20
4	4	2.5	28
5	5	3	36

The addition of the resultant standardized values will give a series of relative values which in themselves are pretty meaningless and they, therefore, need to be related to the possible range of outcomes. We do this by postulating the minimum and maximum possible values (in the standardized form). The sum of the four smallest values is $1+1+1+1 = 4$, whilst the maximum possible outcome is $5+5+5+5 = 20$. The range of all outcomes is therefore 16, from 4 to 20. So the 'factor of quality', for any ascent is the sum of the four standardized variables, less 4 and divided by 16. This will generate a series of values between 0 and 1 and so that it might be slightly easier to read them we simply multiply them by 100. The resultant 'Quality Index' values for all the ascents in the seven guide books lie within a range from 3 to 95 and the minimum, maximum, and average for each book is in Table 12.

The full distribution of all 759 ascents is given in the Table 13 showing the number of occasions each value occurs within each decile between 0 and 100 and for each of the seven guide books.

TABLE 12: **Quality Indices – Summary**

BOOK		MINIMUM	MAXIMUM	AVERAGE
1	EASTERN FELLS	9	73	39
2	FAR EASTERN FELLS	13	73	30
3	CENTRAL FELLS	17	73	44
4	SOUTHERN FELLS	25	95	62
5	NORTHERN FELLS	3	94	49
6	NORTH WESTERN FELLS	25	80	48
7	WESTERN FELLS	14	94	52
ALL BOOKS				**46**

TABLE 13: **Distribution of Quality – Indices of Ascents**

GUIDE BOOK NUMBER

INDEX RANGE	1	2	3	4	5	6	7	ALL
0–10	4	0	0	0	1	0	0	5
11–20	8	24	5	0	3	0	3	43
21–30	30	42	14	1	18	13	15	133
31–40	20	29	19	8	21	10	14	121
41–50	12	17	23	13	19	26	36	146
51–60	14	10	22	32	10	29	19	136
61–70	14	0	6	23	16	12	8	79
71–80	5	2	9	25	2	5	9	57
81–90	0	0	0	2	10	0	4	16
91–100	0	0	0	7	6	0	10	23
ALL ASCENTS	**107**	**124**	**98**	**111**	**106**	**95**	**118**	**759**

VALUE FOR EFFORT

As has been said previously, quality must not be confused with quantity and many climbs of modest height are amongst the best in the Lake District. The Quality Index, above, tends to assign more value to the higher fells because the views are better and there are, typically, more pages assigned to the description.

Thus, in an attempt to make comparisons which even out these differences, it is possible to divide the Quality Factor by the effort required to ascend the fell. For these purposes, the measurement of 'effort' used is the combination of distance and height of ascent in the foregoing data, assuming the near-equal effect between height and distance implied by the Naismith Rule. The 'faster' time calculation has been used although the 'slower' time would produce the same index of 'Value For Effort'. In order to relate the resultant values to the range of possible outcomes, the numbers are divided by the highest possible value, that is where the quality factor is 1 and the time of ascent is at its shortest (0.38 hours, SOUR HOWES from Garburn Pass).

The distribution of the resultant values is shown for each of the seven guide books and, below that, the combined result. An examination of the distribution will show that the average index of 'Value For Effort' is 10 and that the averages for the guide books vary from 13 for NORTH WESTERN to 7 for FAR EASTERN FELLS. First, the minimum, maximum, and average for each book is shown:

TABLE 14: **Value For Effort Indices – Summary**

BOOK		MINIMUM	MAXIMUM	AVERAGE
1	EASTERN FELLS	2	28	8
2	FAR EASTERN FELLS	2	28	7
3	CENTRAL FELLS	3	25	11
4	SOUTHERN FELLS	5	24	11
5	NORTHERN FELLS	1	24	11
6	NORTH WESTERN FELLS	5	40	13
7	WESTERN FELLS	3	31	12
ALL BOOKS				**10**

TABLE 15: **Distribution of Value For Effort – Indices of Ascents**

GUIDE BOOK NUMBER

INDEX RANGE	1	2	3	4	5	6	7	ALL
0–10	22	57	10	0	9	0	8	106
6–10	65	40	37	48	34	30	40	294
11–15	16	19	22	51	45	37	46	236
16–20	2	5	23	9	15	21	18	93
21–25	1	2	5	3	3	4	2	20
26–30	1	1	1	0	0	1	3	7
31–35	0	0	0	0	0	1	1	2
36–40	0	0	0	0	0	1	0	1
ALL ASCENTS	**107**	**124**	**98**	**111**	**106**	**95**	**118**	**759**

The previous chapter explores the delights of the Lakeland mountain ridges. These ridges share all the same 'quality' and 'value for effort' attributes as the ascents, except that of the quality of the ascent itself. The initial fell climbed from the starting point, of course, has all the attributes. If the three remaining variables of summit, view and pages are used to calculate an index for the fells and if the effort for traversing the ridge to the adjacent fell is measured by reference to the time taken, it will be seen that the indices of 'Value for Effort' are considerably higher than those of the individual fells; this is, as any fellwalker will know, because the work done is largely in the ascent.

Indeed, the more fells that are added to the ridge walk, the higher is the average value for effort until the law of diminishing returns comes into effect. In order to achieve an overall view, it is customary to average out a number of samples than just take one. The table below shows the effect of examining the results of the six sample ridges contained within *Wainwright's Tour In The Lake District*, see chapter 4. The ambitious tour contains ridges of at least 7 fells on each of the six days and the highest number in one day is 13. It will be seen in Table 16 that the average value for the first fell is 9. As further fells are added to the ridge walk, the value for effort increases to 21 at its highest value after 10 fells. Thereafter, the Value for Effort index gradually declines.

TABLE 16: **Cumulative Value For Effort on Ridge Routes**

FELLS IN RIDGE	1	2	3	4	5	6	7	8	9	10	11	12	13
VALUE FOR EFFORT INDEX	9	13	16	18	18	19	19	20	20	21	20	19	19

The Value for Effort data which follows is given in two different ways. The first appears in alphabetical order of fell, and within each fell the order is in the descending VFE for each ascent of that fell. This will tell you, for example, that the most rewarding ascent of Helvellyn is from Wythburn via Whelpside Gill.

The second set of tables appears in alphabetical order of starting point and, within each starting point, the fells which can be visited from that particular location are listed in the descending order of Value for Effort. Therefore, it will be seen that if you are staying in Ambleside and have just one day for a walk then Loughrigg Fell, via Browhead Farm, will give you the best VFE.

QUALITATIVE ANALYSIS
listed in 'Value for Effort' order by Fell in alphabetical order

FELL NAME STARTING POINT & ROUTE	BOOK & FELL NO	QUALITY OF			INDEX OF QUALITY	VALUE FOR EFFORT
		ASCENT (1–5)	VIEW (1–5)	SUMMIT (1–5)		
ALLEN CRAGS	4.12					
Seatoller via Allen Gill		2	3	4	47	7
Seatoller direct		2	3	4	47	7
ANGLETARN PIKES	2.26					
Patterdale via Freeze Beck		1	4	3	34	10
Patterdale direct		1	4	3	34	10
Martindale via Angle Tarn		2	4	3	47	10
Martindale via Bedafell Knott		2	4	3	47	10
ARD CRAGS	6.17					
Rigg Beck		2	4	4	52	17
ARMBOTH FELL	3.18					
Thirlmere via Launchy Gill		1	2	3	20	9
Thirlmere via Fisher Gill		1	2	3	20	9
Thirlmere via Brown Rigg		1	2	3	20	8
Thirlmere via Dob Gill		1	2	3	20	6
ARNISON CRAG	1.35					
Patterdale direct		1	2	4	25	14
Patterdale via Trough Head		1	2	4	25	9
ARTHUR'S PIKE	2.28					
Howtown		1	4	3	33	7
BAKESTALL	5.12					
Dash Falls via Birkett Edge		1	2	3	23	13
Bassenthwaite village		2	2	3	36	6
High Side		2	2	3	36	6
BANNERDALE CRAGS	5.10					
Mungrisdale via east ridge		2	3	3	42	11
Mungrisdale via The Tongue		2	3	3	42	9
Scales direct		1	3	3	30	7
Scales via Glendermackin col		1	3	3	30	7
BARF	6.22					
Thornthwaite, Swan Hotel via The Bishop		2	4	3	48	22
Thornthwaite, Swan Hotel via Beckstones Plantation		1	4	3	36	14
BARROW	6.23					
Braithwaite direct		2	4	3	47	16
Braithwaite via Barrow door		2	4	3	47	14
Stair		1	4	3	34	10
BASE BROWN	7.17					
Seathwaite		3	3	2	47	13

FELL NAME STARTING POINT & ROUTE	BOOK & FELL NO	QUALITY OF			INDEX OF QUALITY	VALUE FOR EFFORT
		ASCENT (1–5)	VIEW (1–5)	SUMMIT (1–5)		
BEDA FELL	2.31					
Boardale		2	2	2	27	9
Martindale		1	2	2	14	5
BINSEY	5.23					
Binsey Lodge		1	4	4	41	24
High Ireby		1	4	4	41	18
Bewaldeth		1	4	4	41	15
BIRKHOUSE MOOR	1.19					
Glenridding via north-east ridge		2	2	2	28	7
Patterdale via Grisedale		2	2	2	28	5
Glenridding via Mires Beck		1	2	2	16	4
BIRKS	1.24					
Patterdale via Trough Head		3	4	2	52	12
Patterdale via Thornhow End		2	4	2	39	11
BLACK FELL	4.29					
Borwick Lodge via Iron Keld		1	3	3	25	13
BLAKE FELL	7.23					
Loweswater via High Nook Tarn		2	5	3	53	11
Loweswater via Carling Knott		2	5	3	53	11
Lamplugh		2	5	3	53	11
BLEABERRY FELL	3.10					
Borrowdale road		2	2	3	36	10
Dale Bottom		2	2	3	36	8
Keswick direct		1	2	3	23	4
Keswick via Brown Knotts		1	2	3	23	4
Keswick via Dale Bottom		1	2	3	23	3
BLEA RIGG	3.14					
Dungeon Ghyll New Hotel via Whitegill Crag		2	4	4	56	17
Dungeon Ghyll New Hotel via Tarn Crag		2	4	4	56	15
Grasmere		1	4	4	44	8
BLENCATHRA	5.2					
Scales via Doddick Fell		3	5	4	94	21
Threlkeld via Blease Gill		3	5	4	94	19
Threlkeld via Middle Tongue		3	5	4	94	19
Threlkeld via Hall's Fell		3	5	4	94	19
Threlkeld via Gategill Fell		3	5	4	94	19
Scales via Scaley Beck		2	5	4	81	18
Scales via Sharp Edge		3	5	4	94	17
Scales via Scales Fell		2	5	4	81	17
Threlkeld via Doddick Gill		2	5	4	81	16
Threlkeld via Blease Fell		2	5	4	81	15
Mungrisdale		2	5	4	81	13
Threlkeld via Roughten Gill		2	5	4	81	11

FELL NAME STARTING POINT & ROUTE	BOOK & FELL NO	QUALITY OF			INDEX OF QUALITY	VALUE FOR EFFORT
		ASCENT (1–5)	VIEW (1–5)	SUMMIT (1–5)		
BONSCALE PIKE	2.29					
Howtown via the breast		1	3	2	20	8
Howtown direct		1	3	2	20	8
BOWFELL	4.4					
Mickleden sheepfold		2	5	5	75	16
Dungeon Ghyll Old Hotel direct		2	5	5	75	12
Dungeon Ghyll Old Hotel via Three Tarns		2	5	5	75	12
Wasdale Head via ESK PIKE		2	5	5	75	9
Stonethwaite via Stake Beck		2	5	5	75	8
Stonethwaite via Angletarn Gill		2	5	5	75	8
Boot via Three Tarns		2	5	5	75	7
Boot via Ore Gap		2	5	5	75	7
BOWSCALE FELL	5.8					
Mungrisdale via The Tongue		3	4	4	67	17
Mungrisdale via old bridle path		2	4	4	55	14
Mungrisdale via Bullfell Beck		2	4	4	55	14
Bowscale		2	4	4	55	13
Mungrisdale via east ridge		2	4	4	55	13
BRAE FELL	5.17					
Greenhead		1	4	3	33	10
Fell Side		1	4	3	33	9
BRANDRETH	7.12					
Black Sail Youth Hostel via Loft Beck		2	4	2	42	12
Black Sail Youth Hostel via The Tongue		2	4	2	42	12
Seathwaite		2	4	2	42	10
Honister Pass		1	4	2	30	9
Gatesgarth via Dubbs Quarry		2	4	2	42	8
Gatesgarth via Warnscale Bottom		2	4	2	42	8
BRANSTREE	2.13					
Mardale Head		1	2	2	16	5
Mardale road		1	2	2	16	5
Haweswater Hotel		1	2	2	16	3
Sadgill		1	2	2	16	3
BRIM FELL	4.10					
Coniston direct		2	3	3	39	7
Coniston via Gill Cove		2	3	3	39	6
BROCK CRAGS	2.27					
Hartsop direct		2	3	2	31	12
Hartsop via the filter house		1	3	2	19	5
BROOM FELL	6.21					
High Lorton		1	4	2	28	6
Wythop Mill		1	4	2	28	5

FELL NAME STARTING POINT & ROUTE	BOOK & FELL NO	QUALITY OF			INDEX OF QUALITY	VALUE FOR EFFORT
		ASCENT (1–5)	VIEW (1–5)	SUMMIT (1–5)		
BUCKBARROW	7.31					
Harrow Head		1	3	3	25	11
BURNBANK FELL	7.30					
Lamplugh		1	2	2	14	5
Fangs		1	2	2	14	4
Waterend		1	2	2	14	3
CALF CRAG	3.15					
Wythburn		1	2	3	22	4
Grasmere via Far Easedale		1	2	3	22	4
Grasmere via Green Burn		1	2	3	22	4
CARL SIDE	5.4					
High Side		3	4	3	61	11
Millbeck via White Stones		2	4	3	48	11
Millbeck via Carsleddam		2	4	3	48	11
Millbeck via Slades Beck		2	4	3	48	11
Little Crosthwaite		2	4	3	48	10
Millbeck via cliffs of Doups		1	4	3	36	8
CARROCK FELL	5.13					
Stone Ends		2	4	5	63	21
Mosedale direct		2	4	5	63	17
Mosedale via east peak		2	4	5	63	17
Calebrack		2	4	5	63	13
CASTLE CRAG	6.29					
Grange		1	4	4	41	18
Rosthwaite		1	4	4	41	18
CATBELLS	6.24					
Little Town		1	5	3	42	17
Stair via Skelgill		1	5	3	42	15
Hawse End		1	5	3	42	14
Grange		1	5	3	42	12
CATSTYCAM	1.3					
Glenridding via north-west ridge		2	4	4	53	8
Glenridding via Redtarn Beck		1	4	4	41	6
CAUDALE MOOR	2.7					
Kirkstone Pass		2	3	1	33	9
Troutbeck via Sad Gill		2	3	1	33	5
Brothers Water		1	3	1	20	4
Troutbeck via Woundale		1	3	1	20	3
Troutbeck via St Ravens Edge		1	3	1	20	2
Troutbeck via Threshthwaite Mouth		1	3	1	20	2

| FELL NAME | | QUALITY OF | | | INDEX | VALUE |
STARTING POINT & ROUTE	BOOK & FELL NO	ASCENT (1–5)	VIEW (1–5)	SUMMIT (1–5)	OF QUALITY	FOR EFFORT
CAUSEY PIKE	6.14					
Stair via Rowling End		3	5	5	80	22
Stair direct		2	5	5	67	19
Braithwaite via Sail Pass		2	5	5	67	10
Braithwaite direct		1	5	5	55	8
CAW FELL	7.13					
Low Gillerthwaite		2	2	3	38	8
Blengdale		2	2	3	38	5
Kinniside Stone Circle		2	2	3	38	5
Gosforth		2	2	3	38	4
CLOUGH HEAD	1.18					
Wanthwaite direct		3	5	3	66	15
Wanthwaite via Hause Well		3	5	3	66	13
COLD PIKE	4.19					
Wrynose Pass		1	4	4	38	16
Wrynose Bottom		1	4	4	38	12
CONISTON OLD MAN	4.8					
Coniston via Church Beck		2	5	4	67	12
Coniston via Boo Tarn		2	5	4	67	12
Coniston direct		2	5	4	67	11
Torver direct		2	5	4	67	11
Torver via Goat's Hause		2	5	4	67	11
CRAG FELL	7.26					
Ennerdale Bridge via Anglers' Crag		1	3	3	27	7
Ennerdale Bridge direct		1	3	3	27	7
CRINKLE CRAGS	4.6					
Wrynose Pass		2	4	4	63	14
Cockley Beck Bridge		3	4	4	75	13
Dungeon Ghyll Old Hotel via Oxendale		3	4	4	75	12
Dungeon Ghyll Old Hotel via Red Tarn direct		2	4	4	63	9
Dungeon Ghyll Old Hotel via Red Tarn and Isaac Gill		2	4	4	63	9
Dungeon Ghyll Old Hotel via Hell Gill and Three Tarns		2	4	4	63	9
Dungeon Ghyll Old Hotel via The Band and Three Tarns		2	4	4	63	9
Boot via Rest Gill		2	4	4	63	6
Boot via Swinsty Gill		2	4	4	63	6
Boot via Three Tarns		2	4	4	63	6
DALE HEAD	6.7					
Honister Pass		1	5	4	52	18
Seatoller		2	5	4	64	11
Little Town via Copper Mine		2	5	4	64	11

FELL NAME STARTING POINT & ROUTE	BOOK & FELL NO	QUALITY OF			INDEX OF QUALITY	VALUE FOR EFFORT
		ASCENT (1–5)	VIEW (1–5)	SUMMIT (1–5)		
DALE HEAD *(continued)*	6.7					
Little Town via Dalehead Tarn		2	5	4	64	10
Rosthwaite		2	5	4	64	10
DODD	5.21					
Millbeck		1	2	4	33	11
Dancing Gate		1	2	4	33	11
Little Crosthwaite		1	2	4	33	8
DOLLYWAGGON PIKE	1.7					
Dunmail Raise via Birkside Gill		2	4	3	50	11
Dunmail Raise via Raise Beck		2	4	3	50	11
Dunmail Raise via Reggle Knott		1	4	3	38	8
Patterdale via Grisedale		3	4	3	63	8
Grasmere via Little Tongue Gill		1	4	3	38	5
Grasmere via Tongue Gill		1	4	3	38	5
DOVE CRAG	1.12					
Patterdale direct		3	4	2	55	8
Ambleside via Scandale and High Bakestones		3	4	2	55	7
Ambleside via HIGH PIKE		3	4	2	55	7
Patterdale via Black Brow		2	4	2	42	6
Ambleside via Scandale		2	4	2	42	5
DOW CRAG	4.14					
Coniston via Goat's Hause		3	3	5	69	10
Coniston via Walna Scar Pass		3	3	5	69	10
Torver via Walna Scar Pass		2	3	5	56	9
Torver via Goat's Hause		2	3	5	56	9
Seathwaite (Duddon Valley) via Walna Scar Pass		1	3	5	44	7
Seathwaite (Duddon Valley) via Seathwaite Tarn		1	3	5	44	6
EAGLE CRAG	3.17					
Stonethwaite direct		2	2	3	33	9
Stonethwaite via Greenup path		1	2	3	20	5
EEL CRAG	6.2					
Coledale Hause via the pools		2	4	3	50	25
Coledale Hause direct		1	4	3	38	19
Stair via the mine road		3	4	3	63	9
Rannerdale		2	4	3	50	9
Braithwaite via Tower Ridge		2	4	3	50	8
Stair via Causey Pike		2	4	3	50	7
Braithwaite via Shelf Route		2	4	3	50	7
ESK PIKE	4.5					
Dungeon Ghyll Old Hotel via Ore Gap		3	5	4	77	10
Dungeon Ghyll Old Hotel via Esk Hause		3	5	4	77	10
Seatoller		3	5	4	77	10

FELL NAME		QUALITY OF			INDEX OF QUALITY	VALUE FOR EFFORT
STARTING POINT & ROUTE	BOOK & FELL NO	ASCENT (1–5)	VIEW (1–5)	SUMMIT (1–5)		
ESK PIKE *(continued)*	4.5					
Wasdale Head		2	5	4	64	9
Boot via Cam Spout		3	5	4	77	6
Boot via Lingcove Bridge		2	5	4	64	6
FAIRFIELD	1.5					
Patterdale via Greenhow End		3	4	3	64	8
Patterdale via Deepdale Hause		2	4	3	52	6
Grasmere via Little Tongue Gill		1	4	2	33	5
Grasmere via Tongue Gill		1	4	2	33	5
FELLBARROW	7.32					
Thackthwaite (Lorton Vale) direct		1	3	3	28	12
Thackthwaite (Lorton Vale) via Watching Crag		1	3	3	28	9
Low Lorton		1	3	3	28	7
FLEETWITH PIKE	7.16					
Honister Pass via the old tramway		2	4	3	47	16
Gatesgarth		2	4	3	47	14
Honister Pass via the old Drum House		1	4	3	34	12
FROSWICK	2.12					
Troutbeck via Blue Gill		2	2	3	31	5
Kentmere via the reservoir		2	2	3	31	5
GAVEL FELL	7.25					
Croasdale direct		2	2	3	34	10
Croasdale via Banna Fell		2	2	3	34	10
Loweswater via the drove road		1	2	3	22	5
Loweswater via Highnook Beck		1	2	3	22	5
GIBSON KNOTT	3.21					
Grasmere		1	3	2	19	3
GLARAMARA	4.13					
Rosthwaite via Comb Gill		2	4	3	50	8
Rosthwaite via Thornythwaite Fell		2	4	3	50	8
Stonethwaite via Langstrath and Tray Dub		1	4	3	38	5
Stonethwaite via Langstrath and shepherd's track		1	4	3	38	5
GLENRIDDING DODD	1.34					
Glenridding		2	4	4	50	23
GOWBARROW FELL	1.32					
Dockray direct		1	4	3	34	20
Park Brow Foot via Aira Force		1	4	3	34	13
Park Brow Foot via Yew Crag		1	4	3	34	10

FELL NAME		QUALITY OF			INDEX	VALUE
STARTING POINT & ROUTE	BOOK & FELL NO	ASCENT (1–5)	VIEW (1–5)	SUMMIT (1–5)	OF QUALITY	FOR EFFORT
GRANGE FELL	3.22					
Watendlath to Brund Fell		1	4	4	41	25
Grange to King's How only		2	4	4	53	21
Rosthwaite to King's How, direct		2	4	4	53	20
Rosthwaite to Brund Fell via Hazel Bank		2	4	4	53	19
Grange to King's How via Troutdale		2	4	4	53	17
Rosthwaite to Brund Fell via the bridle path		2	4	4	53	17
Grange to Brund Fell via King's How		2	4	4	53	15
Grange to Brund Fell via Troutdale and King's How		2	4	4	53	14
GRASMOOR	6.1					
Coledale Hause		1	3	3	34	16
Lanthwaite Green direct		3	3	3	59	14
Rannerdale via Red Gill		2	3	3	47	11
Rannerdale via Lad Hows		2	3	3	47	10
Lanthwaite Green via Dove Crags		2	3	3	47	10
GRAY CRAG	2.15					
Hartsop direct		1	3	3	27	6
Hartsop via Threshthwaite Mouth		2	3	2	33	5
GRAYSTONES	6.25					
Scawgill Bridge		1	3	3	30	16
Armaside via Kirk Fell		2	3	3	42	11
Embleton Church		1	3	3	30	8
Armaside direct		1	3	3	30	7
GREAT BORNE	7.20					
Ennerdale Bridge via Floutern Pass		2	4	4	52	9
Ennerdale Bridge direct		2	4	4	52	9
GREAT CALVA	5.9					
Skiddaw House direct		1	3	3	30	10
Skiddaw House via Dead Beck		1	3	3	30	10
Orthwaite direct		1	3	3	30	6
Orthwaite via Brockle Crag		1	3	3	30	6
GREAT CARRS	4.11					
Little Langdale village via Wet Side Edge		2	5	3	53	8
Little Langdale village via Broad Slack		1	5	3	41	6
GREAT COCKUP	5.19					
Orthwaite		1	4	2	27	9
GREAT CRAG	3.20					
Watendlath		1	4	4	39	17
Stonethwaite via Knotts		2	3	4	45	16
Stonethwaite via Dock Tarn		2	3	4	45	16

FELL NAME		QUALITY OF			INDEX OF QUALITY	VALUE FOR EFFORT
STARTING POINT & ROUTE	BOOK & FELL NO	ASCENT (1–5)	VIEW (1–5)	SUMMIT (1–5)		
GREAT DODD	1.8					
Legburthwaite		1	3	2	25	5
Fornside		1	3	2	25	5
Dockray direct		1	3	2	25	4
Dockray via Groove Beck		1	3	2	25	4
GREAT END	4.3					
Sty Head		2	5	4	66	24
Seathwaite via Sty Head		2	5	4	66	10
Wasdale Head via Sty Head		2	5	4	66	10
Seatoller		3	5	4	78	10
Dungeon Ghyll Old Hotel		3	5	4	78	10
Wasdale Head via Corridor Route		2	5	4	66	9
GREAT GABLE	7.1					
Sty Head		2	5	5	81	31
Black Sail Youth Hostel via Windy Gap		3	5	5	94	20
Black Sail Youth Hostel via Beck Head		3	5	5	94	20
Wasdale Head via Gavel Neese and Beck Head		3	5	5	94	16
Wasdale Head via Gavel Neese and Moses' Finger		3	5	5	94	16
Seathwaite direct		3	5	5	94	16
Honister Pass via GREEN GABLE		2	5	5	81	16
Honister Pass via Beck Head		2	5	5	81	16
Seathwaite via Sty Head and the Breast Route		3	5	5	94	15
Seathwaite via Aaron Slack and Windy Gap		3	5	5	94	15
Wasdale Head via Sty Head		3	5	5	94	14
Gatesgarth via GREEN GABLE		3	5	5	94	13
Gatesgarth via Beck Head		3	5	5	94	13
GREAT MELL FELL	1.27					
Troutbeck Old Railway Station		1	2	2	13	6
GREAT RIGG	1.15					
Grasmere via STONE ARTHUR		2	3	4	45	8
Grasmere via Greenhead Gill		1	3	4	33	6
GREAT SCA FELL	5.15					
Fell Side via Roughton Gill		2	2	3	36	8
Fell Side via Ward Steel		2	2	3	36	8
Orthwaite direct		2	2	3	36	7
Orthwaite via Brockle Crag		2	2	3	36	7
Longlands direct		1	2	3	23	6
Longlands via the bridle road		1	2	3	23	5
GREEN CRAG	4.27					
Woolpack Inn via Crook Crag		2	4	4	50	12
Woolpack Inn via Low Birker Tarn		2	4	4	50	12

FELL NAME STARTING POINT & ROUTE	BOOK & FELL NO	QUALITY OF			INDEX OF QUALITY	VALUE FOR EFFORT
		ASCENT (1–5)	VIEW (1–5)	SUMMIT (1–5)		
GREEN GABLE	7.9					
Styhead Gill via Aaron Slack		2	5	4	61	27
Styhead Gill via Mitchell Cove		2	5	4	61	27
Black Sail Youth Hostel via The Tongue		2	5	4	61	15
Black Sail Youth Hostel via River Liza		2	5	4	61	15
Honister Pass		2	5	4	61	14
Seathwaite		2	5	4	61	12
GREY CRAG	2.22					
Sadgill		2	3	3	41	12
Kendal-Shap road (summit)		1	3	3	28	5
Hucks Bridge		1	3	3	28	4
Jungle Cafe		1	3	3	28	4
Selside		1	3	3	28	3
GREY FRIAR	4.15					
Wrynose Bottom		1	4	4	42	12
Troutal		2	4	4	55	12
Wrynose Pass		1	4	4	42	11
Seathwaite (Duddon Valley)		2	4	4	55	9
GREY KNOTTS	7.14					
Honister Pass direct		1	4	3	36	15
Honister Pass via the old Drum House		1	4	3	36	14
Seathwaite		2	4	3	48	13
Seatoller		2	4	3	48	10
GRIKE	7.29					
Kinniside Stone Circle		1	3	3	27	9
Ennerdale Bridge		1	3	3	27	7
GRISEDALE PIKE	6.3					
Coledale Hause		1	4	3	41	20
Whinlatter Pass		2	4	3	53	13
Braithwaite		2	4	3	53	9
Thornthwaite via north-east ridge		2	4	3	53	9
Thornthwaite via north ridge		2	4	3	53	8
HALLIN FELL	2.35					
Martindale		1	4	2	25	18
HARD KNOTT	4.25					
Hardknott Pass		1	4	3	33	24
HARRISON STICKLE	3.3					
Dungeon Ghyll New Hotel via Pike How		3	4	4	73	18
Dungeon Ghyll New Hotel via Stickle Tarn		3	4	4	73	17
Dungeon Ghyll Old Hotel via The Ravines		3	4	4	73	17
Dungeon Ghyll Old Hotel via Thorn Crag		3	4	4	73	16
Dungeon Ghyll Old Hotel via Stickle Tarn		3	4	4	73	16

| FELL NAME | | QUALITY OF | | | INDEX | VALUE |
STARTING POINT & ROUTE	BOOK & FELL NO	ASCENT (1-5)	VIEW (1-5)	SUMMIT (1-5)	OF QUALITY	FOR EFFORT
HARRISON STICKLE *(continued)*	3.3					
Stonethwaite via HIGH RAISE and THUNACAR KNOTT		2	4	4	61	8
Grasmere via BLEA RIGG and Stickle Tarn		2	4	4	61	8
Grasmere via SERGEANT MAN and THUNACAR KNOTT		2	4	4	61	8
Stonethwaite via Langstrath, Stake Pass and PIKE O'STICKLE		2	4	4	61	7
HART CRAG	1.11					
Rydal via Rydal Head		3	2	3	48	7
Rydal direct		3	2	3	48	7
Patterdale via Wallend		2	2	3	36	5
Patterdale via HARTSOP ABOVE HOW		2	2	3	36	5
HART SIDE	1.16					
Dockray via Dowthwaitehead		3	2	1	34	6
Dockray via Brown Hills		1	2	1	9	2
HARTER FELL	2.6					
Mardale Head		1	2	2	20	5
Kentmere via KENTMERE PIKE		2	2	2	33	5
Kentmere via Nan Bield Pass		2	2	2	33	4
Sadgill via Wren Gill		1	2	2	20	3
Sadgill via Gatescarth Pass		1	2	2	20	3
HARTER FELL	4.20					
Hardknott Pass		1	4	4	41	16
Boot		2	4	4	53	9
HARTSOP ABOVE HOW	1.26					
Patterdale		1	4	2	25	6
HARTSOP DODD	2.23					
Hartsop		3	4	2	52	17
Caudale Bridge direct		1	4	2	27	11
Caudale Bridge via Caudale Beck		1	4	2	27	8
HAYCOCK	7.8					
Low Gillerthwaite		2	4	3	48	9
Netherbeck Bridge via Little Lad Crag		2	4	3	48	7
Netherbeck Bridge via Ladcrag Beck		2	4	3	48	7
Greendale		2	4	3	48	7
HAYSTACKS	7.22					
Black Sail Youth Hostel		2	5	5	69	29
Gatesgarth via Scarth Gap		2	5	5	69	19
Gatesgarth via Warnscale		3	5	5	81	18
Honister Pass		1	5	5	56	17
HELM CRAG	3.23					
Grasmere		2	4	5	61	2

FELL NAME STARTING POINT & ROUTE	BOOK & FELL NO	QUALITY OF			INDEX OF QUALITY	VALUE FOR EFFORT
		ASCENT (1–5)	VIEW (1–5)	SUMMIT (1–5)		
HELVELLYN	1.1					
Wythburn via Whelpside Gill		2	4	3	61	11
Wythburn via Comb Gill		2	4	3	61	11
Wythburn via old lead mine		2	4	3	61	11
Wythburn via Birk Side		2	4	3	61	11
Thirlspot via the 'White Stones' Route		2	4	3	61	9
Thirlspot via Helvellyn Gill		2	4	3	61	9
Patterdale via Nethermost Cove and NETHERMOST PIKE		3	4	3	73	9
Patterdale via Striding Edge		3	4	3	73	9
Thirlspot via the old pony-route		2	4	3	61	9
Patterdale via Red Tarn and Swirral Edge		3	4	3	73	9
Patterdale via Ruthwaite cove and DOLLYWAGGON PIKE		3	4	3	73	8
Glenridding via Red Tarn and Swirral Edge		2	4	3	61	8
Patterdale via Grisedale Tarn		3	4	3	73	7
Glenridding via the old pony-route and Keppel Cove		2	4	3	61	7
Grasmere		2	4	3	61	6
HEN COMB	7.28					
Loweswater direct		1	3	3	25	6
Loweswater via Little Dodd		1	3	3	25	6
HERON PIKE	1.25					
Grasmere, Swan Hotel via Alcock Tarn		1	4	2	25	7
Rydal via NAB SCAR		1	4	2	25	7
Rydal via Blind Cove		1	4	2	25	6
HIGH CRAG	7.11					
Black Sail Youth Hostel		2	4	3	47	13
Gatesgarth via Scarth Gap		2	4	3	47	11
Gatesgarth direct		2	4	3	47	11
Buttermere		2	4	3	47	9
HIGH HARTSOP DODD	1.28					
Hartsop Hall		2	2	2	25	11
HIGH PIKE	1.21					
Ambleside		2	3	3	39	6
HIGH PIKE	5.14					
Fell Side		2	4	2	45	11
Nether Row via Sandbed Mine		1	4	2	33	8
Nether Row via Potts Gill Mine		1	4	2	33	8
Calebrack		1	4	2	33	8
HIGH RAISE	2.2					
Riggindale via Mardale		2	3	4	52	11
Measand via Long Grain		2	3	4	52	9
Hartsop		2	3	4	52	9

FELL NAME STARTING POINT & ROUTE	BOOK & FELL NO	QUALITY OF			INDEX OF QUALITY	VALUE FOR EFFORT
		ASCENT (1–5)	VIEW (1–5)	SUMMIT (1–5)		
HIGH RAISE *(continued)*	2.2					
Martindale		2	3	4	52	7
Patterdale		2	3	4	52	7
HIGH RAISE	3.1					
Dungeon Ghyll New Hotel		3	3	3	56	11
Stonethwaite		2	3	3	44	7
Wythburn		2	3	3	44	6
Grasmere		2	3	3	44	6
HIGH RIGG	3.26					
St John's-in-the-Vale Church		1	3	3	25	24
HIGH SEAT	3.9					
Ashness Bridge via the falls		2	4	3	47	13
Watendlath via HIGH TOVE		1	4	3	34	10
Watendlath via Raise Gill		1	4	3	34	10
Armboth		1	4	3	34	9
Ashness Bridge via Dodd		1	4	3	34	9
Dale Bottom via Mere Gill		1	4	3	34	6
Dale Bottom via Litt's Memorial		1	4	3	34	6
Keswick via Ashness Bridge		1	4	3	34	5
Keswick via Dale Bottom		1	4	3	34	4
HIGH SPY	6.13					
Grange via High White Rake		2	4	4	56	13
Seatoller		2	4	4	56	1
Rosthwaite		2	4	4	56	12
Grange via Narrow Moor		2	4	4	56	12
Little Town		2	4	4	56	10
HIGH STILE	7.6					
Gatesgarth		3	4	4	72	15
Buttermere direct		2	4	4	59	12
Buttermere via north-east ridge		2	4	4	59	12
High Gillerthwaite		2	4	4	59	12
HIGH STREET	2.1					
Mardale Head via Blea Water		2	3	2	39	7
Mardale Head via Rough Crag		2	3	2	39	7
Kentmere via Hall Cove		2	3	2	39	5
Kentmere via Lingmell End		2	3	2	39	5
Kentmere via Nan Bield Pass		2	3	2	39	5
Troutbeck		2	3	2	39	5
Hartsop		1	3	2	27	4
Patterdale		1	3	2	27	3
HIGH TOVE	3.16					
Watendlath		1	3	2	19	10
Armboth		1	3	2	19	7

FELL NAME		QUALITY OF			INDEX OF QUALITY	VALUE FOR EFFORT
STARTING POINT & ROUTE	BOOK & FELL NO	ASCENT (1–5)	VIEW (1–5)	SUMMIT (1–5)		
HINDSCARTH	6.9					
Newlands Church		2	4	4	55	11
Gatesgarth via Littledale Edge		2	4	4	55	10
Gatesgarth via Hindscarth Edge		2	4	4	55	10
HOLME FELL	4.30					
Yew Tree House		1	4	4	38	20
HOPEGILL HEAD	6.6					
Coledale Hause via Hobcarton Crag		2	4	4	58	40
Coledale Hause via Sand Hill		1	4	4	45	31
Whinlatter Pass		3	4	4	70	15
Hopebeck		3	4	4	70	14
High Lorton		3	4	4	70	11
ILL BELL	2.9					
Kentmere Reservoir		3	4	5	73	28
Garburn Pass		1	4	5	48	14
Troutbeck via Hagg Gill		3	4	5	73	13
ILLGILL HEAD	4.22					
Eskdale Green via WHIN RIGG		3	4	5	72	10
Boot via old corpse-road		2	4	5	59	9
Wasdale Head		1	4	5	47	8
KENTMERE PIKE	2.11					
Sadgill		2	3	2	36	7
Kentmere		1	3	2	23	5
KIDSTY PIKE	2.5					
Mardale Head		2	4	4	52	10
KIRK FELL	7.7					
Black Sail Youth Hostel		3	4	3	59	17
Wasdale Head		3	4	3	59	14
KNOTT	5.7					
Fell Side		2	2	2	31	6
Orthwaite direct		2	2	2	31	6
Orthwaite via Brockle Crag		2	2	2	31	6
Longlands		1	2	2	19	4
Mosedale		1	2	2	19	3
KNOTT RIGG	6.19					
Keskadale direct		2	3	3	39	16
Keskadale via the ridge		2	3	3	39	16
Newlands Hause		1	3	3	27	15
Keskadale via Ill Gill		1	3	3	27	11
THE KNOTT	2.10					
Hartsop		2	4	2	38	9
Patterdale		1	4	2	25	4

FELL NAME STARTING POINT & ROUTE	BOOK & FELL NO	QUALITY OF			INDEX OF QUALITY	VALUE FOR EFFORT
		ASCENT (1–5)	VIEW (1–5)	SUMMIT (1–5)		
LANK RIGG	7.24					
Coldfell road		1	3	3	28	7
Coldfell Gate		1	3	3	28	6
LATRIGG	5.24					
Keswick		1	4	3	36	10
Threlkeld		1	4	3	36	9
LING FELL	6.26					
Wythop Mill		1	3	3	25	10
LINGMELL	4.7					
Wasdale Head via The Shoulder		3	5	4	73	14
Wasdale Head via Brown Tongue		3	5	4	73	13
Wasdale Head via Piers Gill		3	5	4	73	12
LINGMOOR FELL	4.28					
Dale End		2	5	3	55	20
Dungeon Ghyll Old Hotel direct		2	5	3	55	16
Dungeon Ghyll Old Hotel via Bleatarn House		2	5	3	55	16
Chapel Stile		2	5	3	55	14
Elterwater		2	5	3	55	14
Dungeon Ghyll Old Hotel via Side Pike		2	5	3	55	13
LITTLE HART CRAG	1.23					
Patterdale via Scandale Pass		2	3	3	39	6
Patterdale via HIGH HARTSOP DODD		2	3	3	39	6
Patterdale via Hogget Gill		2	3	3	39	6
Ambleside		1	3	3	27	4
LITTLE MELL FELL	1.29					
Mellfell House		1	3	2	19	14
Thackthwaite		1	3	3	25	13
LOADPOT HILL	2.18					
Moor Divock		2	2	2	33	6
Howtown		1	2	2	20	5
Bampton		1	2	2	20	3
Helton		1	2	2	20	3
Pooley Bridge		1	2	2	20	3
Askham		1	2	2	20	3
LOFT CRAG	3.8					
Dungeon Ghyll Old Hotel		3	3	4	59	16
Dungeon Ghyll New Hotel		3	3	4	59	14
LONGLANDS FELL	5.22					
Longlands		1	3	3	27	12

FELL NAME		QUALITY OF			INDEX OF	VALUE FOR
STARTING POINT & ROUTE	BOOK & FELL NO	ASCENT (1–5)	VIEW (1–5)	SUMMIT (1–5)	QUALITY	EFFORT
LONG SIDE	5.5					
Ravenstone		2	4	4	53	11
Little Crosthwaite via Longside Edge		2	4	4	53	11
Little Crosthwaite via Gable Gill		2	4	4	53	11
LONSCALE FELL	5.6					
Skiddaw House to East Peak		3	4	2	55	19
Skiddaw House via Burnt Horse Ridge		2	4	2	42	15
Keswick via Lonscale Crags		2	4	2	42	6
Keswick via Whit Beck		1	4	2	30	5
Keswick via the central approach		1	4	2	30	5
Keswick via shepherd's tracks		1	4	2	30	5
LORD'S SEAT	6.18					
Whinlatter Pass		1	3	3	31	11
Thornthwaite		2	3	3	44	10
High Lorton		2	3	3	44	8
LOUGHRIGG FELL	3.27					
White Moss		1	3	4	41	16
Ambleside via Browhead Farm		2	3	4	53	15
Skelwith Bridge		1	3	4	41	14
Grasmere		1	3	4	41	13
Rydal		1	3	4	41	12
Clappersgate		1	3	4	41	11
Ambleside via Fox Gill		1	3	4	41	10
LOW FELL	7.33					
Thackthwaite via Watching Gill		2	4	3	45	15
Thackthwaite via the drove road		2	4	3	45	13
Loweswater direct		1	4	3	33	10
Loweswater via Darling Fell		1	4	3	33	7
LOW PIKE	1.30					
Ambleside via Low Sweden Bridge		2	2	2	25	6
Ambleside via High Sweden Bridge		2	2	2	25	6
Rydal		1	2	2	13	3
MAIDEN MOOR	6.15					
Little Town direct		2	3	3	41	14
Grange via Peace How		2	3	3	41	11
Little Town via Hause Gate		1	3	3	28	8
Grange via Manesty		1	3	3	28	7
MARDALE ILL BELL	2.8					
Mardale Head via Blea Water		3	3	3	55	12
Mardale Head via Small Water		2	3	3	42	11
Kentmere via Lingmell End		1	3	3	30	4
Kentmere via Nan Bield Pass		1	3	3	30	4
MEAL FELL	5.18					
Longlands via Trusmadoor		2	3	4	45	13
Orthwaite direct		2	3	4	45	11

FELL NAME STARTING POINT & ROUTE	BOOK & FELL NO	QUALITY OF			INDEX OF QUALITY	VALUE FOR EFFORT
		ASCENT (1–5)	VIEW (1–5)	SUMMIT (1–5)		
MEAL FELL *(continued)*	5.18					
Orthwaite via Brockle Crag		2	3	4	45	11
Longlands via Lowthwaite Fell		1	3	4	33	10
MELLBREAK	7.27					
Crummock Water to the north top		2	4	3	48	20
Crummock Water to the south top		2	4	3	48	17
Loweswater to the north top direct		2	4	3	48	17
Buttermere to the south top		2	4	3	48	12
Loweswater to the north top via the scree		1	4	3	36	10
Loweswater to the north top via the valley path		1	4	3	36	10
MIDDLE DODD	1.22					
Hartsop Hall		2	4	3	44	11
MIDDLE FELL	7.21					
Greendale		2	4	4	52	15
MUNGRISDALE COMMON	5.16					
Threlkeld via Sinen Gill		2	2	2	27	5
Threlkeld via The Stake and Cloven Stone		2	2	2	27	4
Mungrisdale via Glendermackin col		1	2	2	14	3
NAB SCAR	1.33					
Rydal		2	3	2	31	13
Grasmere, Swan Hotel		1	3	2	19	6
THE NAB	2.25					
Martindale		1	3	2	19	4
NETHERMOST PIKE	1.2					
Wythburn		2	3	3	42	9
Patterdale via Grisedale		3	3	3	55	7
OUTERSIDE	6.16					
Stair		1	3	3	28	7
Braithwaite		1	3	3	28	6
PAVEY ARK	3.7					
Dungeon Ghyll New Hotel via Jack's Rake		3	4	5	73	18
Dungeon Ghyll New Hotel via south-west ridge		3	4	5	73	17
Dungeon Ghyll New Hotel via Easy Gully		3	4	5	73	17
Dungeon Ghyll New Hotel via North Rake		3	4	5	73	17
PIKE O'BLISCO	4.18					
Wrynose Pass		1	4	4	42	17

FELL NAME STARTING POINT & ROUTE	BOOK & FELL NO	QUALITY OF			INDEX OF QUALITY	VALUE FOR EFFORT
		ASCENT (1–5)	VIEW (1–5)	SUMMIT (1–5)		
PIKE O'BLISCO *(continued)*	4.18					
Dungeon Ghyll Old Hotel via Wall End		2	4	4	55	12
Dungeon Ghyll Old Hotel via Stool End		2	4	4	55	11
Fell Foot via Little Langdale		1	4	4	42	9
PIKE O'STICKLE	3.6					
Stake Pass		1	4	4	41	18
Dungeon Ghyll Old Hotel via Mickleden		2	4	4	53	13
Mickleden via Troughton Beck		2	4	4	53	10
PILLAR	7.2					
Memorial Footbridge		3	5	4	80	20
Black Sail Youth Hostel direct		3	5	4	80	16
Black Sail Youth Hostel via High Level Route		3	5	4	80	15
High Gillerthwaite via the north-west ridge		3	5	4	80	14
High Gillerthwaite via Wind Gap		3	5	4	80	13
Wasdale Head via Wind Gap		3	5	4	80	12
Wasdale Head via Black Sail Pass		3	5	4	80	11
PLACE FELL	2.20					
Sandwick via Sleet Fell		3	3	3	55	12
Patterdale direct		2	3	3	42	11
Patterdale via The Knight		2	3	3	42	11
Patterdale via Boardale Hause		2	3	3	42	11
Sandwick via High Dodd		2	3	3	42	10
Sandwick via Scalehow Beck		2	3	3	42	10
Sandwick via Nettleslack		2	3	3	42	9
RAISE	1.4					
Glenridding direct		2	3	2	36	5
Glenridding via Sticks Pass		2	3	2	36	5
Stanah		1	3	2	23	4
Thirlspot direct		1	3	2	23	4
Thirlspot via Brund Gill		1	3	2	23	4
RAMPSGILL HEAD	2.3					
Hartsop		2	3	3	42	8
Patterdale		2	3	3	42	6
Mardale Head		1	3	3	30	5
RANNERDALE KNOTTS	6.28					
Rannerdale		1	4	4	38	22
Buttermere		1	4	4	38	15
RAVEN CRAG	3.19					
Thirlmere Dam		1	4	3	31	15
RED PIKE (Buttermere)	7.10					
High Gillerthwaite		2	4	3	50	12
Buttermere via Bleaberry Tarn		2	4	3	50	11
Buttermere via Far Ruddy Beck		2	4	3	50	10

FELL NAME STARTING POINT & ROUTE	BOOK & FELL NO	QUALITY OF			INDEX OF QUALITY	VALU FOR EFFO
		ASCENT (1–5)	VIEW (1–5)	SUMMIT (1–5)		
RED PIKE (Buttermere) *(continued)*	7.10					
Buttermere via Lingcomb Edge		2	4	3	50	10
Buttermere via Scale Force		2	4	3	50	8
RED PIKE (Wasdale)	7.4					
Wasdale Head		2	3	4	48	9
Overbeck Bridge via Dore Head		2	3	4	48	8
Overbeck Bridge via Low Tarn		2	3	4	48	8
RED SCREES	1.14					
Kirkstone Pass		2	4	4	56	28
Ambleside via Kirkstone Pass road		2	4	4	56	8
Ambleside via Scandale Pass		2	4	4	56	7
Patterdale		2	4	4	56	7
REST DODD	2.16					
Hartsop		1	2	2	14	4
Patterdale		1	2	2	14	3
ROBINSON	6.8					
Newlands Hause		3	3	3	56	19
Hassness		2	3	3	44	11
Newlands Church via Scope Beck		3	3	3	56	11
Newlands Church via High Snab Bank		3	3	3	56	11
Buttermere		2	3	3	44	9
Gatesgarth		2	3	3	44	8
ROSSETT PIKE	4.21					
Mickleden sheepfold via Rossett Gill		2	3	3	41	12
Mickleden sheepfold via Littlegill Head		2	3	3	41	12
ROSTHWAITE FELL	4.24					
Stonethwaite		3	3	3	52	16
SAIL	6.5					
Braithwaite		3	5	3	64	10
Stair		2	5	3	52	9
SAINT SUNDAY CRAG	1.10					
Grisedale Tarn		1	2	2	17	6
Patterdale via Thornhow End		2	2	2	30	5
Patterdale via east ridge		2	2	2	30	5
Patterdale via Trough Head		1	2	2	17	3
SALE FELL	6.27					
Wythop Mill		1	4	4	44	19
Bassenthwaite Lake Station direct		2	4	4	56	19
Bassenthwaite Lake Station via Dodd Crag		2	4	4	56	19
SALLOWS	2.30					
Kentmere		1	3	3	25	8

FELL NAME STARTING POINT & ROUTE	BOOK & FELL NO	QUALITY OF			INDEX OF QUALITY	VALUE FOR EFFORT
		ASCENT (1–5)	VIEW (1–5)	SUMMIT (1–5)		
CAFELL	4.2					
Wasdale Head via Brown Tongue		3	5	4	78	12
Wasdale Head via Green How		3	5	4	78	11
Boot direct		3	5	4	78	8
Boot via Cam Spout Crag		3	5	4	78	8
Boot via Cam Spout and Foxes Tarn		2	5	4	66	6
CAFELL PIKE	4.1					
Wasdale Head via Brown Tongue and Mickledore		3	5	5	95	14
Wasdale Head via Piers Gill and Broad Crag col		3	5	5	95	13
Wasdale Head via Brown Tongue and Lingmell col		2	5	5	83	12
Wasdale Head via Piers Gill and Lingmell col		2	5	5	83	11
Seatoller via Esk Hause		3	5	5	95	11
Seatoller via Sty Head		3	5	5	95	10
Dungeon Ghyll Old Hotel via Esk Hause		3	5	5	95	10
Boot via Mickledore		3	5	5	95	9
Boot via Broad Crag col		3	5	5	95	9
CAR CRAGS	6.11					
Stair		2	4	3	44	8
COAT FELL	7.3					
Wasdale Head		3	3	3	55	9
Low Gillerthwaite direct		2	3	3	42	7
Low Gillerthwaite via Deep Gill		2	3	3	42	7
Netherbeck Bridge direct		2	3	3	42	6
Netherbeck Bridge via Scoat Tarn		2	3	3	42	6
EAT SANDAL	1.17					
Dunmail Raise		1	3	3	28	8
Grasmere via Little Tongue Gill		2	3	3	41	7
Grasmere via Tongue Gill		2	3	3	41	7
Grasmere via south ridge		1	3	3	28	5
EATALLAN	7.15					
Greendale		2	3	4	47	11
Netherbeck Bridge		2	3	4	47	9
Strands		2	3	4	47	7
Strands via BUCKBARROW		2	3	4	47	7
EATHWAITE FELL	4.23					
Seathwaite via Black Waugh		2	4	4	50	14
Seathwaite via Styhead Gill		2	4	4	50	14
ELSIDE PIKE	2.21					
Swindale Head via north-east ridge		1	2	2	14	5
Swindale Head via Mosedale path		1	2	2	14	4

FELL NAME		QUALITY OF			INDEX OF	VALU FOR
STARTING POINT & ROUTE	BOOK & FELL NO	ASCENT (1–5)	VIEW (1–5)	SUMMIT (1–5)	QUALITY	EFFOR
SERGEANT MAN	3.2					
Dungeon Ghyll New Hotel direct		3	4	4	69	14
Dungeon Ghyll New Hotel via Stickle Tarn		2	4	4	56	12
Grasmere via Easedale Tarn		2	4	4	56	9
Grasmere by Codale Tarn		2	4	4	56	8
Wythburn via Far Easedale		2	4	4	56	8
Grasmere via Far Easedale		2	4	4	56	7
SERGEANT'S CRAG	3.11					
Stonethwaite		1	3	3	27	4
SHEFFIELD PIKE	1.20					
Glencoyne via HERON PIKE		2	2	1	22	5
Glenridding via south-east ridge		1	2	1	9	2
Glencoyne via Nick Head		1	2	1	9	2
Glenridding via Lead Mine		1	2	1	9	2
SHIPMAN KNOTTS	2.24					
Sadgill		2	3	2	31	10
Kentmere		2	3	2	31	8
SILVER HOW	3.24					
Chapel Stile direct		2	3	3	42	17
Grasmere direct		2	3	3	42	15
Grasmere via Wray Gill		2	3	3	42	15
Chapel Stile via Spedding Crag		2	3	3	42	14
Elterwater		2	3	3	42	12
SKIDDAW	5.1					
Dash Falls via the Skiddaw House road		2	4	4	69	17
Skiddaw House via Sale How		2	4	4	69	16
Skiddaw House via Hare Crag		2	4	4	69	14
Millbeck		3	4	4	81	13
High Side via north-west ridge		3	4	4	81	13
High Side via Southerndale		3	4	4	81	12
Melbecks		2	4	4	69	12
High Side via Barkbethdale		3	4	4	81	11
Applethwaite direct		2	4	4	69	11
Applethwaite via Howgill Tongue		2	4	4	69	11
Bassenthwaite village via north-west ridge		2	4	4	69	10
Bassenthwaite village via Southerndale		2	4	4	69	9
Bassenthwaite village via Barkbethdale		2	4	4	69	9
Keswick		2	4	4	69	8
SKIDDAW LITTLE MAN	5.3					
Millbeck via the two boulders		3	5	3	70	15
Millbeck via south-west arete		3	5	3	70	15
Applethwaite direct		2	5	3	58	12
Skiddaw House		1	5	3	45	12
Applethwaite via Howgill Tongue		2	5	3	58	12
Keswick		2	5	3	58	8

FELL NAME STARTING POINT & ROUTE	BOOK & FELL NO	QUALITY OF			INDEX OF QUALITY	VALUE FOR EFFORT
		ASCENT (1–5)	VIEW (1–5)	SUMMIT (1–5)		
LIGHT SIDE	4.17					
Boot		2	5	4	56	8
SOUR HOWES	2.33					
Garburn Pass		1	3	2	19	19
High Borrans		1	3	2	19	7
Ings via Grassgarth		1	3	2	19	4
Ings via Hugill Hall		1	3	2	19	4
Windermere		1	3	2	19	4
Staveley via Browfoot		1	3	2	19	3
SOUTHER FELL	5.20					
Mungrisdale		1	3	2	22	9
Scales		1	3	2	22	7
STARLING DODD	7.18					
Loweswater		2	3	3	39	6
STEEL FELL	3.12					
Dunmail Raise		1	2	2	17	8
Grasmere		2	2	2	30	6
Wythburn		1	2	2	17	5
STEEL KNOTTS	2.34					
Howtown		2	4	3	44	21
Martindale		1	4	3	31	19
Lanty Tarn		1	4	3	31	17
STEEPLE	7.5					
Low Gillerthwaite		3	4	5	72	13
STONE ARTHUR	1.31					
Grasmere, Swan Hotel		1	3	2	19	7
STYBARROW DODD	1.9					
Stanah via Stanah Gill		2	3	3	42	8
Dockray via Green Side		2	3	3	42	6
Stanah via Sticks Pass		1	3	3	30	6
Dockray via Deep Dale		1	3	3	30	4
SWIRL HOW	4.9					
Coniston via Levers Hause		3	4	4	67	11
Coniston via Swirl Hause		2	4	4	55	9
Little Langdale via Greenburn Tarn		2	4	4	55	8
Little Langdale via Long Crag levels		2	4	4	55	8
TARN CRAG	2.19					
Sadgill		2	2	3	34	9
Kendal-Shap road (summit) via GREY CRAG		1	2	3	22	3
Hucks Bridge via GREY CRAG		1	2	3	22	3
Shap via Peat Hill and Brunt Tongue		1	2	3	22	3

FELL NAME STARTING POINT & ROUTE	BOOK & FELL NO	QUALITY OF			INDEX OF QUALITY	VALUE FOR EFFORT
		ASCENT (1–5)	VIEW (1–5)	SUMMIT (1–5)		
TARN CRAG *(continued)*	2.19					
Rosgill via Swindale and Brunt Tongue		1	2	3	22	3
Jungle Cafe via GREY CRAG		1	2	3	22	3
Selside via GREY CRAG		1	2	3	22	2
TARN CRAG	3.13					
Grasmere via Sour Milk Gill		2	3	4	48	10
Grasmere via Stythwaite Steps		2	3	4	48	9
Grasmere via Deer Bield Crag		2	3	4	48	9
Grasmere via the east ridge		1	3	4	36	8
THORNTHWAITE CRAG	2.4					
Kentmere Reservoir via Gavel Crag		2	3	3	44	11
Kentmere Reservoir via Hall Cove		2	3	3	44	11
Hartsop via Threshthwaite Mouth		3	3	3	56	10
Hartsop via GRAY CRAG		2	3	3	44	8
Hartsop via Hayeswater Gill		1	3	3	31	5
Troutbeck via Scot Rake		1	3	3	31	4
Troutbeck via Threshthwaite Mouth		1	3	3	31	4
THUNACAR KNOTT	3.5					
Dungeon Ghyll New Hotel		3	3	3	52	11
TROUTBECK TONGUE	2.36					
Troutbeck Park Farm		1	2	2	13	8
Troutbeck Park Farm via the Tongue		1	2	2	13	4
ULLOCK PIKE	5.11					
Ravenstone		1	5	4	48	12
High Side		1	5	4	48	10
Bassenthwaite village		1	5	4	48	9
ULLSCARF	3.4					
Watendlath		2	3	2	39	8
Wythburn via West Head		2	3	2	39	7
Stonethwaite via Coldbarrow Fell		2	3	2	39	7
Stonethwaite via Lining Crag		2	3	2	39	7
WALLA CRAG	3.25					
Borrowdale road		2	4	4	52	24
Keswick		1	4	4	39	11
WANDOPE	6.4					
Buttermere via the Addacomb Ridge		3	3	3	55	9
Buttermere direct		2	3	3	42	8
Buttermere via Third Gill		2	3	3	42	8
WANSFELL	2.32					
Ambleside via Stock Ghyll Force		2	3	2	36	9
Troutbeck		1	3	2	23	8
Ambleside via Blue Hill road		1	3	2	23	6

FELL NAME STARTING POINT & ROUTE	BOOK & FELL NO	QUALITY OF			INDEX OF QUALITY	VALUE FOR EFFORT
		ASCENT (1–5)	VIEW (1–5)	SUMMIT (1–5)		
WATSON'S DODD	1.13					
Legburthwaite		1	3	3	27	6
WETHER HILL	2.17					
Martindale		1	2	1	13	3
Howtown		1	2	1	13	3
Burn Banks direct		1	2	1	13	2
Burn Banks via Measand Beck		1	2	1	13	2
Bampton		1	2	1	13	2
WETHERLAM	4.16					
Tilberthwaite		3	4	4	70	16
Little Langdale via High Fellside Quarry		2	4	4	58	10
Little Langdale via Greenburn Copper Works		2	4	4	58	10
Coniston via Red Dell Copper Works		2	4	4	58	9
Coniston via Lad Stones		2	4	4	58	9
WHIN RIGG	4.26					
Woodhow Farm		2	4	4	55	14
Eskdale Green		2	4	4	55	10
WHINLATTER	6.20					
Whinlatter Pass		1	3	3	27	11
WHITELESS PIKE	6.12					
Buttermere		2	4	2	39	10
WHITESIDE	6.10					
Lanthwaite Green		3	5	4	75	20
Beck House		2	5	4	63	17
Hopebeck via Dodd		2	5	4	63	14
Hopebeck via Cold Gill		2	5	4	63	14
Hopebeck via Penn		2	5	4	63	14
WHITE SIDE	1.6					
Thirlspot		1	3	3	30	6
Glenridding		1	3	3	30	4
YEWBARROW	7.19					
Overbeck Bridge		3	3	3	54	14
Wasdale Head		2	3	3	41	9
YOKE	2.14					
Garburn Pass		1	4	2	30	11
Kentmere direct		1	4	2	30	7
Kentmere via Garburn Pass		1	4	2	30	6

QUALITATIVE ANALYSIS
listed in 'Value for Effort' order by starting point

STARTING POINT FELL NAME AND ROUTE	BOOK & FELL NO	QUALITY OF			INDEX OF QUALITY (1–5)	VALUE FOR EFFORT (1–5)
		ASCENT	VIEW	SUMMIT (1–5)		
Ambleside						
LOUGHRIGG FELL via Browhead Farm	3.27	2	3	4	53	15
LOUGHRIGG FELL via Fox Gill	3.27	1	3	4	41	10
WANSFELL via Stock Ghyll Force	2.32	2	3	2	36	9
RED SCREES via Kirkstone Pass road	1.14	2	4	4	56	8
RED SCREES via Scandale Pass	1.14	2	4	4	56	7
DOVE CRAG via Scandale and High Bakestones	1.12	3	4	2	55	7
DOVE CRAG via HIGH PIKE	1.12	3	4	2	55	7
HIGH PIKE	1.21	2	3	3	39	6
LOW PIKE via Low Sweden Bridge	1.30	2	2	2	25	6
LOW PIKE via High Sweden Bridge	1.30	2	2	2	25	6
WANSFELL via Blue Hill road	2.32	1	3	2	23	6
DOVE CRAG via Scandale	1.12	2	4	2	42	5
LITTLE HART CRAG	1.23	1	3	3	27	4
Applethwaite						
SKIDDAW LITTLE MAN direct	5.3	2	5	3	58	12
SKIDDAW LITTLE MAN via Howgill Tongue	5.3	2	5	3	58	12
SKIDDAW direct	5.1	2	4	4	69	11
SKIDDAW via Howgill Tongue	5.1	2	4	4	69	11
Armaside						
GRAYSTONES via Kirk Fell	6.25	2	3	3	42	11
GRAYSTONES direct	6.25	1	3	3	30	7
Armboth						
HIGH SEAT	3.9	1	4	3	34	9
HIGH TOVE	3.16	1	3	2	19	7
Ashness Bridge						
HIGH SEAT via the falls	3.9	2	4	3	47	13
HIGH SEAT via Dodd	3.9	1	4	3	34	9
Askham						
LOADPOT HILL	2.18	1	2	2	20	3
Bampton						
LOADPOT HILL	2.18	1	2	2	20	3
WETHER HILL	2.17	1	2	1	13	2
Bassenthwaite Lake Station						
SALE FELL direct	6.27	2	4	4	56	19
SALE FELL via Dodd Crag	6.27	2	4	4	56	19
Bassenthwaite village						
SKIDDAW via north-west ridge	5.1	2	4	4	69	10
SKIDDAW via Southerndale	5.1	2	4	4	69	9

| FELL NAME | | QUALITY OF | | | INDEX OF | VALUE FOR |
FELL NAME AND ROUTE	BOOK & FELL NO	ASCENT (1–5)	VIEW (1–5)	SUMMIT (1–5)	QUALITY	EFFORT
Bassenthwaite village *(continued)*						
SKIDDAW via Barkbethdale	5.1	2	4	4	69	9
ULLOCK PIKE	5.11	1	5	4	48	9
BAKESTALL	5.12	2	2	3	36	6
Beck House						
WHITESIDE	6.10	2	5	4	63	17
Bewaldeth						
BINSEY	5.23	1	4	4	41	15
Binsey Lodge						
BINSEY	5.23	1	4	4	41	24
Black Sail Youth Hostel						
HAYSTACKS	7.22	2	5	5	69	29
GREAT GABLE via Windy Gap	7.1	3	5	5	94	20
GREAT GABLE via Beck Head	7.1	3	5	5	94	20
KIRK FELL	7.7	3	4	3	59	17
PILLAR direct	7.2	3	5	4	80	16
PILLAR via High Level Route	7.2	3	5	4	80	15
GREEN GABLE via The Tongue	7.9	2	5	4	61	15
GREEN GABLE via River Liza	7.9	2	5	4	61	15
HIGH CRAG	7.11	2	4	3	47	13
BRANDRETH via Loft Beck	7.12	2	4	2	42	12
BRANDRETH via The Tongue	7.12	2	4	2	42	12
Blengdale						
CAW FELL	7.13	2	2	3	38	5
Boardale						
BEDA FELL	2.31	2	2	2	27	9
Boot						
SCAFELL PIKE via Mickledore	4.1	3	5	5	95	9
SCAFELL PIKE via Broad Crag col	4.1	3	5	5	95	9
ILLGILL HEAD via old corpse-road	4.22	2	4	5	59	9
HARTER FELL	4.20	2	4	4	53	9
SCAFELL direct	4.2	3	5	4	78	8
SCAFELL via Cam Spout Crag	4.2	3	5	4	78	8
SLIGHT SIDE	4.17	2	5	4	56	8
BOWFELL via Three Tarns	4.4	2	5	5	75	7
BOWFELL via Ore Gap	4.4	2	5	5	75	7
ESK PIKE via Cam Spout	4.5	3	5	4	77	6
SCAFELL via Cam Spout and Foxes Tarn	4.2	2	5	4	66	6
ESK PIKE via Lingcove Bridge	4.5	2	5	4	64	6
CRINKLE CRAGS via Rest Gill	4.6	2	4	4	63	6
CRINKLE CRAGS via Swinsty Gill	4.6	2	4	4	63	6
CRINKLE CRAGS via Three Tarns	4.6	2	4	4	63	6
Borrowdale road						
WALLA CRAG	3.25	2	4	4	52	24
BLEABERRY FELL	3.10	2	2	3	36	10

FELL NAME AND ROUTE	BOOK & FELL NO	QUALITY OF			INDEX OF QUALITY	VALUE FOR EFFORT
		ASCENT (1–5)	VIEW (1–5)	SUMMIT (1–5)		
Borwick Lodge						
BLACK FELL via Iron Keld	4.29	1	3	3	25	13
Bowscale						
BOWSCALE FELL	5.8	2	4	4	55	13
Braithwaite						
BARROW direct	6.23	2	4	3	47	16
BARROW via Barrow door	6.23	2	4	3	47	14
CAUSEY PIKE via Sail Pass	6.14	2	5	5	67	10
SAIL	6.5	3	5	3	64	10
GRISEDALE PIKE	6.3	2	4	3	53	9
CAUSEY PIKE direct	6.14	1	5	5	55	8
EEL CRAG via Tower Ridge	6.2	2	4	3	50	8
EEL CRAG via Shelf Route	6.2	2	4	3	50	7
OUTERSIDE	6.16	1	3	3	28	6
Brothers Water						
CAUDALE MOOR	2.7	1	3	1	20	4
Burn Banks						
WETHER HILL direct	2.17	1	2	1	13	2
WETHER HILL via Measand Beck	2.17	1	2	1	13	2
Buttermere						
RANNERDALE KNOTTS	6.28	1	4	4	38	15
HIGH STILE direct	7.6	2	4	4	59	12
HIGH STILE via north-east ridge	7.6	2	4	4	59	12
MELLBREAK to the south top	7.27	2	4	3	48	12
RED PIKE (Buttermere) via Bleaberry Tarn	7.10	2	4	3	50	11
RED PIKE (Buttermere) via Far Ruddy Beck	7.10	2	4	3	50	10
RED PIKE (Buttermere) via Lingcomb Edge	7.10	2	4	3	50	10
WHITELESS PIKE	6.12	2	4	2	39	10
WANDOPE via the Addacomb Ridge	6.4	3	3	3	55	9
HIGH CRAG	7.11	2	4	3	47	9
ROBINSON	6.8	2	3	3	44	9
RED PIKE (Buttermere) via Scale Force	7.10	2	4	3	50	8
WANDOPE direct	6.4	2	3	3	42	8
WANDOPE via Third Gill	6.4	2	3	3	42	8
Calebrack						
CARROCK FELL	5.13	2	4	5	63	13
HIGH PIKE	5.14	1	4	2	33	8
Caudale Bridge						
HARTSOP DODD direct	2.23	1	4	2	27	11
HARTSOP DODD via Caudale Beck	2.23	1	4	2	27	8

FELL NAME FELL NAME AND ROUTE	BOOK & FELL NO	QUALITY OF			INDEX OF QUALITY	VALUE FOR EFFORT
		ASCENT (1–5)	VIEW (1–5)	SUMMIT (1–5)		
Chapel Stile						
SILVER HOW direct	3.24	2	3	3	42	17
LINGMOOR FELL	4.28	2	5	3	55	14
SILVER HOW via Spedding Crag	3.24	2	3	3	42	14
Clappersgate						
LOUGHRIGG FELL	3.27	1	3	4	41	11
Cockley Beck Bridge						
CRINKLE CRAGS	4.6	3	4	4	75	13
Coldfell Gate						
LANK RIGG	7.24	1	3	3	28	6
Coldfell road						
LANK RIGG	7.24	1	3	3	28	7
Coledale Hause						
HOPEGILL HEAD via Hobcarton Crag	6.6	2	4	4	58	40
HOPEGILL HEAD via Sand Hill	6.6	1	4	4	45	31
EEL CRAG via the pools	6.2	2	4	3	50	25
GRISEDALE PIKE	6.3	1	4	3	41	20
EEL CRAG direct	6.2	1	4	3	38	19
GRASMOOR	6.1	1	3	3	34	16
Coniston						
CONISTON OLD MAN via Church Beck	4.8	2	5	4	67	12
CONISTON OLD MAN via Boo Tarn	4.8	2	5	4	67	12
CONISTON OLD MAN direct	4.8	2	5	4	67	11
SWIRL HOW via Levers Hause	4.9	3	4	4	67	11
DOW CRAG via Goat's Hause	4.14	3	3	5	69	10
DOW CRAG via Walna Scar Pass	4.14	3	3	5	69	10
WETHERLAM via Red Dell Copper Works	4.16	2	4	4	58	9
WETHERLAM via Lad Stones	4.16	2	4	4	58	9
SWIRL HOW via Swirl Hause	4.9	2	4	4	55	9
BRIM FELL direct	4.10	2	3	3	39	7
BRIM FELL via Gill Cove	4.10	2	3	3	39	6
Croasdale						
GAVEL FELL direct	7.25	2	2	3	34	10
GAVEL FELL via Banna Fell	7.25	2	2	3	34	10
Crummock Water						
MELLBREAK to the north top	7.27	2	4	3	48	20
MELLBREAK to the south top	7.27	2	4	3	48	17
Dale Bottom						
BLEABERRY FELL	3.10	2	2	3	36	8
HIGH SEAT via Mere Gill	3.9	1	4	3	34	6
HIGH SEAT via Litt's Memorial	3.9	1	4	3	34	6

FELL NAME AND ROUTE	BOOK & FELL NO	QUALITY OF			INDEX OF QUALITY	VALUE FOR EFFORT
		ASCENT (1–5)	VIEW (1–5)	SUMMIT (1–5)		
Dale End						
LINGMOOR FELL	4.28	2	5	3	55	20
Dancing Gate						
DODD	5.21	1	2	4	33	11
Dash Falls						
SKIDDAW via the Skiddaw House road	5.1	2	4	4	69	17
BAKESTALL via Birkett Edge	5.12	1	2	3	23	13
Dockray						
GOWBARROW FELL direct	1.32	1	4	3	34	20
STYBARROW DODD via Green Side	1.9	2	3	3	42	6
HART SIDE via Dowthwaitehead	1.16	3	2	1	34	6
STYBARROW DODD via Deep Dale	1.9	1	3	3	30	4
GREAT DODD direct	1.8	1	3	2	25	4
GREAT DODD via Groove Beck	1.8	1	3	2	25	4
HART SIDE via Brown Hills	1.16	1	2	1	9	2
Dungeon Ghyll New Hotel						
PAVEY ARK via Jack's Rake	3.7	3	4	5	73	18
HARRISON STICKLE via Pike How	3.3	3	4	4	73	18
PAVEY ARK via south-west ridge	3.7	3	4	5	73	17
PAVEY ARK via Easy Gully	3.7	3	4	5	73	17
PAVEY ARK via North Rake	3.7	3	4	5	73	17
HARRISON STICKLE via Stickle Tarn	3.3	3	4	4	73	17
BLEA RIGG via Whitegill Crag	3.14	2	4	4	56	17
BLEA RIGG via Tarn Crag	3.14	2	4	4	56	15
SERGEANT MAN direct	3.2	3	4	4	69	14
LOFT CRAG	3.8	3	3	4	59	14
SERGEANT MAN via Stickle Tarn	3.2	2	4	4	56	12
THUNACAR KNOTT	3.5	3	3	3	52	11
HIGH RAISE	3.1	3	3	3	56	11
Dungeon Ghyll Old Hotel						
HARRISON STICKLE via The Ravines	3.3	3	4	4	73	17
HARRISON STICKLE via Thorn Crag	3.3	3	4	4	73	16
LOFT CRAG	3.8	3	3	4	59	16
LINGMOOR FELL direct	4.28	2	5	3	55	16
LINGMOOR FELL via Bleatarn House	4.28	2	5	3	55	16
HARRISON STICKLE via Stickle Tarn	3.3	3	4	4	73	16
LINGMOOR FELL via Side Pike	4.28	2	5	3	55	13
PIKE O'STICKLE via Mickleden	3.6	2	4	4	53	13
BOWFELL direct	4.4	2	5	5	75	12
BOWFELL via Three Tarns	4.4	2	5	5	75	12
CRINKLE CRAGS via Oxendale	4.6	3	4	4	75	12
PIKE O'BLISCO via Wall End	4.18	2	4	4	55	12
PIKE O'BLISCO via Stool End	4.18	2	4	4	55	11
SCAFELL PIKE via Esk Hause	4.1	3	5	5	95	10
GREAT END	4.3	3	5	4	78	10
ESK PIKE via Ore Gap	4.5	3	5	4	77	10

FELL NAME FELL NAME AND ROUTE	BOOK & FELL NO	QUALITY OF			INDEX OF QUALITY	VALUE FOR EFFORT
		ASCENT (1–5)	VIEW (1–5)	SUMMIT (1–5)		
Dungeon Ghyll Old Hotel *(continued)*						
ESK PIKE via Esk Hause	4.5	3	5	4	77	10
CRINKLE CRAGS via Red Tarn direct	4.6	2	4	4	63	9
CRINKLE CRAGS via Red Tarn and Isaac Gill	4.6	2	4	4	63	9
CRINKLE CRAGS via Hell Gill and Three Tarns	4.6	2	4	4	63	9
CRINKLE CRAGS via The Band and Three Tarns	4.6	2	4	4	63	9
Dunmail Raise						
DOLLYWAGGON PIKE via Birkside Gill	1.7	2	4	3	50	11
DOLLYWAGGON PIKE via Raise Beck	1.7	2	4	3	50	11
DOLLYWAGGON PIKE via Reggle Knott	1.7	1	4	3	38	8
SEAT SANDAL	1.17	1	3	3	28	8
STEEL FELL	3.12	1	2	2	17	8
Elterwater						
LINGMOOR FELL	4.28	2	5	3	55	14
SILVER HOW	3.24	2	3	3	42	12
Embleton Church						
GRAYSTONES	6.25	1	3	3	30	8
Ennerdale Bridge						
GREAT BORNE via Floutern Pass	7.20	2	4	4	52	9
GREAT BORNE direct	7.20	2	4	4	52	9
GRIKE	7.29	1	3	3	27	7
CRAG FELL via Anglers' Crag	7.26	1	3	3	27	7
CRAG FELL direct	7.26	1	3	3	27	7
Eskdale Green						
ILLGILL HEAD via WHIN RIGG	4.22	3	4	5	72	10
WHIN RIGG	4.26	2	4	4	55	10
Fangs						
BURNBANK FELL	7.30	1	2	2	14	4
Fell Foot						
PIKE O'BLISCO via Little Langdale	4.18	1	4	4	42	9
Fell Side						
HIGH PIKE	5.14	2	4	2	45	11
BRAE FELL	5.17	1	4	3	33	9
GREAT SCA FELL via Roughton Gill	5.15	2	2	3	36	8
GREAT SCA FELL via Ward Steel	5.15	2	2	3	36	8
KNOTT	5.7	2	2	2	31	6
Fornside						
GREAT DODD	1.8	1	3	2	25	5

FELL NAME AND ROUTE	BOOK & FELL NO	QUALITY OF			INDEX OF QUALITY	VALUE FOR EFFORT
		ASCENT (1–5)	VIEW (1–5)	SUMMIT (1–5)		
Garburn Pass						
SOUR HOWES	2.33	1	3	2	19	19
ILL BELL	2.9	1	4	5	48	14
YOKE	2.14	1	4	2	30	11
Gatesgarth						
HAYSTACKS via Scarth Gap	7.22	2	5	5	69	19
HAYSTACKS via Warnscale	7.22	3	5	5	81	18
HIGH STILE	7.6	3	4	4	72	15
FLEETWITH PIKE	7.16	2	4	3	47	14
GREAT GABLE via GREEN GABLE	7.1	3	5	5	94	13
GREAT GABLE via Beck Head	7.1	3	5	5	94	13
HIGH CRAG via Scarth Gap	7.11	2	4	3	47	11
HIGH CRAG direct	7.11	2	4	3	47	11
HINDSCARTH via Littledale Edge	6.9	2	4	4	55	10
HINDSCARTH via Hindscarth Edge	6.9	2	4	4	55	10
ROBINSON	6.8	2	3	3	44	8
BRANDRETH via Dubbs Quarry	7.12	2	4	2	42	8
BRANDRETH via Warnscale Bottom	7.12	2	4	2	42	8
Glencoyne						
SHEFFIELD PIKE via HERON PIKE	1.20	2	2	1	22	5
SHEFFIELD PIKE via Nick Head	1.20	1	2	1	9	2
Glenridding						
GLENRIDDING DODD	1.34	2	4	4	50	23
HELVELLYN via Red Tarn and Swirral Edge	1.1	2	4	3	61	8
CATSTYCAM via north-west ridge	1.3	2	4	4	53	8
HELVELLYN via the old pony-route and Keppel Cove	1.1	2	4	3	61	7
BIRKHOUSE MOOR via north-east ridge	1.19	2	2	2	28	7
CATSTYCAM via Redtarn Beck	1.3	1	4	4	41	6
RAISE direct	1.4	2	3	2	36	5
RAISE via Sticks Pass	1.4	2	3	2	36	5
WHITE SIDE	1.6	1	3	3	30	4
BIRKHOUSE MOOR via Mires Beck	1.19	1	2	2	16	4
SHEFFIELD PIKE via south-east ridge	1.20	1	2	1	9	2
SHEFFIELD PIKE via Lead Mine	1.20	1	2	1	9	2
Gosforth						
CAW FELL	7.13	2	2	3	38	4
Grange						
GRANGE FELL to King's How only	3.22	2	4	4	53	21
CASTLE CRAG	6.29	1	4	4	41	18
GRANGE FELL to King's How via Troutdale	3.22	2	4	4	53	17
GRANGE FELL to Brund Fell via King's How	3.22	2	4	4	53	15
GRANGE FELL to Brund Fell via Troutdale and King's How	3.22	2	4	4	53	14
HIGH SPY via High White Rake	6.13	2	4	4	56	13

| FELL NAME | | QUALITY OF | | | INDEX OF | VALUE FOR |
FELL NAME AND ROUTE	BOOK & FELL NO	ASCENT (1–5)	VIEW (1–5)	SUMMIT (1–5)	QUALITY	EFFORT
Grange (*continued*)						
HIGH SPY via Narrow Moor	6.13	2	4	4	56	12
CATBELLS	6.24	1	5	3	42	12
MAIDEN MOOR via Peace How	6.15	2	3	3	41	11
MAIDEN MOOR via Manesty	6.15	1	3	3	28	7
Grasmere						
HELM CRAG	3.23	2	4	5	61	22
SILVER HOW direct	3.24	2	3	3	42	15
SILVER HOW via Wray Gill	3.24	2	3	3	42	15
LOUGHRIGG FELL	3.27	1	3	4	41	13
TARN CRAG via Sour Milk Gill	3.13	2	3	4	48	10
SERGEANT MAN via Easedale Tarn	3.2	2	4	4	56	9
TARN CRAG via Stythwaite Steps	3.13	2	3	4	48	9
TARN CRAG via Deer Bield Crag	3.13	2	3	4	48	9
BLEA RIGG	3.14	1	4	4	44	8
HARRISON STICKLE via BLEA RIGG and Stickle Tarn	3.3	2	4	4	61	8
HARRISON STICKLE via SERGEANT MAN and THUNACAR KNOTT	3.3	2	4	4	61	8
SERGEANT MAN by Codale Tarn	3.2	2	4	4	56	8
GREAT RIGG via STONE ARTHUR	1.15	2	3	4	45	8
TARN CRAG via the east ridge	3.13	1	3	4	36	8
SERGEANT MAN via Far Easedale	3.2	2	4	4	56	7
SEAT SANDAL via Little Tongue Gill	1.17	2	3	3	41	7
SEAT SANDAL via Tongue Gill	1.17	2	3	3	41	7
HELVELLYN	1.1	2	4	3	61	6
HIGH RAISE	3.1	2	3	3	44	6
GREAT RIGG via Greenhead Gill	1.15	1	3	4	33	6
STEEL FELL	3.12	2	2	2	30	6
DOLLYWAGGON PIKE via Little Tongue Gill	1.7	1	4	3	38	5
DOLLYWAGGON PIKE via Tongue Gill	1.7	1	4	3	38	5
FAIRFIELD via Little Tongue Gill	1.5	1	4	2	33	5
FAIRFIELD via Tongue Gill	1.5	1	4	2	33	5
SEAT SANDAL via south ridge	1.17	1	3	3	28	5
CALF CRAG via Far Easedale	3.15	1	2	3	22	4
CALF CRAG via Green Burn	3.15	1	2	3	22	4
GIBSON KNOTT	3.21	1	3	2	19	3
Grasmere, Swan Hotel						
HERON PIKE via Alcock Tarn	1.25	1	4	2	25	7
STONE ARTHUR	1.31	1	3	2	19	7
NAB SCAR	1.33	1	3	2	19	7
Greendale						
MIDDLE FELL	7.21	2	4	4	52	15
SEATALLAN	7.15	2	3	4	47	11
HAYCOCK	7.8	2	4	3	48	7
Greenhead						
BRAE FELL	5.17	1	4	3	33	10

| FELL NAME | | QUALITY OF | | | INDEX | VALUE |
FELL NAME AND ROUTE	BOOK & FELL NO	ASCENT (1–5)	VIEW (1–5)	SUMMIT (1–5)	OF QUALITY	FOR EFFORT
Grisedale Tarn						
SAINT SUNDAY CRAG	1.10	1	2	2	17	6
Hardknott Pass						
HARD KNOTT	4.25	1	4	3	33	24
HARTER FELL	4.20	1	4	4	41	16
Harrow Head						
BUCKBARROW	7.31	1	3	3	25	11
Hartsop						
HARTSOP DODD	2.23	3	4	2	52	17
BROCK CRAGS direct	2.27	2	3	2	31	12
THORNTHWAITE CRAG via Threshthwaite Mouth	2.4	3	3	3	56	10
HIGH RAISE	2.2	2	3	4	52	9
THE KNOTT	2.10	2	4	2	38	9
THORNTHWAITE CRAG via GRAY CRAG	2.4	2	3	3	44	8
RAMPSGILL HEAD	2.3	2	3	3	42	8
GRAY CRAG direct	2.15	1	3	3	27	7
GRAY CRAG via Threshthwaite Mouth	2.15	2	3	2	33	5
THORNTHWAITE CRAG via Hayeswater Gill	2.4	1	3	3	31	5
BROCK CRAGS via the filter house	2.27	1	3	2	19	5
HIGH STREET	2.1	1	3	2	27	4
REST DODD	2.16	1	2	2	14	4
Hartsop Hall						
MIDDLE DODD	1.22	2	4	3	44	11
HIGH HARTSOP DODD	1.28	2	2	2	25	11
Hassness						
ROBINSON	6.8	2	3	3	44	11
Haweswater Hotel						
BRANSTREE	2.13	1	2	2	16	3
Hawse End						
CATBELLS	6.24	1	5	3	42	14
Helton						
LOADPOT HILL	2.18	1	2	2	20	3
High Borrans						
SOUR HOWES	2.33	1	3	2	19	7
High Gillerthwaite						
PILLAR via the north-west ridge	7.2	3	5	4	80	14
PILLAR via Wind Gap	7.2	3	5	4	80	13
HIGH STILE	7.6	2	4	4	59	12
RED PIKE (Buttermere)	7.10	2	4	3	50	12

FELL NAME FELL NAME AND ROUTE	BOOK & FELL NO	QUALITY OF			INDEX OF QUALITY	VALUE FOR EFFORT
		ASCENT (1–5)	VIEW (1–5)	SUMMIT (1–5)		
High Ireby						
BINSEY	5.23	1	4	4	41	18
High Lorton						
HOPEGILL HEAD	6.6	3	4	4	70	11
LORD'S SEAT	6.18	2	3	3	44	8
BROOM FELL	6.21	1	4	2	28	6
High Side						
SKIDDAW via north-west ridge	5.1	3	4	4	81	13
SKIDDAW via Southerndale	5.1	3	4	4	81	12
SKIDDAW via Barkbethdale	5.1	3	4	4	81	11
CARL SIDE	5.4	3	4	3	61	11
ULLOCK PIKE	5.11	1	5	4	48	10
BAKESTALL	5.12	2	2	3	36	6
Honister Pass						
DALE HEAD	6.7	1	5	4	52	18
HAYSTACKS	7.22	1	5	5	56	17
GREAT GABLE via GREEN GABLE	7.1	2	5	5	81	16
GREAT GABLE via Beck Head	7.1	2	5	5	81	16
FLEETWITH PIKE via the old tramway	7.16	2	4	3	47	16
GREY KNOTTS direct	7.14	1	4	3	36	15
GREEN GABLE	7.9	2	5	4	61	14
GREY KNOTTS via the old Drum House	7.14	1	4	3	36	14
FLEETWITH PIKE via the old Drum House	7.16	1	4	3	34	12
BRANDRETH	7.12	1	4	2	30	9
Hopebeck						
HOPEGILL HEAD	6.6	3	4	4	70	14
WHITESIDE via Dodd	6.10	2	5	4	63	14
WHITESIDE via Cold Gill	6.10	2	5	4	63	14
WHITESIDE via Penn	6.10	2	5	4	63	14
Howtown						
STEEL KNOTTS	2.34	2	4	3	44	21
ARTHUR'S PIKE	2.28	1	4	3	33	7
BONSCALE PIKE via the breast	2.29	1	3	2	20	8
BONSCALE PIKE direct	2.29	1	3	2	20	8
LOADPOT HILL	2.18	1	2	2	20	5
WETHER HILL	2.17	1	2	1	13	3
Hucks Bridge						
GREY CRAG	2.22	1	3	3	28	4
TARN CRAG via GREY CRAG	2.19	1	2	3	22	3
Ings						
SOUR HOWES via Grassgarth	2.33	1	3	2	19	4
SOUR HOWES via Hugill Hall	2.33	1	3	2	19	4
Jungle Cafe						
GREY CRAG	2.22	1	3	3	28	4
TARN CRAG via GREY CRAG	2.19	1	2	3	22	3

FELL NAME AND ROUTE	BOOK & FELL NO	QUALITY OF			INDEX OF QUALITY	VALUE FOR EFFORT
		ASCENT (1–5)	VIEW (1–5)	SUMMIT (1–5)		
Kendal-Shap road (summit)						
GREY CRAG	2.22	1	3	3	28	5
TARN CRAG via GREY CRAG	2.19	1	2	3	22	3
Kentmere						
SHIPMAN KNOTTS	2.24	2	3	2	31	8
SALLOWS	2.30	1	3	3	25	8
YOKE direct	2.14	1	4	2	30	7
YOKE via Garburn Pass	2.14	1	4	2	30	6
HIGH STREET via Hall Cove	2.1	2	3	2	39	5
HIGH STREET via Lingmell End	2.1	2	3	2	39	5
HIGH STREET via Nan Bield Pass	2.1	2	3	2	39	5
HARTER FELL via KENTMERE PIKE	2.6	2	2	2	33	5
FROSWICK via the reservoir	2.12	2	2	3	31	5
KENTMERE PIKE	2.11	1	3	2	23	5
HARTER FELL via Nan Bield Pass	2.6	2	2	2	33	4
MARDALE ILL BELL via Lingmell End	2.8	1	3	3	30	4
MARDALE ILL BELL via Nan Bield Pass	2.8	1	3	3	30	4
Kentmere Reservoir						
ILL BELL	2.9	3	4	5	73	28
THORNTHWAITE CRAG via Gavel Crag	2.4	2	3	3	44	11
THORNTHWAITE CRAG via Hall Cove	2.4	2	3	3	44	11
Keskadale						
KNOTT RIGG direct	6.19	2	3	3	39	16
KNOTT RIGG via the ridge	6.19	2	3	3	39	16
KNOTT RIGG via Ill Gill	6.19	1	3	3	27	11
Keswick						
WALLA CRAG	3.25	1	4	4	39	11
LATRIGG	5.24	1	4	3	36	10
SKIDDAW	5.1	2	4	4	69	8
SKIDDAW LITTLE MAN	5.3	2	5	3	58	8
LONSCALE FELL via Lonscale Crags	5.6	2	4	2	42	6
HIGH SEAT via Ashness Bridge	3.9	1	4	3	34	5
LONSCALE FELL via Whit Beck	5.6	1	4	2	30	5
LONSCALE FELL via the central approach	5.6	1	4	2	30	5
LONSCALE FELL via shepherd's tracks	5.6	1	4	2	30	5
HIGH SEAT via Dale Bottom	3.9	1	4	3	34	4
BLEABERRY FELL direct	3.10	1	2	3	23	4
BLEABERRY FELL via Brown Knotts	3.10	1	2	3	23	4
BLEABERRY FELL via Dale Bottom	3.10	1	2	3	23	3
Kinniside Stone Circle						
GRIKE	7.29	1	3	3	27	9
CAW FELL	7.13	2	2	3	38	5
Kirkstone Pass						
RED SCREES	1.14	2	4	4	56	28
CAUDALE MOOR	2.7	2	3	1	33	9

FELL NAME FELL NAME AND ROUTE	BOOK & FELL NO	QUALITY OF			INDEX OF QUALITY	VALUE FOR EFFORT
		ASCENT (1–5)	VIEW (1–5)	SUMMIT (1–5)		
Lamplugh						
BLAKE FELL	7.23	2	5	3	53	11
BURNBANK FELL	7.30	1	2	2	14	5
Lanthwaite Green						
WHITESIDE	6.10	3	5	4	75	20
GRASMOOR direct	6.1	3	3	3	59	14
GRASMOOR via Dove Crags	6.1	2	3	3	47	10
Lanty Tarn						
STEEL KNOTTS	2.34	1	4	3	31	17
Legburthwaite						
WATSON'S DODD	1.13	1	3	3	27	6
GREAT DODD	1.8	1	3	2	25	5
Little Crosthwaite						
LONG SIDE via Longside Edge	5.5	2	4	4	53	11
LONG SIDE via Gable Gill	5.5	2	4	4	53	11
CARL SIDE	5.4	2	4	3	48	10
DODD	5.21	1	2	4	33	8
Little Langdale						
WETHERLAM via High Fellside Quarry	4.16	2	4	4	58	10
WETHERLAM via Greenburn Copper Works	4.16	2	4	4	58	10
SWIRL HOW via Greenburn Tarn	4.9	2	4	4	55	8
SWIRL HOW via Long Crag levels	4.9	2	4	4	55	8
Little Langdale village						
GREAT CARRS via Wet Side Edge	4.11	2	5	3	53	8
GREAT CARRS via Broad Slack	4.11	1	5	3	41	6
Little Town						
CATBELLS	6.24	1	5	3	42	17
MAIDEN MOOR direct	6.15	2	3	3	41	14
DALE HEAD via Copper Mine	6.7	2	5	4	64	11
DALE HEAD via Dalehead Tarn	6.7	2	5	4	64	10
HIGH SPY	6.13	2	4	4	56	10
MAIDEN MOOR via Hause Gate	6.15	1	3	3	28	8
Longlands						
MEAL FELL via Trusmadoor	5.18	2	3	4	45	13
LONGLANDS FELL	5.22	1	3	3	27	12
MEAL FELL via Lowthwaite Fell	5.18	1	3	4	33	10
GREAT SCA FELL direct	5.15	1	2	3	23	6
GREAT SCA FELL via the bridle road	5.15	1	2	3	23	5
KNOTT	5.7	1	2	2	19	4
Low Gillerthwaite						
STEEPLE	7.5	3	4	5	72	13
HAYCOCK	7.8	2	4	3	48	9
CAW FELL	7.13	2	2	3	38	8

FELL NAME		QUALITY OF			INDEX	VALUE
	BOOK &				OF	FOR
FELL NAME AND ROUTE	FELL NO	ASCENT VIEW SUMMIT			QUALITY	EFFORT
		(1–5)	(1–5)	(1–5)		
Low Gillerthwaite *(continued)*						
SCOAT FELL direct	7.3	2	3	3	42	7
SCOAT FELL via Deep Gill	7.3	2	3	3	42	7
Low Lorton						
FELLBARROW	7.32	1	3	3	28	7
Loweswater						
MELLBREAK to the north top direct	7.27	2	4	3	48	17
BLAKE FELL via High Nook Tarn	7.23	2	5	3	53	11
BLAKE FELL via Carling Knott	7.23	2	5	3	53	11
LOW FELL direct	7.33	1	4	3	33	10
MELLBREAK to the north top via the scree	7.27	1	4	3	36	10
MELLBREAK to the north top via the valley path	7.27	1	4	3	36	10
LOW FELL via Darling Fell	7.33	1	4	3	33	7
STARLING DODD	7.18	2	3	3	39	6
HEN COMB direct	7.28	1	3	3	25	6
HEN COMB via Little Dodd	7.28	1	3	3	25	6
GAVEL FELL via the drove road	7.25	1	2	3	22	5
GAVEL FELL via Highnook Beck	7.25	1	2	3	22	5
Mardale Head						
MARDALE ILL BELL via Blea Water	2.8	3	3	3	55	12
MARDALE ILL BELL via Small Water	2.8	2	3	3	42	11
KIDSTY PIKE	2.5	2	4	4	52	10
HIGH STREET via Blea Water	2.1	2	3	2	39	7
HIGH STREET via Rough Crag	2.1	2	3	2	39	7
RAMPSGILL HEAD	2.3	1	3	3	30	5
HARTER FELL	2.6	1	2	2	20	5
BRANSTREE	2.13	1	2	2	16	5
Mardale Road						
BRANSTREE	2.13	1	2	2	16	5
Martindale						
STEEL KNOTTS	2.34	1	4	3	31	19
HALLIN FELL	2.35	1	4	2	25	18
ANGLETARN PIKES via Angle Tarn	2.26	2	4	3	47	10
ANGLETARN PIKES via Bedafell Knott	2.26	2	4	3	47	10
HIGH RAISE	2.2	2	3	4	52	7
BEDA FELL	2.31	1	2	2	14	5
THE NAB	2.25	1	3	2	19	4
WETHER HILL	2.17	1	2	1	13	3
Measand						
HIGH RAISE via Long Grain	2.2	2	3	4	52	9
Melbecks						
SKIDDAW	5.1	2	4	4	69	12
Mellfell House						
LITTLE MELL FELL	1.29	1	3	2	19	15

FELL NAME FELL NAME AND ROUTE	BOOK & FELL NO	QUALITY OF			INDEX OF QUALITY	VALUE FOR EFFORT
		ASCENT (1–5)	VIEW (1–5)	SUMMIT (1–5)		
Memorial Footbridge						
PILLAR	7.2	3	5	4	80	20
Mickleden						
PIKE O'STICKLE via Troughton Beck	3.6	2	4	4	53	10
Mickleden sheepfold						
BOWFELL	4.4	2	5	5	75	16
ROSSETT PIKE via Rossett Gill	4.21	2	3	3	41	12
ROSSETT PIKE via Littlegill Head	4.21	2	3	3	41	12
Millbeck						
SKIDDAW LITTLE MAN via the two boulders	5.3	3	5	3	70	15
SKIDDAW LITTLE MAN via south-west arete	5.3	3	5	3	70	15
SKIDDAW	5.1	3	4	4	81	13
CARL SIDE via White Stones	5.4	2	4	3	48	11
CARL SIDE via Carsleddam	5.4	2	4	3	48	11
CARL SIDE via Slades Beck	5.4	2	4	3	48	11
DODD	5.21	1	2	4	33	11
CARL SIDE via cliffs of Doups	5.4	1	4	3	36	8
Moor Divock						
LOADPOT HILL	2.18	2	2	2	33	6
Mosedale						
CARROCK FELL direct	5.13	2	4	5	63	17
CARROCK FELL via east peak	5.13	2	4	5	63	17
KNOTT	5.7	1	2	2	19	3
Mungrisdale						
BOWSCALE FELL via The Tongue	5.8	3	4	4	67	17
BOWSCALE FELL via old bridle path	5.8	2	4	4	55	14
BOWSCALE FELL via Bullfell Beck	5.8	2	4	4	55	14
BLENCATHRA	5.2	2	5	4	81	13
BOWSCALE FELL via east ridge	5.8	2	4	4	55	13
BANNERDALE CRAGS via east ridge	5.10	2	3	3	42	11
BANNERDALE CRAGS via The Tongue	5.10	2	3	3	42	9
SOUTHER FELL	5.20	1	3	2	22	9
MUNGRISDALE COMMON via Glendermackin col	5.16	1	2	2	14	3
Nether Row						
HIGH PIKE via Sandbed Mine	5.14	1	4	2	33	8
HIGH PIKE via Potts Gill Mine	5.14	1	4	2	33	8
Netherbeck Bridge						
SEATALLAN	7.15	2	3	4	47	9
HAYCOCK via Little Lad Crag	7.8	2	4	3	48	7
HAYCOCK via Ladcrag Beck	7.8	2	4	3	48	7
SCOAT FELL direct	7.3	2	3	3	42	6
SCOAT FELL via Scoat Tarn	7.3	2	3	3	42	6

FELL NAME AND ROUTE	BOOK & FELL NO	QUALITY OF			INDEX OF QUALITY	VALUE FOR EFFORT
		ASCENT (1–5)	VIEW (1–5)	SUMMIT (1–5)		
Newlands Church						
ROBINSON via Scope Beck	6.8	3	3	3	56	11
ROBINSON via High Snab Bank	6.8	3	3	3	56	11
HINDSCARTH	6.9	2	4	4	55	11
Newlands Hause						
ROBINSON	6.8	3	3	3	56	19
KNOTT RIGG	6.19	1	3	3	27	15
Orthwaite						
MEAL FELL direct	5.18	2	3	4	45	11
MEAL FELL via Brockle Crag	5.18	2	3	4	45	11
GREAT COCKUP	5.19	1	4	2	27	9
GREAT SCA FELL direct	5.15	2	2	3	36	7
GREAT SCA FELL via Brockle Crag	5.15	2	2	3	36	7
KNOTT direct	5.7	2	2	2	31	6
KNOTT via Brockle Crag	5.7	2	2	2	31	6
GREAT CALVA direct	5.9	1	3	3	30	6
GREAT CALVA via Brockle Crag	5.9	1	3	3	30	6
Overbeck Bridge						
YEWBARROW	7.19	3	3	3	54	14
RED PIKE (Wasdale) via Dore Head	7.4	2	3	4	48	8
RED PIKE (Wasdale) via Low Tarn	7.4	2	3	4	48	8
Park Brow Foot						
GOWBARROW FELL via Aira Force	1.32	1	4	3	34	13
GOWBARROW FELL via Yew Crag	1.32	1	4	3	34	10
Patterdale						
ARNISON CRAG direct	1.35	1	2	4	25	14
BIRKS via Trough Head	1.24	3	4	2	52	12
PLACE FELL direct	2.20	2	3	3	42	11
PLACE FELL via The Knight	2.20	2	3	3	42	11
PLACE FELL via Boardale Hause	2.20	2	3	3	42	11
BIRKS via Thornhow End	1.24	2	4	2	39	11
ANGLETARN PIKES via Freeze Beck	2.26	1	4	3	34	10
ANGLETARN PIKES direct	2.26	1	4	3	34	10
HELVELLYN via Nethermost Cove and NETHERMOST PIKE	1.1	3	4	3	73	9
HELVELLYN via Striding Edge	1.1	3	4	3	73	9
HELVELLYN via Red Tarn and Swirral Edge	1.1	3	4	3	73	9
ARNISON CRAG via Trough Head	1.35	1	2	4	25	9
HELVELLYN via Ruthwaite cove and DOLLYWAGGON PIKE	1.1	3	4	3	73	8
FAIRFIELD via Greenhow End	1.5	3	4	3	64	8
DOLLYWAGGON PIKE via Grisedale	1.7	3	4	3	63	8
DOVE CRAG direct	1.12	3	4	2	55	8
HELVELLYN via Grisedale Tarn	1.1	3	4	3	73	7
RED SCREES	1.14	2	4	4	56	7
NETHERMOST PIKE via Grisedale	1.2	3	3	3	55	7

FELL NAME AND ROUTE	BOOK & FELL NO	QUALITY OF			INDEX OF QUALITY	VALUE FOR EFFORT
		ASCENT (1–5)	VIEW (1–5)	SUMMIT (1–5)		

Patterdale *(continued)*

FELL NAME AND ROUTE	BOOK & FELL NO	ASCENT	VIEW	SUMMIT	INDEX	VALUE
HIGH RAISE	2.2	2	3	4	52	7
FAIRFIELD via Deepdale Hause	1.5	2	4	3	52	7
RAMPSGILL HEAD	2.3	2	3	3	42	6
DOVE CRAG via Black Brow	1.12	2	4	2	42	6
LITTLE HART CRAG via Scandale Pass	1.23	2	3	3	39	6
LITTLE HART CRAG via HIGH HARTSOP DODD	1.23	2	3	3	39	6
LITTLE HART CRAG via Hogget Gill	1.23	2	3	3	39	6
HARTSOP ABOVE HOW	1.26	1	4	2	25	6
HART CRAG via Wallend	1.11	2	2	3	36	5
HART CRAG via HARTSOP ABOVE HOW	1.11	2	2	3	36	5
SAINT SUNDAY CRAG via Thornhow End	1.10	2	2	2	30	5
SAINT SUNDAY CRAG via east ridge	1.10	2	2	2	30	5
BIRKHOUSE MOOR via Grisedale	1.19	2	2	2	28	5
THE KNOTT	2.10	1	4	2	25	4
HIGH STREET	2.1	1	3	2	27	3
SAINT SUNDAY CRAG via Trough Head	1.10	1	2	2	17	3
REST DODD	2.16	1	2	2	14	3

Pooley Bridge

FELL NAME AND ROUTE	BOOK & FELL NO	ASCENT	VIEW	SUMMIT	INDEX	VALUE
LOADPOT HILL	2.18	1	2	2	20	3

Rannerdale

FELL NAME AND ROUTE	BOOK & FELL NO	ASCENT	VIEW	SUMMIT	INDEX	VALUE
RANNERDALE KNOTTS	6.28	1	4	4	38	22
GRASMOOR via Red Gill	6.1	2	3	3	47	11
GRASMOOR via Lad Hows	6.1	2	3	3	47	10
EEL CRAG	6.2	2	4	3	50	9

Ravenstone

FELL NAME AND ROUTE	BOOK & FELL NO	ASCENT	VIEW	SUMMIT	INDEX	VALUE
ULLOCK PIKE	5.11	1	5	4	48	12
LONG SIDE	5.5	2	4	4	53	11

Rigg Beck

FELL NAME AND ROUTE	BOOK & FELL NO	ASCENT	VIEW	SUMMIT	INDEX	VALUE
ARD CRAGS	6.17	2	4	4	52	17

Riggindale

FELL NAME AND ROUTE	BOOK & FELL NO	ASCENT	VIEW	SUMMIT	INDEX	VALUE
HIGH RAISE via Mardale	2.2	2	3	4	52	11

Rosgill

FELL NAME AND ROUTE	BOOK & FELL NO	ASCENT	VIEW	SUMMIT	INDEX	VALUE
TARN CRAG via Swindale and Brunt Tongue	2.19	1	2	3	22	3

Rosthwaite

FELL NAME AND ROUTE	BOOK & FELL NO	ASCENT	VIEW	SUMMIT	INDEX	VALUE
GRANGE FELL to King's How, direct	3.22	2	4	4	53	20
GRANGE FELL to Brund Fell via Hazel Bank	3.22	2	4	4	53	19
CASTLE CRAG	6.29	1	4	4	41	18
GRANGE FELL to Brund Fell via the bridle path	3.22	2	4	4	53	17

FELL NAME AND ROUTE	BOOK & FELL NO	QUALITY OF			INDEX OF QUALITY	VALUE FOR EFFORT
		ASCENT (1–5)	VIEW (1–5)	SUMMIT (1–5)		
Rosthwaite *(continued)*						
HIGH SPY	6.13	2	4	4	56	12
DALE HEAD	6.7	2	5	4	64	10
GLARAMARA via Comb Gill	4.13	2	4	3	50	8
GLARAMARA via Thornythwaite Fell	4.13	2	4	3	50	8
Rydal						
NAB SCAR	1.33	2	3	2	31	13
LOUGHRIGG FELL	3.27	1	3	4	41	12
HART CRAG via Rydal Head	1.11	3	2	3	48	7
HART CRAG direct	1.11	3	2	3	48	7
HERON PIKE via NAB SCAR	1.25	1	4	2	25	7
HERON PIKE via Blind Cove	1.25	1	4	2	25	6
LOW PIKE	1.30	1	2	2	13	3
Sadgill						
GREY CRAG	2.22	2	3	3	41	12
SHIPMAN KNOTTS	2.24	2	3	2	31	10
TARN CRAG	2.19	2	2	3	34	9
KENTMERE PIKE	2.11	2	3	2	36	7
HARTER FELL via Wren Gill	2.6	1	2	2	20	3
HARTER FELL via Gatescarth Pass	2.6	1	2	2	20	3
BRANSTREE	2.13	1	2	2	16	3
Sandwick						
PLACE FELL via Sleet Fell	2.20	3	3	3	55	12
PLACE FELL via High Dodd	2.20	2	3	3	42	10
PLACE FELL via Scalehow Beck	2.20	2	3	3	42	10
PLACE FELL via Nettleslack	2.20	2	3	3	42	9
Scales						
BLENCATHRA via Doddick Fell	5.2	3	5	4	94	21
BLENCATHRA via Scaley Beck	5.2	2	5	4	81	18
BLENCATHRA via Sharp Edge	5.2	3	5	4	94	17
BLENCATHRA via Scales Fell	5.2	2	5	4	81	17
BANNERDALE CRAGS direct	5.10	1	3	3	30	7
BANNERDALE CRAGS via Glendermackin col	5.10	1	3	3	30	7
SOUTHER FELL	5.20	1	3	2	22	7
Scawgill Bridge						
GRAYSTONES	6.25	1	3	3	30	16
Seathwaite						
GREAT GABLE direct	7.1	3	5	5	94	16
GREAT GABLE via Sty Head and the Breast Route	7.1	3	5	5	94	15
GREAT GABLE via Aaron Slack and Windy Gap	7.1	3	5	5	94	15
SEATHWAITE FELL via Black Waugh	4.23	2	4	4	50	14

FELL NAME		QUALITY OF			INDEX OF QUALITY	VALUE FOR EFFORT
FELL NAME AND ROUTE	BOOK & FELL NO	ASCENT (1–5)	VIEW (1–5)	SUMMIT (1–5)		

FELL NAME AND ROUTE	BOOK & FELL NO	ASCENT (1–5)	VIEW (1–5)	SUMMIT (1–5)	INDEX OF QUALITY	VALUE FOR EFFORT
Seathwaite *(continued)*						
SEATHWAITE FELL via Styhead Gill	4.23	2	4	4	50	14
GREY KNOTTS	7.14	2	4	3	48	13
BASE BROWN	7.17	3	3	2	47	13
GREEN GABLE	7.9	2	5	4	61	12
GREAT END via Sty Head	4.3	2	5	4	66	10
BRANDRETH	7.12	2	4	2	42	10
Seathwaite (Duddon Valley)						
GREY FRIAR	4.15	2	4	4	55	9
DOW CRAG via Walna Scar Pass	4.14	1	3	5	44	7
DOW CRAG via Seathwaite Tarn	4.14	1	3	5	44	6
Seatoller						
HIGH SPY	6.13	2	4	4	56	12
SCAFELL PIKE via Esk Hause	4.1	3	5	5	95	11
DALE HEAD	6.7	2	5	4	64	11
SCAFELL PIKE via Sty Head	4.1	3	5	5	95	10
GREAT END	4.3	3	5	4	78	10
ESK PIKE	4.5	3	5	4	77	10
GREY KNOTTS	7.14	2	4	3	48	10
ALLEN CRAGS via Allen Gill	4.12	2	3	4	47	7
ALLEN CRAGS direct	4.12	2	3	4	47	7
Selside						
GREY CRAG	2.22	1	3	3	28	3
TARN CRAG via GREY CRAG	2.19	1	2	3	22	2
Shap						
TARN CRAG via Peat Hill and Brunt Tongue	2.19	1	2	3	22	3
Skelwith Bridge						
LOUGHRIGG FELL	3.27	1	3	4	41	14
Skiddaw House						
LONSCALE FELL to East Peak	5.6	3	4	2	55	19
SKIDDAW via Sale How	5.1	2	4	4	69	16
LONSCALE FELL via Burnt Horse Ridge	5.6	2	4	2	42	15
SKIDDAW via Hare Crag	5.1	2	4	4	69	14
SKIDDAW LITTLE MAN	5.3	1	5	3	45	12
GREAT CALVA direct	5.9	1	3	3	30	10
GREAT CALVA via Dead Beck	5.9	1	3	3	30	10
St John's-in-the-Vale Church						
HIGH RIGG	3.26	1	3	3	25	24
Stair						
CAUSEY PIKE via Rowling End	6.14	3	5	5	80	22
CAUSEY PIKE direct	6.14	2	5	5	67	19
CATBELLS via Skelgill	6.24	1	5	3	42	15

FELL NAME FELL NAME AND ROUTE	BOOK & FELL NO	QUALITY OF			INDEX OF QUALITY	VALUE FOR EFFORT
		ASCENT (1–5)	VIEW (1–5)	SUMMIT (1–5)		
Stair *(continued)*						
BARROW	6.23	1	4	3	34	10
EEL CRAG via the mine road	6.2	3	4	3	63	9
SAIL	6.5	2	5	3	52	9
SCAR CRAGS	6.11	2	4	3	44	8
EEL CRAG via Causey Pike	6.2	2	4	3	50	7
OUTSIDE	6.16	1	3	3	28	7
Stake Pass						
PIKE O'STICKLE	3.6	1	4	4	41	18
Stanah						
STYBARROW DODD via Stanah Gill	1.9	2	3	3	42	8
STYBARROW DODD via Sticks Pass	1.9	1	3	3	30	6
RAISE	1.4	1	3	2	23	4
Staveley						
SOUR HOWES via Browfoot	2.33	1	3	2	19	3
Stone Ends						
CARROCK FELL	5.13	2	4	5	63	21
Stonethwaite						
ROSTHWAITE FELL	4.24	3	3	3	52	16
GREAT CRAG via Knotts	3.20	2	3	4	45	16
GREAT CRAG via Dock Tarn	3.20	2	3	4	45	16
EAGLE CRAG direct	3.17	2	2	3	33	9
BOWFELL via Stake Beck	4.4	2	5	5	75	8
BOWFELL via Angletarn Gill	4.4	2	5	5	75	8
HARRISON STICKLE via HIGH RAISE and THUNACAR KNOTT	3.3	2	4	4	61	8
HARRISON STICKLE via Langstrath, Stake Pass and PIKE O'STICKLE	3.3	2	4	4	61	7
HIGH RAISE	3.1	2	3	3	44	7
ULLSCARF via Coldbarrow Fell	3.4	2	3	2	39	7
ULLSCARF via Lining Crag	3.4	2	3	2	39	7
GLARAMARA via Langstrath and Tray Dub	4.13	1	4	3	38	5
GLARAMARA via Langstrath and shepherd's track	4.13	1	4	3	38	5
EAGLE CRAG via Greenup path	3.17	1	2	3	20	5
SERGEANT'S CRAG	3.11	1	3	3	27	4
Strands						
SEATALLAN	7.15	2	3	4	47	7
SEATALLAN via BUCKBARROW	7.15	2	3	4	47	7
Sty Head						
GREAT GABLE	7.1	2	5	5	81	31
GREAT END	4.3	2	5	4	66	24

FELL NAME FELL NAME AND ROUTE	BOOK & FELL NO	QUALITY OF			INDEX OF QUALITY	VALUE FOR EFFORT
		ASCENT (1–5)	VIEW (1–5)	SUMMIT (1–5)		
Styhead Gill						
GREEN GABLE via Aaron Slack	7.9	2	5	4	61	27
GREEN GABLE via Mitchell Cove	7.9	2	5	4	61	27
Swindale Head						
SELSIDE PIKE via north-east ridge	2.21	1	2	2	14	5
SELSIDE PIKE via Mosedale path	2.21	1	2	2	14	4
Thackthwaite						
LITTLE MELL FELL	1.29	1	3	3	25	13
Thackthwaite (Lorton Vale)						
LOW FELL via Watching Gill	7.33	2	4	3	45	15
LOW FELL via the drove road	7.33	2	4	3	45	13
FELLBARROW direct	7.32	1	3	3	28	12
FELLBARROW via Watching Crag	7.32	1	3	3	28	9
Thirlmere						
ARMBOTH FELL via Launchy Gill	3.18	1	2	3	20	9
ARMBOTH FELL via Fisher Gill	3.18	1	2	3	20	9
ARMBOTH FELL via Brown Rigg	3.18	1	2	3	20	8
ARMBOTH FELL via Dob Gill	3.18	1	2	3	20	6
Thirlmere Dam						
RAVEN CRAG	3.19	1	4	3	31	15
Thirlspot						
HELVELLYN via the 'White Stones' Route	1.1	2	4	3	61	9
HELVELLYN via Helvellyn Gill	1.1	2	4	3	61	9
HELVELLYN via the old pony-route	1.1	2	4	3	61	9
WHITE SIDE	1.6	1	3	3	30	6
RAISE direct	1.4	1	3	2	23	4
RAISE via Brund Gill	1.4	1	3	2	23	4
Thornthwaite						
LORD'S SEAT	6.18	2	3	3	44	10
GRISEDALE PIKE via north-east ridge	6.3	2	4	3	53	9
GRISEDALE PIKE via north ridge	6.3	2	4	3	53	8
Thornthwaite, Swan Hotel						
BARF via The Bishop	6.22	2	4	3	48	22
BARF via Beckstones Plantation	6.22	1	4	3	36	14
Threlkeld						
BLENCATHRA via Blease Gill	5.2	3	5	4	94	19
BLENCATHRA via Middle Tongue	5.2	3	5	4	94	19
BLENCATHRA via Hall's Fell	5.2	3	5	4	94	19
BLENCATHRA via Gategill Fell	5.2	3	5	4	94	19
BLENCATHRA via Doddick Gill	5.2	2	5	4	81	16
BLENCATHRA via Blease Fell	5.2	2	5	4	81	15
BLENCATHRA via Roughten Gill	5.2	2	5	4	81	11
LATRIGG	5.24	1	4	3	36	9

FELL NAME FELL NAME AND ROUTE	BOOK & FELL NO	QUALITY OF			INDEX OF QUALITY	VALUE FOR EFFORT
		ASCENT (1–5)	VIEW (1–5)	SUMMIT (1–5)		
Threlkeld *(continued)*						
MUNGRISDALE COMMON via Sinen Gill	5.16	2	2	2	27	5
MUNGRISDALE COMMON via The Stake and Cloven Stone	5.16	2	2	2	27	4
Tilberthwaite						
WETHERLAM	4.16	3	4	4	70	16
Torver						
CONISTON OLD MAN direct	4.8	2	5	4	67	11
CONISTON OLD MAN via Goat's Hause	4.8	2	5	4	67	11
DOW CRAG via Walna Scar Pass	4.14	2	3	5	56	9
DOW CRAG via Goat's Hause	4.14	2	3	5	56	9
Troutal						
GREY FRIAR	4.15	2	4	4	55	12
Troutbeck						
ILL BELL via Hagg Gill	2.9	3	4	5	73	13
WANSFELL	2.32	1	3	2	23	8
HIGH STREET	2.1	2	3	2	39	5
CAUDALE MOOR via Sad Gill	2.7	2	3	1	33	5
FROSWICK via Blue Gill	2.12	2	2	3	31	5
THORNTHWAITE CRAG via Scot Rake	2.4	1	3	3	31	4
THORNTHWAITE CRAG via Threshthwaite Mouth	2.4	1	3	3	31	4
CAUDALE MOOR via Woundale	2.7	1	3	1	20	3
CAUDALE MOOR via St Ravens Edge	2.7	1	3	1	20	2
CAUDALE MOOR via Threshthwaite Mouth	2.7	1	3	1	20	2
Troutbeck Old Railway Station						
GREAT MELL FELL	1.27	1	2	2	13	7
Troutbeck Park Farm						
TROUTBECK TONGUE	2.36	1	2	2	13	8
TROUTBECK TONGUE via the Tongue	2.36	1	2	2	13	4
Wanthwaite						
CLOUGH HEAD direct	1.18	3	5	3	66	15
CLOUGH HEAD via Hause Well	1.18	3	5	3	66	13
Wasdale Head						
GREAT GABLE via Gavel Neese and Beck Head	7.1	3	5	5	94	16
GREAT GABLE via Gavel Neese and Moses' Finger	7.1	3	5	5	94	16
GREAT GABLE via Sty Head	7.1	3	5	5	94	14
KIRK FELL	7.7	3	4	3	59	14
LINGMELL via The Shoulder	4.7	3	5	4	73	14
SCAFELL PIKE via Brown Tongue and Mickledore	4.1	3	5	5	95	14

FELL NAME FELL NAME AND ROUTE	BOOK & FELL NO	QUALITY OF			INDEX OF QUALITY	VALUE FOR EFFORT
		ASCENT (1–5)	VIEW (1–5)	SUMMIT (1–5)		
Wasdale Head *(continued)*						
LINGMELL via Brown Tongue	4.7	3	5	4	73	13
SCAFELL PIKE via Piers Gill and Broad Crag col	4.1	3	5	5	95	13
SCAFELL PIKE via Brown Tongue and Lingmell col	4.1	2	5	5	83	12
PILLAR via Wind Gap	7.2	3	5	4	80	12
SCAFELL via Brown Tongue	4.2	3	5	4	78	12
LINGMELL via Piers Gill	4.7	3	5	4	73	12
SCAFELL PIKE via Piers Gill and Lingmell col	4.1	2	5	5	83	11
PILLAR via Black Sail Pass	7.2	3	5	4	80	11
SCAFELL via Green How	4.2	3	5	4	78	11
GREAT END via Sty Head	4.3	2	5	4	66	10
BOWFELL via ESK PIKE	4.4	2	5	5	75	9
GREAT END via Corridor Route	4.3	2	5	4	66	9
ESK PIKE	4.5	2	5	4	64	9
SCOAT FELL	7.3	3	3	3	55	9
RED PIKE (Wasdale)	7.4	2	3	4	48	9
YEWBARROW	7.19	2	3	3	41	9
ILLGILL HEAD	4.22	1	4	5	47	8
Watendlath						
GRANGE FELL to Brund Fell	3.22	1	4	4	41	25
GREAT CRAG	3.20	1	4	4	39	17
HIGH SEAT via HIGH TOVE	3.9	1	4	3	34	10
HIGH SEAT via Raise Gill	3.9	1	4	3	34	10
HIGH TOVE	3.16	1	3	2	19	10
ULLSCARF	3.4	2	3	2	39	8
Waterend						
BURNBANK FELL	7.30	1	2	2	14	3
Whinlatter Pass						
HOPEGILL HEAD	6.6	3	4	4	70	15
GRISEDALE PIKE	6.3	2	4	3	53	13
LORD'S SEAT	6.18	1	3	3	31	11
WHINLATTER	6.20	1	3	3	27	11
White Moss						
LOUGHRIGG FELL	3.27	1	3	4	41	16
Windermere						
SOUR HOWES	2.33	1	3	2	19	4
Woodhow Farm						
WHIN RIGG	4.26	2	4	4	55	14
Woolpack Inn						
GREEN CRAG via Crook Crag	4.27	2	4	4	50	12
GREEN CRAG via Low Birker Tarn	4.27	2	4	4	50	12

FELL NAME FELL NAME AND ROUTE	BOOK & FELL NO	QUALITY OF			INDEX OF QUALITY	VALUE FOR EFFORT
		ASCENT (1–5)	VIEW (1–5)	SUMMIT (1–5)		
Wrynose Bottom						
GREY FRIAR	4.15	1	4	4	42	12
COLD PIKE	4.19	1	4	4	38	12
Wrynose Pass						
PIKE O'BLISCO	4.18	1	4	4	42	17
COLD PIKE	4.19	1	4	4	38	16
CRINKLE CRAGS	4.6	2	4	4	63	14
GREY FRIAR	4.15	1	4	4	42	11
Wythburn						
HELVELLYN via Whelpside Gill	1.1	2	4	3	61	11
HELVELLYN via Comb Gill	1.1	2	4	3	61	11
HELVELLYN via old lead mine	1.1	2	4	3	61	11
HELVELLYN via Birk Side	1.1	2	4	3	61	11
NETHERMOST PIKE	1.2	2	3	3	42	9
SERGEANT MAN via Far Easedale	3.2	2	4	4	56	8
ULLSCARF via West Head	3.4	2	3	2	39	7
HIGH RAISE	3.1	2	3	3	44	6
STEEL FELL	3.12	1	2	2	17	5
CALF CRAG	3.15	1	2	3	22	4
Wythop Mill						
SALE FELL	6.27	1	4	4	44	19
LING FELL	6.26	1	3	3	25	10
BROOM FELL	6.21	1	4	2	28	5
Yew Tree House						
HOLME FELL	4.30	1	4	4	38	20

Haweswater
from the third cairn

aWainwright
THE PICTORIAL GUIDES

The hills are eternal.
Always there will be
the lonely ridge, the
dancing beck, the silent
forest; always there
will be the
exhilaration
of the summits.

from Penny Hill

Published by MICHAEL JOSEPH
and available, together with other
Wainwright sketchbooks, through
leading bookshops.